THE SECRET
SERVICE
WEBSITE
FORMULA

https://secretservice.biz
Secret Service Business Pty Ltd (publisher)
de Lacy, Laura (author)
Secret Service Business Series, Book Two
The Secret Service Website Formula: 3 Steps to a Lead Machine Website for Small Skill-or-Service Business Owners, their Web Designers & Content Creators
ISBN Paperback: 978-0-6450683-2-0
ISBN eBook: 978-0-6450683-3-7
BUSINESS

https://greenhillpublishing.com.au/

Typeset Calluna 10/16
Cover Image by Adobe Stock
Editing by Isabelle Russell, New Zealand
Interior illustrations by
Tatsiana Teush, Poland
Cover and book design by
Green Hill Publishing

A catalogue record for this book is available from the National Library of Australia

THE SECRET SERVICE WEBSITE FORMULA

3 Steps to a Lead Machine Website for Small Skill-or-Service Business Owners, their Web Designers & Content Creators

LAURA DE LACY

THE WORD ON THE STREET...

"My business has absolutely boomed with this system. It's amazing... really quite ridiculous."
Andrew Matthias, Landscaper, Adelaide

"This website is honestly the best thing I've ever done for my business. Leads just keep rolling in and I don't have to compete on price anymore."
Peter Beggs, Building Inspector, Blue Mountains

"I get all my work from my website and get so many comments about it, all these years later. It's the best investment I've ever made."
Damien Beveridge, Builder, Newcastle Region

For business owners, web designers and content creators who've endured the expense, frustration, shame or guilt of websites that just don't work.

READ THIS FIRST

This book is one of three in the *Secret Service Business Series*:

1. ***Secret Service Marketing:*** *The Underground Guide to Modern Marketing for Small Skill-or-Service Businesses*
2. ***The Secret Service Website Formula:*** *3 Steps to a Lead Machine Website for Small Skill-or-Service Business Owners, their Web Designers & Content Creators*
3. ***The Modern Marketing Arsenal:*** *Ways & Means to Promote a Small Skill-or-Service Business (& Which to Choose to Get the Most Bang for Your Marketing Buck)*

To reap the best possible results, reading the books in the above order is recommended. As tempting as it may be to skip ahead, *Secret Service Marketing* lays critical foundations to give your marketing tools and activities (including your next website) the best possible chance; reducing the time and money you'll need to spend on them in the future.

Reading *Secret Service Marketing* first is all the more important if you've been struggling to cultivate a winning business concept or convert a worthy concept into a viable business model.

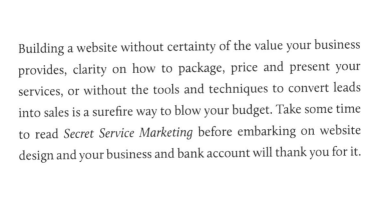

Building a website without certainty of the value your business provides, clarity on how to package, price and present your services, or without the tools and techniques to convert leads into sales is a surefire way to blow your budget. Take some time to read *Secret Service Marketing* before embarking on website design and your business and bank account will thank you for it.

CONTENTS

ACHY BREAKY HEART: CONFESSIONS OF A LOST SSB SOUL

On a sunny Monday morning in March 2007, I leaned back on my new, leather-look office chair with a satisfied smile, admiring the DIY handiwork in my freshly painted home office (formerly known as *bedroom 3*).

Having resigned from full time employment two weeks earlier, it was the first day of the rest of my life. I was 26 years old and my own boss, on a mission to 'change the face of marketing and design for small businesses in southern Adelaide' – whatever that meant.

Working for myself, from home, was a dream come true. Equipped with a marketing degree, a client on a small retainer (the hotel I had worked at for five years), the services of a talented designer (a lifelong friend), an articulate business plan and, of course, a fully equipped spare bedroom/home office, I had all my ducks in a row...

Or so I thought.

Unfortunately, it was only a matter of months before I realised that little from my studies applied to the real world of small business. Trying to apply corporate strategies for branding and business growth to small business clients on a tight budget was like trying to cook pancakes with Pythagoras' Theorem.

What's more, I must have been off sick the day my Bachelor of Management taught me how to manage. Of course I'd learned management principles, but they applied to teams of people in corporate offices, not the management of highly creative, off-site freelancers.

Beyond that, there's one thing you need in business that no university degree can teach: self-confidence... and mine was severely lacking. I was scared of everyone – my clients, my subcontractors, my family and friends – and what they would think if they knew how much I was struggling to make this business thing work. The result was me giving too much away for free, not taking credit for my work and settling for results that didn't meet my high standards.

Less than a year down the track, my retainer client fell through. Due to a paralysing fear of conflict, my extremely passionate then-husband, Billy, stepped in (in somewhat dramatic fashion) after having enough of me 'being taken advantage of'. We were fired on the spot and I was devastated. A week later, I was hired back at twice the rate. A win and a big 'I told you so' for Billy, but it was on a casual basis and things were never the same. The casual rate relationship died a gradual death and I was left with no fall-back retainer. *Shit*.

Working with my lifelong friend as sole designer was fun and exciting, but more challenging than I'd anticipated. A highly talented visual artist, her design style was vastly different to mine; artistic and uninhibited – always beautiful and intricately detailed but difficult for my logical business brain to accept. Of the two of us though, she was the experienced web designer, so I would second-guess myself; suppressing my business intuition to avoid offending her. As my technical knowledge grew, so did my ability to communicate what I needed, but constraining her talent to meet simple briefs and tight budgets felt awkward and cruel. After working together on a range of branding and web design projects (time and experiences I am forever grateful for) our paths gradually separated.

As for my business plan, well... let's just say it oozed youthful exuberance and wishful thinking. In hindsight, it lacked a depth of insight that can only come from experience-based mastery of your field.

Being a qualified marketer, my business plan had a carefully considered marketing section but the strategies I'd excitedly outlined didn't pack a punch in the real world. My biggest blunder was our pricing strategy, summed up in a single sentence: *Projects will be quoted on an individual basis.* This turned out to be a drastic oversimplification. From day one, quoting was the bane of my existence. I would rarely quote the 'right' amount. My prices were either too low, attracting difficult clients and giving our services away at a loss (in the vague hope of building a stronger portfolio), or too high (so I believed), causing us to miss out on projects altogether. Living in a state of desperation and high-functioning anxiety, I would take on any project that came our way – whether we were technically equipped to handle it or not – partly to appease Billy and partly to avoid hammering the final nail of failure into my coffin of self-employment.

As a result of taking on projects for the wrong reasons or at too low a price, I lacked drive and procrastinated badly, particularly when it came to prospecting for new sales and preparing quotes. I was completely conflicted – my head knew we needed sales to keep the business afloat... my heart felt heavy and hindered at the thought. This compounded my feelings of failure. Ashamed of not coming close to achieving its pie-in-the-sky targets, I relegated my business plan to the back of the filing cabinet and there it stayed.

Seeing how overworked and underpaid I was, Billy concluded we needed a pool of borrowed funds to draw on to give us some financial breathing room. I reluctantly agreed and we successfully applied for a line of credit – essentially a big, low-rate credit card with our home as collateral. Although this gave us the breathing room we needed and sustained us through some particularly hard times, it was a massive burden. In my mind, we were living in debt, which meant feeling immense guilt at the prospect of spending any money. I would scrimp and save wherever I could – rarely buying new clothes, let alone spoiling myself – all the while applying the *fake it 'til you make it* formula. I presented myself to everyone but Billy as calm, happy and more successful than I actually was. Friends who earned far more than I did were envious of my 'cool job' and the perceived freedom and flexibility of working from home. Little did they know that beneath the calm façade, I was working a minimum of 70 hours a week, earning less than I would on the dole, riddled with anxiety and racked with guilt.

Unlike other service-based businesses I'd encountered, the web design industry was a minefield. There seemed to be no precedent for success; no 'best practice' approach to build a viable business. In hindsight, I'd entered one of the newest, most convoluted and rapidly evolving industries on the planet with no industry-specific experience, training or technical skills. Not the wisest of strategies.

To make matters worse, I had established my business in a tough market. Adelaide, South Australia, is a brilliant city but renowned for being more reserved and cautious than most. As such, it's often used as a testing ground for new concepts by businesses bold enough to challenge the unwritten law: 'If it works in Adelaide, it'll work anywhere.' My business concept was *not* working. Not in Adelaide. Not anywhere.

Sales fluctuated wildly from one year to the next. There was no consistency... only chaos. Every marketing and website project was unique, which meant operations couldn't be streamlined and, because I couldn't develop websites myself, I felt completely out of control. The sweet sensation of making a sale was soured by a feeling of dread – not knowing if I could rely on my team to deliver the project to the standard I strived for, within the budget they'd helped me set. Back then, there were only a handful of projects that were genuinely profitable if I were to factor in my own time – which I avoided, opting to bury my head in the sand for sanity's sake.

Knowing I had to change something but having lost all faith in my own business intelligence, I looked to anyone and everyone for answers or alternative paths to success. From starting time-sapping side-ventures with strangers to inadvertently joining and recruiting for a commercial cult, it's safe to say my business journey has not run smoothly...

... and thank God for that.

If not for these challenges, feelings of inadequacy, isolation, falsity and failure, along with a few monumental errors in judgement, the Secret Service Website Formula would not exist. Just as a diamond is born under pressure, the formula came to be – after seven years of relentless stress and strain, having exhausted all excuses, plan Bs and bright shiny objects and found no one to provide the answers I desperately sought. I had no choice but to roll up my sleeves and dig for the diamonds myself.

Of course, during those years, I'd had some little wins – the odd revelation, result or reward that was just enough to keep me believing that the struggle and sacrifice would one day prove worthwhile. But it was never enough to feel like I was gaining ground.

Then one day, figuratively speaking, I tripped over something in the dirt; something I'd dug up years earlier but disregarded amid my other disorderly business diggings, thinking it was just a pretty rock. *It* was the slidedeck (PowerPoint presentation) for a training workshop I'd once developed for a local business association, which I'd called *More than just a website: How to make the most of the web to benefit your business.*

The workshop had been a paid gig – a blessing in more ways than one. Secure in the knowledge I was being paid for it, I'd been liberated to share my best, money-saving, marketing advice for local businesses. There was no risk of being taken advantage of by giving too much away for free, as was my natural inclination (a trait I'd been trying to suppress, given it never seemed to serve me well). I could finally be myself and give as much away as I wanted – so I had, and delivered the workshop to rave reviews. Other than my then-unbridled phobia of public speaking turning my legs into jackhammers and my voice to vibrato for the first half-hour, I chalked it up as a rare success and thought little more of it. However, I did keep a printout of the slides in a pile on my desk to savour the sense of satisfaction I got from sharing my knowledge with no agenda or expectation of return. It was that printout I fatefully stumbled across that day.

With a whole lot of polishing over the coming months – in conjunction with some major tweaks to my business model (detailed in *Secret Service Marketing*) – my little slidedeck transformed into something pretty special... an approach to marketing and web design which would change the game for my business, and those I elected to work with, from that point on.

Small skill-or-service businesses (SSBs) became my focus for a couple of reasons. For as long as I could remember, I'd been fascinated by SSB owners – their stories, struggles, extraordinary skills and inspiring successes, often cloaked in quiet humility. In my mind, they were the businesses that should be enjoying the easiest, most immediate benefits from internet marketing but from what I'd seen, they were struggling the most and benefiting least.

Born from this underlying passion, my web design and content formula produced sites for clients that they were not only proud of, but that actually worked. They experienced real-world results – leads flowing in on autopilot, day after day, month after month. This gave them the power to cherry-pick the customers and projects they took on, without dropping their prices or profit margins to compete.

The formula worked like a charm – for one client, then another... then another, until we had a waitlist of hundreds of SSBs. But I still wasn't satisfied. Amid a series of other major life-changes – including having a baby and, three months later, separating from my husband – I arrived at a crossroad in my business journey. I could veer left – accepting the advice of well-meaners to keep the formula under wraps and grow Cyberstart into a large digital agency. Or I could veer right – somehow sharing it en masse; empowering SSB owners and web designers across the globe to take the formula, run with it and prosper for themselves.

Instinctively, I knew that the bigger we grew, the more diluted our ability to apply the formula for individual clients would become. And even if we did manage to retain our small business soul, our reach would be limited. I would not be helping the little guy... and certainly not en masse.

Sharing the formula became my only option. Even if it meant packing it all in at some point and getting a job to support myself and my baby boy (which I eventually did), the vision and, more importantly, the sense of satisfaction I'd get from finally being myself, seemed worth the risk.

And it has been. Nine years, a pandemic and three 'book babies' later, my decision to share the formula turned out to be the most illuminating, liberating and healing decision of my life.

I am sharing all this for a reason – to demonstrate that pain and pressure are an SSB owner's rite of passage to clarity of purpose and personal fulfilment. Like digging for diamonds, it takes blood, sweat, tears, time and tenacity to identify the business model that resonates with us; to pinpoint the business path that aligns with our personality, passion and purpose. The harder, more desolate the path, the greater our potential to improve or enrich the world through service to others – and to be rewarded and remunerated accordingly.

No book, course or coach can make the journey of business ownership a walk in the park, however for those with the noble intent of building a service-based business, the *Secret Service Business Series* can make the journey a whole lot smoother. Read with an open mind, attention to detail and a willingness to follow through, these three books can avert years of aimless stumbling in the entrepreneurial wilderness – transforming your business brain into a finely tuned GPS that directs you to SSB success via the fastest possible route.

That said, *The Secret Service Website Formula* is powerful in its own right. It was not only the diamond in the rough and saving grace of *my* business but many of our SSB clients, who had been digging aimlessly in the marketing dirt for years. It's my hope that the formula will be the diamond in the rough you're seeking too – skyrocketing your sales potential through the development of a *Lead Machine*, while unravelling the mysteries of modern marketing and design. Above all else, I hope the formula does for you what it did for me... rekindle the romance between you and your business, leading to the ultimate SSB satisfaction – thriving in the service of others.

PART ONE

FEELING THE LOVE: THE LOGIC OF A LEAD MACHINE

CHAPTER 1.

BRIDGING THE DIGITAL DIVIDE

Of all developments in human history, the internet is the most widespread and rapidly evolving. Used by over 87% of people in advanced economies and 44% in those still emerging, the web has transformed the way we seek and share information, and forever changed the way we communicate, problem-solve and transact.[1]

Yet, for the owners of small skill-or-service businesses (SSBs), the internet's monolithic scale and rapid-fire pace can be daunting. Despite good intentions, as many as 51% of small businesses don't have a website.[2] That's up to half of us who are missing a central piece of the modern marketing puzzle; perpetuating a cycle of struggle and self-doubt by underestimating the role that the internet plays in SSB success.

WHAT IS AN SSB?

To recap from the first book of the Secret Service Business Series, a small skill-or-service business (SSB) is one that:

- Has 0 to 19 employees;
- Draws on a body of skills, knowledge and/or resources in a particular area of expertise to satisfy customer needs or expectations;
- Primarily sells information, advice or assistance, manual labour, the use or benefit of physical resources, an experience, or a unique, handmade or customised end product to customers in its local area.

Note: A customised end product is a product tailored to suit the specific needs of a customer. In other words, it is made to order, not made to stock. That means the product would not appear, exist or function in its finished form without drawing on human know-how – usually through a process of consultation, assessment, design, development, installation and/or calibration. A building renovation, an irrigation system or air conditioner installation, the tailoring of a suit, creation of a floral bouquet or design and manufacture of a sail for a yacht, for example, are all reliant on human know-how and skill to determine, process and satisfy individual customer requirements. That's why, for the purposes of marketing, a business that sells a customised end product falls squarely under the SSB banner.

Of SSB owners *with* a website, most have an interesting tale to tell. Many have tried it all – dabbling with DIY development, calling in favours from design- or tech-savvy family or friends, exploring cheap offshore outsourcing and engaging high-priced agencies – all in the desperate pursuit of one seemingly simple thing: a website that works as a marketing tool for their business, driving leads to their inbox and sales to their door. But, sadly, this result is rare.

The more common outcome is a feeling of disappointment, disillusionment or full-blown resentment toward the web design industry. While these feelings may be warranted, they have contributed to a great divide of anguish and frustration between SSB owners and their web designers; a modern marketing stand-off preventing us from working together to achieve our professional potential. SSB owners are frustrated by a perceived lack of input and accountability from web designers, while web designers are frustrated by a perceived lack of understanding and appreciation from SSB clients. This paradox has made it near impossible to determine what marketing strategies we need to achieve our business goals without a costly, ongoing process of trial and error. For too long, it has stood in the way of progress in the SSB marketing field and inhibited the survival and growth of millions of businesses worldwide.

ECHOES OF THE DIGITAL DIVIDE

Things SSB owners say about websites and web designers:

'Websites don't work for my business.'

'I spent thousands on a website but haven't had a single enquiry from it.'

'Our website is only really there so we're taken seriously when we're quoting for new work but we don't get any leads from it.'

'My website is nothing like I'd hoped... I'm so disappointed.'

'As soon as I paid the designer, they forgot all about me.'

'My designer is AWOL most of the time – they never get back to me.'

'Web designers are a necessary evil.'

Things web designers say about their SSB clients:

'Clients expect a new website to fix all their problems – it doesn't work like that. A website is an online brochure, not a silver bullet.'

'I can create any website – big or small. The client just needs to tell me what they want.'

'They don't know what they want – it makes the whole process so hard' or the opposite... 'They know exactly what they want... who am I to argue?'

'Clients don't appreciate the time that goes into building a website.'

'Clients are never happy.'

'Getting content from clients is so frustrating.'

'Clients are a necessary evil.'

The key to ending the stand-off between SSB owners and web designers is acknowledging each other's challenges and frustrations. Only by putting the shoe on the other foot can we move past our feelings of resentment and join forces for the greater good, creating websites geared to drive SSB success.

The Secret Life of Web Workers

Since internet marketing emerged, website designers, developers and internet marketers have been flying by the seat of their pants. Just when they think they've got the techy stuff down pat (platforms, programming and other digital delights), the next cyber-tsunami of technological change rolls in. From *cascading stylesheets* and *content management systems* to the nuances of *responsive web design* and *Google algorithm updates*, they often find themselves at the bottom of a steep learning curve. Of course, they have the choice to close their eyes, hold their breath and duck – hoping the wave passes without impact. But those who do usually experience a barrage of passive-aggressive, disgruntled clients and, sooner or later, get swept out to sea.

Amid these giant waves of change, self-employed web designers experience stormy seas on a day-to-day basis. Web design is a tough, unregulated and unprecedented industry. Anyone can enter it but few stand the test of time. Between navigating the challenges of a service-based, time-for-money business, making ends meet in a highly competitive, global market, scrounging to collect useful website content from clients (the process of which – if you're doing it wrong – can be like pulling teeth), all the while trying to retain some semblance of artistic integrity, a career in freelance web design is not for the faint-hearted. It can be a painstaking, poor-paying pursuit of passion.

Why Web Workers Go AWOL

The intense pressure web designers exist under can cause even the most honourable to drop the ball. The struggle to stay afloat tends to manifest as poor communication, failure to follow through or non-existent follow-up.

I say this from experience.

Before refining the Secret Service Website Formula, I distanced myself from website clients as soon as possible after their site had gone live. I'd reply to emails and fix any bugs but I'd become difficult to reach by phone and under no circumstances would I initiate a discussion about whether a website was driving leads or boosting sales. I preferred not to know if it was working, for three reasons:

- **Budgets were too tight to do anything about it.**
  The prices we charged for websites rarely reflected the true value of the time and energy required to build them. This left little room in the budget to add value, provide additional support or go the extra mile.
- **I was just following orders.**
  When clients came along who confidently stated what they wanted, I'd take their lead, working with

ill-advised instructions and poor-quality content without question or comment – even if I knew the resultant website wouldn't engage its users. This was a subconscious self-defence mechanism. If I was merely following client orders, I couldn't be blamed for the site's poor performance.

- **Accountability was a heavy cross to bear.**
  In the state of constant stress I existed under, trying to hold myself accountable for the results of each website we developed (when I was spread too thin to figure out how to get predictable results for any one type of business, let alone all of them) was too much to bear. Instead, I buried my head in the sand and hoped for the best.

These feelings were not unique to me. To this day, they are the reason many web designers abandon clients after sites have gone live and bills have been paid.

Understandable? Yes. Acceptable or sustainable? Of course not. So let's bridge the gap.

The Results Rift

When SSB owners invest in a website (or other marketing endeavour), a monetary return is expected. In other words, *the only reason business owners spend money on a website is to make money.* Few web designers truly understand this; often detaching themselves from the results generated by the websites they build by boxing themselves into the role of *arty designer* or *code junky*. Little do they know that by detaching themselves from the end result, they are missing out on the greatest satisfaction of all... knowing that a website you've created has had a major, measurable impact on the profitability of a struggling business and relieved the burden of marketing from its owner.

Adopting the *arty designer* or *code junky* role can be beneficial in big business but for freelancers striving to make ends meet by designing websites for small businesses, it can spell disaster. Despite what we're led to believe, the effectiveness of a SSB website is *not* determined by the distinctiveness of the design, nor the quality of the code. It's determined by the marketing insight that underpins it.

Marketing is the function of a business concerned with attracting and retaining customers. It's what brings money in, so it's critical. Poor marketing is one of the main causes of stress and struggle for SSB owners and a leading cause of business failure. But much of this pain and heartache can be avoided when web designers are equipped to provide the marketing insight, advice and guidance SSBs so desperately need.

It might seem obvious that web designers need a strong working knowledge of SSB marketing – given that SSBs comprise a whopping 78% of businesses and potential web design clients[3] – but on the most part, it's a foreign concept. This is demonstrated by a quote from a struggling freelancer, captured during a small study I conducted several years ago:

'I've noticed a trend where graphic design roles seem to want the *all round* candidate, i.e. a graphic designer who can also do web design and maybe marketing as well! It's very annoying, as I consider them to be three different roles if they are to be done well.'

Having marketing and design as separate roles may be ideal but it's illogical for the majority of business owners. Why would you hire a marketer, when you're confident that all you need is a decent website? You wouldn't.

Successful web designers are successful because they bridge the marketing/design gap. They see themselves as a blend of several roles, with marketer or internet marketer at the top of the list.

But these all-rounders are a rare breed. Most web designers don't see themselves as marketers, to their own detriment and that of their clients. Even those equipped with the credentials and confidence to call themselves marketers are of little practical help to SSBs.

But it's not their fault.

Here's why…

The Faultline

Every year, thousands of fresh-faced marketers, web workers and graphic designers are churned out from tertiary institutions across the globe. Degrees, diplomas and design portfolios in hand, they are unleashed into the working world, equipped with the technical skills and creative fortitude to embark on a rewarding career in an exciting industry. Little do they know they've been trained to work for big brands and creative agencies (where jobs are few and far between), not to get real-world results for small business clients. Unfortunately for them, at the big end of town, the quantity of graduates far exceeds employment opportunities. Competition is fierce and the likelihood of employment at the end of a degree (for creative art roles at least) is lower than any other field of study.[4]

Through no fault of their own, many marketing, web and design graduates end up with incredibly frustrating freelance careers, spending years or decades trying to force the square peg of *big business know-how* into the round hole of *small business needs*. Anyone in this position will understand the struggle of finding clients, figuring out what to charge, communicating prices without scaring small business owners off and having to constantly compromise their artistic integrity to keep clients happy – all because they've never been taught to work with small businesses, let alone a subset as specific as SSBs.

Educational institutions rarely distinguish between the marketing and design needs of business subsets, at least not in any useful depth. Big business and SSBs usually get lumped together under the one broad banner of *business*, along with online retail, brick-and-mortar retail, NFPs, SaaS and other subsets with specialised requirements. This is causing undue stress and struggle for small business owners the world over, impeding the growth and success of their businesses and unwittingly contributing to the economic paradigm 'the rich get richer and the poor get poorer.'

While thousands of qualified marketers, designers and web workers flap and flounder with small business clients as they wait for their break with a big brand, hundreds of thousands of SSBs are in dire need of help. Unlike the big boys of business, who've had the resources to explore and experiment with the internet as a marketing platform, SSB owners have been left to their own devices; stabbing in the dark, feeling overwhelmed and undergunned, not knowing where to turn or who to trust.

The Unique Needs of SSBs

SSB owners have drastically different marketing and design needs to our corporate cousins, due largely to the depth and breadth of their resources. Big businesses have infinitely bigger budgets which allow for marketing planning, research, design and concept testing, and for going back to the drawing board if a design project or marketing campaign falls flat. SSB owners don't have that luxury. Most of us have one budget for a design or website project; one shot to get it right. Blowing that shot can have devastating consequences on our bank balance and financial reports, mental and physical health, capacity to provide for our families and our business' lifespan. If we don't effectively shoot our shot, it can be years before we can afford to try again... and by then, it may well be too late.

Another crucial difference between the marketing and design needs of SSBs and big business is their reliance on branding. For a sneaky reason, revealed in Chapter 3, big businesses rely heavily on their brands. They need distinct, cutting-edge and often artistic design to cut through the clutter. SSBs don't. Contrary to what most marketing and branding professionals say, fancy design and branding doesn't give an SSB any greater chance of survival – in fact, it can hinder success by being too corporate, cryptic or 'clever'.

A Bridge Over Troubled Water

So, now you know. Web design can be traumatic for web designers and SSB owners alike. Trying to survive as a self-employed web designer without the appropriate marketing insight and training, can be soul-destroying. Trying to survive as the owner of an SSB – desperately needing the insights, advice and skills of a results-driven web/marketing all-rounder, not knowing where to turn or who to trust – is equally so. Now we're even, it's time to build a bridge over the troubled waters of web design to unite in each other's best interests; working together to make the most of the extraordinary marketing opportunities the internet provides.

To the marketers, web designers and content creators reading this book... I am excited you're here. SSBs need you, which means over three quarters of the business population needs you. You have an important role to play, and there's plenty of money to make from it, but it'll require you to disregard much of what you've learned and observed about marketing, design and content to date. There may be some unlearning to do and resentment to drop. When you switch from resenting SSB clients for their limitations (not having a separate budget for marketing, not providing great content, not appreciating highly artistic, creative concepts, etc) to embracing them as welcome challenges, your career can progress in leaps and bounds – becoming more fulfilling and lucrative than you ever thought possible.

So, let's get to it.

CHAPTER 2.

C3 & CUPID'S ARROWS

Amid the action-adventure of building a viable business, developing a website can be a mission in itself – with foreign concepts to consider, daunting decisions to make and obstacles (both online and offline) to overcome. Many of us believe web development to be a highly technical process and, quite naturally, approach it by focusing on the skills and resources we lack... seeking out a web designer, DIY website platform or tech-savvy teenager to fill the gaps. But in getting caught up in the technicality of web design, we can set ourselves up to suffer years of marketing misery; missing the opportunity to build a site geared to streamline the entire marketing function.

Focusing too heavily on the technical side of web design can seal our business' fate because, although essential, it's not what drives leads for SSBs. What *does*, requires a more considered, bigger picture approach.

Every good action-adventure needs a juicy romantic subplot and, for us, the quest to woo website visitors is it. A website plays a critical role in SSB marketing, as illustrated in the ***Secret***

Service Marketing Wheel – the model that underpins the Secret Service methodology, recapped from the first book for quick reference below.[5]

Figure 1: The Secret Service Marketing Wheel

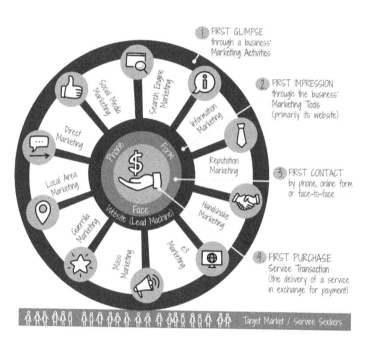

A website comes into play at step two of the Secret Service marketing process (the *first impression* phase), after a potential customer has become aware of our business' existence through one or more marketing activities and is interested enough to take a closer look.

Fatal First Impressions

For a potential customer, visiting a website for the first time is like an encounter with a stranger. Within the blink of an eye, an impression is formed, which sweetens or sours their perception and resultant experience. In a real-world rendezvous, there's time to turn things around if we (the stranger) get off to a shaky start but, online, we don't have that luxury. The decision to stay or leave a website is made in as little as 50 milliseconds of it coming into view[6] – a tiny window of opportunity to make a positive impression. If we miss that opportunity it's as good as over. The visitor will abandon our site to continue their search for a skill-or-service provider elsewhere.

Too often, the first impression made by an SSB website falls a long way short, sparking one or more of five negative emotional responses:

- **Concern** that the website is not safe, secure or legitimate in some way;
- **Confusion** surrounding what the business provides or the applicability of its offerings;
- **Frustration** at having to wait too long for website pages or elements to load;
- **Overwhelm**, having been bombarded by too much, messy or convoluted content – often the case with outdated directories or blogs;
- **Underwhelm**, having been insufficiently engaged by the site's look or feel.

Website visitors tend not to consciously acknowledge that they're concerned, confused, frustrated, overwhelmed or under-whelmed. It happens on an unconscious level, resulting only in a slight feeling of displeasure or detachment. It's like coming away from a first date, not knowing why you're not interested – just that there was no spark.

To function as a ***Lead Machine*** – an SSB website geared to consistently generate high-quality leads – a site needs to ignite a spark similar to what's experienced on a great first date, causing visitors to raise their eyebrows and think 'this might actually be *the one*'.

But how?

Brainpleasers

First impressions aside for a moment, human brains consist of two halves – a left side and a right side. The left brain is the logical, analytical side. It's the home of sequential language and verbal thought, enabling us to do things like read, write, calculate and evaluate. The right side is the emotional, intuitive side. It's where visual thoughts and memories, instinctive awareness (social, spatial, etc), creativity and emotions come from. Much of this is buried deep below the surface in the unconscious mind.

To form a first impression of anyone or anything, the right brain takes the data received through the five sensory inputs of sight, hearing, touch, taste and smell, processes it and generates an emotional or intuitive response. This right brain response heavily influences our thoughts and actions from that point, determining what information, if any, is filtered through to the left brain for conscious analysis.

When browsing online, the right brain's role as an information filter serves a handy purpose – protecting the left brain from getting bogged down with information and options. Without it, internet users would be infinitely more overwhelmed and vulnerable. Thanks to the right brain, we get an inkling as to what is and isn't right for us upfront, which saves a whole lot of time and brainpower.

When planning a website, most SSB owners are quite good at appealing to the logical left side of the brain. We know we need to introduce our business, outline our services, include our contact details and ensure the site looks and functions the way a website should. But that isn't enough. Taking a logical approach to the development of a website generates a lacklustre, logical response from those who visit it. We need more than a lacklustre response.

To create a high-performing site, we need to induce a resoundingly positive *emotional or intuitive response* – the spark mentioned earlier. This is done by appealing to a potential customer's right brain, with an emphasis on the abyss that is their unconscious mind. The equivalent of a *seven-year old child*, the unconscious mind responds best to images and visual cues, information presented in a simple, orderly, yet compelling way and clear, incentivised instructions.[7] This needs to be top of mind when planning and preparing content for an SSB website or it won't light the all-important spark, nor function as a Lead Machine.

Lighting the SSB Spark

For a site to induce a strong enough emotional response from visitors to serve as a Lead Machine, it must – quite consistently – satisfy three cognitive criteria:

1. Surprise and stimulate the right brain;
2. Impress the logical left brain; and

3. Make it easy and rewarding to take a specific, lead-inducing action.

In other words, the website must *connect, convince* and *convert*.

Figure 2: The Secret Service Website Formula (C³)

The Steps Explained

1. Connect

The first step – connecting with website visitors by surprising and stimulating the emotional right brain – is achieved by tapping into our visitors' most basic human need: the need for familial connection or **connectivity**. When potential customers feel a sense of familial connection with a business, a baseline level of trust and camaraderie is formed, which makes them less likely to focus on price and more likely to take action. This reduces the time and effort we need to spend to get sales over the line. Luckily for us, sparking this connection is easier for SSBs than any other type of business (as you'll discover in Chapter 3).

2. Convince

Once an emotional connection has been formed, we get the opportunity to impress our potential customers' logical left brain. Intuitively intrigued, they'll start to explore and analyse our website content. This is our chance to convince them that they've found the business they need and that it would be silly to go elsewhere.

3. Convert

Once they're adequately convinced, visitors warm to the idea of making contact. This can happen at any time, anywhere on the site and, at that point, we have to make it easy and appealing to take action; gently guiding them to contact us like holding the hand of a child to cross the road. No matter how engaged visitors are by our website, the conversion action is what really counts. As long as they are taking action, we are receiving leads, and as long as we are receiving leads, we have the opportunity to make sales – fuelling our business' existence.

Of the three steps that comprise the **Secret Service Website Formula** (*C3 Formula* for short), none require high-end design or complex code but they do require care, consideration and a quiver of 'Cupid's arrows'.

Cupid's Arrows (aka Marketing Amplifiers)

As Cupid has the power to make people fall in love (or so they say), the C^3 Formula has the power to make people who are seeking out a skill-or-service provider – referred to from here as *service seekers* – 'feel the love' for a business. Where Cupid uses a bow and quiver of arrows however, we use a website and a suite of functional competencies called *marketing amplifiers.*

Like Cupid's arrows, marketing amplifiers deliver the magic blow. They give a Lead Machine the ability to evoke a positive emotional response from website visitors – connecting, convincing and converting more potential customers into leads, thereby amplifying the effectiveness of our marketing efforts.

Figure 3: Marketing amplifiers - The functional competencies
underpinning a Lead Machine

Copywriting (Essential)　Photography (Essential)　Videography (Optional)　Web Design (Essential)

Each of the four marketing amplifiers is a profession in itself – a blend of art, science and skill, mastered over many years of education, experience, trial and error. This book is not intended to teach the fundamentals of these professions; it's intended to reveal the approach to take, and specific techniques to apply for each one, to maximise the chances of producing a Lead

Machine. With these insights, you can implement the aspects you feel comfortable with and confidently engage professionals to handle the rest, knowing exactly what to ask of them to put the Secret Service Website Formula into practice.

Copywriting

Copywriting is 'writing to sell'. It uses words – and the formatting of those words – to engage, educate and influence an audience for the purpose of attaining and retaining customers. Advertising headlines, slogans, scripts and the words that comprise brochures, signs and websites are all examples of marketing *copy*.

Copywriting is the aspect of content creation we are most likely to attempt ourselves. Many of us fancy ourselves as writers or, at least, think we're capable of stringing a few pages of website content together. But *writing* and *writing to sell* are two very different things – a difference that's nearly impossible to comprehend, let alone overcome, without the guidance of an experienced copywriter. Chapters 4 and 8–11 provide just that – a framework for producing compelling website copy, with practical steps, rules and resources to guide the writing of every word, whether you're collaborating with a professional copywriter or going it alone.

To avoid any confusion, 'copyright' and 'copywriting' are not related. Copyright is concerned with the protection of intellectual property from plagiarism or misuse, not the act or outcome of copywriting. For the purposes of this book, we are only concerned with the latter.

Photography

Photography is the process of capturing moments in time as still images. The production of high-quality photos requires not only a camera but an intricate knowledge of lighting, staging, timing, editing and more.

Of the four marketing amplifiers, photography is the most powerful in its ability to influence a first impression. The brain is visual, which means it responds quickest and most naturally to visual imagery. A photograph is not read and interpreted with the logical left brain; it is processed and 'felt' with the right brain. Understanding this is critical to the development of an effective website. Photography is key to evoking a positive emotional response from website visitors and passing through the 'first impression' filter.

For SSB owners, professional photography is the most under-rated, underutilised facet of the marketing function. Most of us dismiss it as a corporate luxury or optional extra but in doing so, we miss the main opportunity to spark a connection with potential customers via our marketing materials. Professional photography is as imperative to an SSB's marketing efforts as a phone or business card, and must be prioritised accordingly.

That said, not any professional photo will do. To make an emotional connection with service seekers, we need a specific style of photography, capturing a certain subject at a designated place and time... all for an important reason, revealed in Chapter 5.

Videography

Videography is the production of audio visual files; the planning, recording, editing and publishing of moving pictures accompanied by sound. With the internet as a platform for sharing video, it has become a mainstream marketing function, giving us the power to introduce, educate, demonstrate and even deliver certain services, without a physical audience and without spending a cent.

Like the cherry on a cake, adding the right video to a Lead Machine can make a visitor's experience sweeter and our service offering more enticing. A carefully crafted video can generate a considerable upswing in leads; boosting our website's ability to connect, convince and convert by simultaneously engaging the left and right sides of the brain.

Despite its benefits, video is the optional extra of amplifiers. A video is not necessary for a Lead Machine to work. In fact, it's better to have no video at all than one that's ill-considered or poorly executed. So, if the time or money is not available to produce a high-quality video (as outlined in Chapter 6), it's fine to put it aside and focus on the other amplifiers, secure in the knowledge that a Lead Machine doesn't need a video to reap game-changing results.

Web Design

The term **web design** refers to the graphic design of web pages and the conversion of those page designs (often called *wireframes*) into a finished, functional website. To produce a Lead Machine however, there's a bit more to it.

The Secret Service approach to web design, referred to later as **service-centric design**, is a different take on the traditional web design process, with a swag of benefits for SSB site owners and designers alike. It prioritises marketing effectiveness over all else; drawing on the needs and psychology of service seekers to produce an online marketing tool that is far superior to conventional websites in its ability to connect, convince and convert.

Service-centric web design is born from empathy; putting ourselves in the shoes of service seekers to anticipate their emotional and physical response to each planned page. It considers what they need to see and feel in order to take action. Getting this right requires careful consideration of the service seekers' needs – not just their superficial need for a product or service but their unconscious emotional needs... the needs that make them human (explained in greater detail in Chapter 14 of *Secret Service Marketing*, 'Needs to Know'). As technical or convoluted as this may sound, there's no need to worry. In most cases, these unconscious needs can be met by adhering to the Secret Service Website Formula. They've all been carefully considered and factored into the C^3 steps.

At this stage, the most important thing to know about web design is that it alone can't create a Lead Machine. Equal emphasis must be given to the three essential marketing amplifiers (copywriting, photography and web design) for a site to adequately connect, convince and convert. The role of web design is to bring everything else together and present it in the friendliest, most engaging and effective way – just as a brilliant actor brings out the best in a storyline and is so natural in their role that you forget they're acting.

UX for SSBs – From Confusion to Clarity

Until now, the closest thing to purchasing this book would have been hiring a *user experience (UX)* designer specialising in SSBs... if they existed. UX design and its cousin *user interface (UI)* design are a relatively recent progression in the web design industry, aimed at improving the performance of websites by optimising the experience of those who use them – from the layout and structure of pages to seemingly insignificant details like the colour of buttons and choice of fonts. However, most UX and UI designers work with big businesses and established ecommerce stores – the businesses that can afford to pay for their expertise. As introduced earlier and explored in greater detail shortly, SSBs have vastly different marketing and design needs to other businesses. That means many of the insights that could be offered by corporate UX designers would be irrelevant anyway – and certainly not communicated through an easy to follow, replicable formula.

Since the concept of user experience gained notoriety, web design has progressed in leaps and bounds. But the lack of attention given to the user experience of SSB sites specifically, has left SSB owners stuck with sites developed with a primitive, pre-UX approach. Many of us have had our website redesigned time and time again, in the hope that a newer, 'better' website will hit the mark, only to find that it makes no difference. It might look a bit prettier. It might display better on a mobile phone. But it doesn't drive any more leads or sales than the old one did and we're left wondering where we went wrong.

With this book as your guide, any run of bad web design luck can finally come to an end. *The Secret Service Website Formula* is UX for SSBs made simple. The psychology has been studied, theories developed and tactics tried and tested, then distilled down to a potent blend of design and content specifications. Over the coming chapters, you'll acquire all the UX insight you need to create SSB websites that meet or exceed the expectations of service seekers so, from this point on, you can settle for nothing less than a site that delivers an exceptional user experience.

CHAPTER 3.

WINDOW TO THE SOUL

Before we explore *how* to use the four marketing amplifiers to implement the C³ Formula, it's important to know *why*. As with any elective business endeavour, if we don't know why we're doing it, we can't embody it and our efforts will likely be in vain. But if we know *why*, we can embark on it empowered by purpose and better equipped to navigate any obstacles, making us more likely to follow through.

Why Follow the C³ Formula?

There's an unwritten assumption in the world of business that bigger is better. Big businesses have more resources, customers and clout. If they talk, the market listens. With their strong, well-established brands and multi-million-dollar ad campaigns, they are perceived as far superior to small business – a greater threat and a more solid investment.

That's why, when it comes to marketing and design, most SSB owners look up to big business. We see their bold brands, clever ad campaigns and sophisticated websites and seek to emulate them, assuming that's what it takes to succeed. This assumption leads us to make marketing and design decisions with a *fake it 'til you make it* mentality. Whether it's naming our business to imply we're bigger than we are (a sole trader operating as Global Services, for example), spending thousands of dollars on fancy branding, plastering stock images of non-existent tele-sales staff on our website, or dabbling with ads we can't actually afford, *fake it 'til you make it marketing* is common among SSBs. Many of us strive to present our businesses as corporate enterprises, thinking that – by looking like we should be taken seriously – we'll grow to fill the shoes of the corporate image we've created. But it doesn't work that way.

For SSBs, *fake it 'til you make it marketing* is not an effective approach. In trying to fit in with the big boys, we fail to stand out – like wearing beige against a beige curtain. But nullification of our marketing efforts is not the worst possible outcome. Corporate fakery can have the exact opposite effect to what we intend; driving potential customers away and our business into the ground. Instead of faking it 'til we make it, we can fake it 'til we flop.

So what are SSB owners to do? If following the marketing rules set by the big boys is not in our best interest, whose rules do we follow?

The answer is... our own.

We need a different approach to marketing and design than our corporate cousins because SSBs *are* different. The enormous disparity in our size, scale, reach and resources, means we are playing a different game by default. That's not to say our SSB can't grow *into* a big business but as long as it fits the definition of 'small' (fewer than 20 employees), a corporate approach to marketing and design is not in our best interest. We need an entirely different playbook to stay in the game.

The Big Difference

The key to successful SSB marketing and web design lies buried in a crucial distinction between big businesses and SSBs... the *intention* or *why* of their existence.

Big businesses exist to keep shareholders satisfied by reaping the perks and profits of mass production. Whether producing a good or a service, the more units a business produces, the less it costs to produce each one. This is due to increased efficiencies and buying power and the ability to spread fixed costs (such as rent and salaries) across more units of output. At a mass scale, per-unit costs are reduced to a bare minimum, exponentially increasing profit margins. Maximising efficiencies at scale (producing the highest volume at the lowest cost) is like entering a slipstream in which production and profitability are amplified. This phenomenon – known as *economies of scale* – underlies the existence of big business. Without it, growing so big would be more trouble than it was worth.

The vast majority of SSB owners don't strive to maximise economies of scale. We strive to build a viable business on a foundation of mastery in our chosen field; one which meets customer needs and contributes to the community, while affording us a lifestyle we love. This endeavour is simpler, purer and a whole lot more human than the big business quest for economies of scale and yet we tarnish it by comparing our game to theirs. We become blinded by our limitations and inefficiencies – unable to see the strength of the cards we're holding.

Bigger is *not* better. It's just different. Big businesses need mass resources to make economies of scale possible and mass marketing to make it viable. SSBs don't. What we need is a simple approach to attracting and retaining customers; an approach that derives a healthy return on investment and requires as little of our time and attention as possible, so we can focus on doing what we do best – being of service.

Although SSBs don't have the resources of big businesses, we are no less capable of marketing success relative to the size and scale of our operations. But as long as we see our business size as a hindrance and yearn for resources to compete on a grander scale, this success can remain elusive. Getting sustainable marketing results becomes possible when we accept and embrace our small business limitations and recognise the value of the intangible marketing asset that comes hand in hand with them... our SSB 'soul'.

The Soul of Business

Luckily for us little guys, it's not just the cost-per-unit that drops as big businesses move closer to achieving economies of scale. Beyond a certain point of growth and systemisation, the amount of human influence and intensity (or 'soul') that goes into the production of each unit drops too. The tipping point at which this energetic shift begins differs for every business; it could be a change of leadership (the appointment of a new Managing Director, CEO or Board of Directors), a change in structure or shareholding (instigated by a merger or acquisition, or being floated as a public company), or simply a crackdown on KPIs. Whatever the cause, a good or service begins to lose its soul when the business' scale of priorities tips from a delicate balance of people *and* profits, to profits *over* people.

Figure 4: The Soul Scale

People – The best interest of staff, suppliers and customers

Profits – The money that's left after a business' expenses are deducted from its revenue

Once profits take precedence, the only thing that gives a good or service a sense of soul is its **brand.** For these 'soul*less*' businesses, a brand is a face-plate, worn to mask the sometimes ugly, oily cogs of the profit-churning machine behind it. Big businesses invest so much money on brand development because their brand creates the *perception* of soul. A big business' brand *is* its personality and often, its main point of difference. Without a carefully crafted brand, there is little human energy in a mass produced good or service for consumers to relate to or connect with.

Unlike in businesses that prioritise profits over people, the soul of an SSB does not need to be forced or fabricated via a fancy brand.[8] It exists organically, as a result of the energy and input of the key individuals in the business – particularly that of the owner. As the owner, we are the heart of our business and our distinct blend of *personality*, *passion*, *purpose*, *physical presence* and *technical prowess* is its soul. This unique soul tonic – squalid, sparkling or something in between – filters down through every element of the business, influencing the perceptions and actions of every stakeholder. It attracts warm, personal interactions and repeat patronage, or it repels them.

When harnessed, this sense of soul gives SSBs the ability to meet the most primitive of human needs... the need for **connectivity.** Connectivity is simply connection and interaction with other people for the purpose of getting our needs and wants met. It's utilising and benefiting from the insight, knowledge or skills of others – through a mutually acceptable arrangement of supply, trade or exchange – to survive, create or maintain a suitable lifestyle, and develop as individuals.[9]

From the moment we're born, we rely on other people – usually our family unit – to satisfy our needs. These range from simple physiological needs, such as food and warmth, to complex emotional ones, like affection and achievement. As we grow into independent adults, our needs and wants expand to encompass all manner of goods and services our family unit is no longer equipped to provide. In the modern world, our needs are so vast and varied that we have to transact with others to have them fulfilled. Enter the SSB.

SSBs fill the void of connectivity left by the family unit. As such, our role is not only to fulfil the service-based needs that customers are not capable, equipped or inclined to fulfil themselves, but to *provide a sense of familial warmth, comfort and support*. When we do this, we transform the customer experience from neutral to positive... from beige to blazoned with colour. Our business becomes a safehaven of trust that not only meets customers' surface-level needs but their deepest, most unconscious ones.

SSBs are more capable of connectivity than corporations. When businesses strive to maximise economies of scale, the quantity of customer relationships takes priority over the quality of those relationships, leaving little scope for meaningful connection. Top-tier managers (the 'C-suite') become inaccessible to customers and half-hearted staff come and go. Employees and customers are identified by numbers, which inadvertently dehumanises them, and procedures, protocols, rosters and rotations prevent close working relationships forming between the two. Both may stay seemingly loyal to the machine of big business but this is often only out of a 'better the devil you know' mentality, a lack of suitable alternatives or plain apathy.

In an SSB, top-tier management is us – the owner. We are a constant presence in our business, with a vested interest in its success. We determine its culture and the level of connection between staff and customers. We have the capacity to engage and interact with customers personally and meaningfully, make decisions on the spot without the red tape of corporate enterprise and foster genuine loyalty. Our humanity, coupled with our business' inherent reliance on us, makes our SSB human by association. It's capable of connectivity in ways big business is not.

Connectivity: Love Tonic for the Little Guy

SSBs can leverage connectivity in two ways. The first is *connective operations:* the formation and maintenance of familial relationships with customers in operational interactions. This means treating customers like family – with the warmth, consideration and respect they deserve. Operational connectivity requires us to be fully present and humble in the service of others and to activate our performance persona (explained in Chapter 5 of *Secret Service Marketing*, 'Rally the Troops to Thrill Current Customers') at the start of every workday.

Improving operational connectivity has an array of benefits. It can boost customer spend and retention rates, increase the likelihood of positive reviews and word of mouth, and make running an SSB more meaningful and rewarding. But as beneficial as it is, improving the quality of our interactions with existing customers is not a reliable growth strategy. We can't force them to transact with us regularly, promote our business to others, or spend increasing amounts of money. We can hope they will... but hope is not a strategy.

To grow, an SSB needs more leads in its sales funnel; more opportunities to convert potential customers into paying customers. Contrary to popular belief though, generating more leads doesn't necessarily mean engaging in costly marketing activities like advertising. Often, SSBs get ample exposure to potential customers through organic means. We just fail to convert it into leads by not creating a strong enough connection with potential customers in our marketing communications. This failure cannot be overcome by increasing our marketing activity. Spending more time or money on marketing activity when a lack of activity is not the problem, only multiplies our losses. To fix the underlying problem – low lead conversion rates – we need the second stream of connectivity: *connective marketing.*

Connective marketing uses our small business soul as a lure to catch and keep the interest of potential customers and boost our chances of reeling them in. Like a love tonic, it has the power to amplify our potential customer's natural feelings and alter their course of action. It creates a feeling of comfort and familiarity, which leaves them wanting more... wanting to experience the operational connectivity depicted in our marketing.

Connective marketing is powerful stuff, driving more leads, higher sales and ultimately, business growth. But before we delve deeper into the use of our SSB soul as a lure for leads, there's some confusion around a particular business concept that needs clearing up.

The 'Separate Entity' Marketing Misconception

From the moment we seek advice about starting a business, it's drummed into us that a business owner and their business are two separate entities. For accounting and tax purposes, this *separate entity principle* is both wise and correct – ensuring our *business'* financial affairs are kept separate from our *personal* financial affairs, so our business records aren't tainted with personal transactions. But despite its applicability from a financial perspective, the separate entity principle has no place in the day-to-day operations of an SSB, nor in its marketing.

As SSB owners, we are intrinsically linked to our businesses. Without our involvement at an operational level, the majority of SSBs would cease to exist. Although the consequences are more subtle, the same can be said about marketing. Without factoring ourselves into our marketing communications – infusing them with our profile and personality – marketing effectively and sustainably can be a real struggle; our business will be repeatedly perceived as another beige-coloured, corporate clone. When we present ourselves as one-and-the-same with our business (in a carefully considered and executed way), everything changes... the marketing function becomes a whole lot easier and the pressure of corporate fakery is released.

Connective marketing requires putting ourselves out there in the best interest of our business, which isn't as scary as it might sound. It doesn't have to mean speaking on stage, plastering our face on billboards or magazines, or doing live video feeds on social media (unless we feel driven to do so). For most of us, all it takes to enjoy the benefits of connective marketing is a specific type and style of content stationed on our website.

SSB Website: Window to the Soul

Before the internet, contacting a service provider was a service seeker's only option to move beyond initial awareness. There was no actionable step between seeing a provider's ad, for example, and making two-way contact with them. No way for the service seeker to undertake anonymous research. No way to indulge their curiosity without making themselves known to, or interacting with, the provider they were considering. Although we didn't recognise it back then, this gave us (SSB owners) a distinct advantage. It gave us the opportunity to make a human connection with service seekers during the research phase – influencing them through the cultivation of positive feelings, so their decisions weren't based on logic alone.

But the internet changed all that. Now, service seekers have the ability to investigate and assess service providers anonymously, with no interaction at all. They can indulge their curiosity from a safe distance, with no risk of unwanted sales pressure and no obligation to take further action. As a result, the advantage we didn't know we had, has been lost.

This subtle power shift knocked our marketing efforts off balance. Some SSB owners were knocked so hard their businesses collapsed. Others wobbled but managed to steady themselves. And many are still wobbling – unable to find a sturdy combination of marketing tools and activities to lean on. For those who continue to wobble, the key to regaining balance is realising that the 'online research' phase of seeking out a skill-or-service provider can be used to our advantage, with a website geared to evoke the same feelings that used to be cultivated through that initial two-way communication.

Conventionally, most of us think of our website as an online business card, ad or brochure, displaying a fleshed-out version of our usual marketing messages. This approach may satisfy our visitors' logical left brain but not the unconscious need for connectivity that stems from the emotional right. It might make them think a little bit, but it won't make them feel anything different from the websites of similar businesses.

How we *should* be thinking of our website is as a window to our SSB soul; a platform to showcase our personality, passion, purpose, presence and prowess through the four marketing amplifiers of copywriting, photography, videography and web design. Our marketing messages are still necessary but they must be optimised and balanced with the humanity of who we are and what we do.

When we shine a light on our SSB soul in this way, it breathes life into our marketing communications. The humanity, authenticity and transparency our website conveys, sets the stage for service seekers to feel a connection with us *before* they consider interacting with us, emotionally interrupting their search for a suitable skill-or-service provider. It makes our business infinitely more appealing, boosts the likelihood of service seekers converting into tangible leads and – as an added bonus – differentiates us from every other business in the world.

Prepare to Bare Your Soul

It's natural to feel reluctant about putting yourself in the spotlight for the purposes of connective marketing. The prospect of appearing in photos and videos in particular, can be quite disconcerting, especially for those of us who are at all self-conscious, camera-shy or concerned about the judgements of family and friends. But here's something to consider...

Prior to the emergence of big business in the late 19th century, there was no big business. As recently as the mid-1800s, small business *was* business. At that time, common sense and best practice dictated that an SSB owner should merge their personal identity with that of their business for the purposes of marketing. Due to the limitations of publishing back then, this meant incorporating their personal name into their business name, such as 'William P. Dolliver – Auctioneer and Appraiser',

'John Lloyd's Undertaker's Wareroom', 'Howard's Dining Rooms', etc – a practice which gave the business individuality and credibility.[10]

Somewhere along the way, in the quest for big business growth and greatness, SSB owners started dabbling with corporate fakery. We stopped proudly representing our businesses in our marketing and started hiding behind logos and corporate imagery. In striving to fit in with the big boys, we stopped standing out. We relinquished our connectivity and authenticity – our greatest marketing strengths – disregarding hundreds, perhaps thousands, of years of best practice.

A corporate brand is a façade. SSB owners are not. We are real people with real personalities, real values and the ability to establish real connections with others. When we leverage this through connective marketing and operations, we have the ability to acquire and retain customers by making them want to connect with us as much as they want our product or service, if not more. Baring our SSB soul is just as powerful (relatively speaking) as a corporate brand but far more authentic, and a lot less expensive to build and maintain.

Now that we know this, it's time to return to our roots – reclaiming our connective marketing power uninhibited by the technological limitations of old. Where once an SSB's business name was its main means of connective marketing, we have a suite of tools and technologies at our disposal. All it takes to make the most of them is a willingness to step outside our comfort zone for the greater good.

If the idea of connective marketing makes you deeply uncomfortable, ask yourself *why*. If it's because you feel awkward about appearing in photographs, or inadequate in some other way, push through until Chapter 5. We'll cover this common little sticking-point there. If it's because your business has a poor reputation and you don't want to associate yourself with it, or you don't feel your results are good enough to stand by, then your intuition is telling you something else. Most likely, it's that you need to rework your business model (as per Chapter 11 of *Secret Service Marketing*, 'Agility: Use it or Lose it'), configuring it in such a way that you are proud to be seen as the driving force and connective face of your business.

Associating your personal identity with your business can feel uncomfortable or risky, but when compared to the leap of faith required to start a business in the first place, it's no risk at all. By going out on your own, you chose to go against the societal grain, despite very real risks of judgement and failure. Connective marketing is simply 'backing' that bold decision. It's one of the simplest but most profound contributions we can make to our business, our customers and ourselves. Be brave and bold enough to make the move – like starting a conversation with an attractive stranger – and the rest might be history.

CHAPTER 4.

COMPELLING COPY: THE LOVE LANGUAGE OF A LEAD MACHINE

A website without words is like a tour without a tour guide. With no one explaining what's what and where to go, the best sights, most pertinent information and overall significance of the visit will be lost. But the mere presence of words is not enough. Just as the insight, organisation and attitude of a tour guide can make or break a tour experience, the style, structure and tone of the words on a website can make or break user experience; causing a potential customer to take an excited step towards a service transaction, or cringe and click away.

A website's written content – as with any text-based business communication – exists on a spectrum, from *technical copy* at one extreme to *sales copy* at the other. Technical writing and sales copywriting are like chalk and cheese. They're two very different writing styles that produce very different results.

Technical Writing

Technical writing uses words and sentences to inform and educate, as in a case study, report or user guide. It's the writing style that comes naturally to many of us because it's what we're taught in school. As soon as essay writing becomes necessary, we start to recognise that the aim of the writing game is to make ourselves sound as smart as possible to boost our chances of getting a good grade. We're rewarded for communicating facts as articulately as we can, using sophisticated vocabulary and adhering to strict rules about grammar, sentence structure and formatting. Ideally, these practices become second nature, infiltrating and enhancing our written communications for the rest of our lives.

But technical writing skills can also be a hindrance, particularly when trying to write engaging website content or promotional copy. In its purest form, technical writing is long and detailed, with a plethora of subject-specific jargon. To fully absorb and appreciate it, readers require concentration and commitment. That's fine in certain circumstances but for marketing communications – particularly on SSB sites where attention spans are at a minimum – it's too much to ask. Most service seekers don't want to wade through the technical intricacies of our methodology or materials, at least not on our website's main pages. If our homepage is arduous and boring, it implies we'll be arduous and boring to work with – instantly turning visitors off.

Technical copy on a homepage will start something like this:

'Welcome to Groundgate Plumbing'

Groundgate Plumbing was established in 2008 in response to market demand for a plumbing

> company specialising in the installation and maintenance of septic systems in the broader metropolitan area…'

As you might have experienced reading this yourself, by the end of the first line of body content (at most), attention starts to wane. Reading turns into skim reading or worse, not reading at all. Because the business' point of difference – a clear field of specialisation – is not revealed until the second line, most visitors would overlook it, disregarding the business as 'just another plumber' based on the heading and first line alone.

Needless to say, pure technical writing is not ideal for SSB marketing communications and has no place on the homepage of a Lead Machine.

Sales Copywriting

At the other end of the spectrum, **_sales copywriting_** uses words and the formatting of those words to steer potential customers towards the actions we want them to take, ultimately culminating in sales. Sales copy is more conversational, inclusive and emotive than technical copy, which makes it much easier to read and understand. As a writing style, it's more relaxed and flexible to the extent that many of the most powerful sales copywriting techniques fly in the face of generally accepted writing principles.

However, pure sales copy can be all fluff and no substance. It can ramble on and on (as in an old-school, long-form sales letter), playing on the reader's every fear and hope, with little regard for the time and attention-span of readers. Depending on the demographic of the target market, this can be a highly effective approach but that doesn't make it honourable. For SSB marketing – where integrity, authenticity and transparency are key – pure sales copy is entirely inappropriate.

Compelling Copy: A Blend of Both

To be as effective as possible, SSB marketing communications require a balanced blend of technical and sales writing. Technical content without any sales charisma will fall flat, driving service seekers to distraction. Sales copy without technical substance will come across as shallow, cheesy and even condescending, driving potential customers away for an entirely different reason. For SSBs, the secret to *compelling copy* is to combine the best of both styles; fusing the charisma of sales copywriting with the substance of technical writing to produce copy that's not only insightful and educational but engaging, influential and easy to read.

Compelling copy is particularly vital on an SSB website, where the window of opportunity to connect with potential customers is miniscule. Bombarding visitors with a wall of tiresome technical copy or shallow sales copy squanders the chance to use words to connect, convince and convert. While technical or sales copy at its purest is a barrier to generating online leads, the right combination of both can be a goldmine.

To Write or Not to Write

Compelling copy is critical to the survival of businesses of all sizes but the ability to write it rarely comes naturally. That's why professional copywriters exist. The role of a *copywriter* is to examine a business' objectives and offerings, identify and extract the hidden gold (unique selling proposition, benefits, social proof and more) and craft it into a dazzling piece of written work that's fit to draw the attention, interest, desire and action of its target market – like an eye-catching diamond ring in a jewellery shop window. Ironically, however, the copywriting industry is an understated and undervalued one. Many of us don't know what a copywriter is, let alone that hiring one could be the missing link in our marketing efforts and one of the smartest investments we ever make.

Not realising that outsourcing our content writing is an option, most of us take the DIY approach by default. That might be okay if we were introduced to the purpose and principles of compelling copy before school solidified technical writing as our go-to style... but unfortunately, we're not. So, for the vast majority, a technical style it is; approaching the written content for our website as we'd approach writing a report – in a logical, detached manner – not realising that, from a marketing perspective, we're completely missing the mark.

Typically, it's not for months after seeing our website go live, that we realise it's not having the desired effect. Disillusioned and disappointed, it can be easy to blame the designer, the internet as a marketing medium, or both... when the problem (or one of them, at least) may be our choice of words.

3 Keys to Compelling Copy

Becoming a compelling copy writer requires three key strengths:

1. **Lateral thinking** – A willingness to escape the confines of traditional writing and design principles to write

objectively, with consideration to what will mentally, emotionally and visually stimulate readers. Thinking laterally is also a vital aspect of digging for copywriting gold – asking the right questions and wading through information, features, facts and figures to extract and communicate meaningful benefits.

2. **Empathy** – The ability to put ourselves in the shoes of our *ideal customer* (a hypothetical person we most want to attract and work with) to write from a place of awareness and understanding. Great copywriting involves envisioning the problems, pains, challenges, values, expectations, beliefs, misassumptions, desires, hopes and fears pertaining to a product, then writing to acknowledge and address them. Note that empathic reading is a crucial part of copywriting. It's only when we stop, slip into the shoes of the customer and read back what we've written – visualising their emotional reaction to it – that we can feel if our copy is weak or strong.

3. **Wordsmithery** – The ability to communicate sometimes complex or boring concepts in a way that's concise, meaningful and entertaining for the reader.

The combination of strengths required to write compelling copy rarely come naturally but most of us have the capacity to develop them. It just takes practice. The more you write, the better you get.

As much as I'd love to equip you with a fill-in-the-blanks template for the development of compelling website content, it wouldn't be in your business' best interest. Every SSB is different – with different people, personalities, customers, offerings, goals, resources and values. To be as effective as possible, a business' website content needs to convey these intricacies with a uniquely engaging, personalised and authentic voice. A template would defeat this purpose (not to mention undermine our *search engine optimisation* – aka *SEO* – efforts by breaching Google's 'duplicate content' rule). But that doesn't mean we need to go it alone.

If all this talk of compelling copy has you in a state of panic, outsourcing it to an experienced professional may be your best bet. Even those of us who consider ourselves reasonable writers can benefit from some objective insight and assistance. We all get caught up in the operational intricacies of our businesses, which can make it difficult to see the forest for the trees – an essential aspect of planning and writing content to connect, convince and convert.

Hallmarks of Lead Machine Love Language

Whether you seek the assistance of a copywriter or opt to DIY, there are three principles to bear in mind to boost your chances of creating a Lead Machine.

1. **Prioritise connection over keyword injection**

   Striving to 'rank number one on Google' is a worthy goal for most SSBs, which can have enormous payoffs in terms of website visitors, leads and sales. Unfortunately though, in the quest for higher rankings, many SEO agencies prioritise the injection of commonly searched keywords and phrases into headings and body content above all else. This act of 'keyword stuffing' produces content that is annoyingly repetitive at best and awkwardly nonsensical at worst. When keywords are repeated too many times or injected into sentences with no regard for their readability, a site's content comes across as generic, monotonous and contrived. It won't connect, it won't convince and it certainly won't help convert visitors into leads.

That's not to say that the inclusion of keywords isn't important. Identifying keywords and phrases that potential customers are using to search for our services, then weaving them into our content, is incredibly important. Our website can only be considered relevant to a search engine user, if the terms they search for are featured in its content. If Google can't match the searcher's terminology with the words on our site, it can only deduce that our site is not relevant to their search.

To sum it up, keywords *are* a priority... just not at the expense of well-crafted copy, equipped to connect with, convince and convert website visitors. There's no point using cunning keyword stuffing tactics to drive traffic to a website if the poor quality of its content is going to drive them away.

The injection of keywords in our content is one way to improve our site's performance in search engines but it's not the only way. As outlined in Chapter 3 of *The Modern Marketing Arsenal,* there are various things we can try to boost our SEO without spending any money. Beyond or failing those, respectable SEO consultants have a myriad of tricks up their sleeves to help websites rank higher in search listings. Many of these techniques are implemented behind the scenes, having little bearing on page content, readability or the capacity for potential customers to engage with us through our choice of words.

2. **Remove the mask**

As highlighted in Chapter 3, many of us let ourselves down by depicting our business as a corporate enterprise – whether it's to avoid being perceived as a 'backyarder' or 'one-man band', or to avoid limiting our business' geographic reach. Any fear of being seen as *too small* can be spotted a mile off on an SSB website – reflected in the images chosen to represent the business and the style and tone of its written content. They result in an inauthentic representation of the business; a website that works as a lead repellant, not a Lead Machine.

Contrary to our business size insecurities, service seekers appreciate the benefits of working with micro-businesses more than ever. It's well known that engaging smaller providers can have an array of benefits, stemming from low overheads and flat organisational structures, so many service seekers actively seek SSBs out. But when we present our business as bigger or more corporate than it is, we make this difficult for them – repelling them with a cold, inauthentic image.

To feel a connection with us through our website – a connection strong enough to compel them to take action – service seekers need exposure to the humanity behind our brand. They need to see a human face, hear a human voice (through the tone of our written words) and sense a human soul. This means removing the mask – the characterless corporate image we think we should be conveying – to reveal the driving force of our business: our SSB soul (the alluring blend of personality, passion, purpose, physical presence and technical prowess introduced in Chapter 3).

3. **Hit a home run**

The homepage of our website plays a particularly important role in establishing a connection with service seekers. It's where the majority of visitors enter our site, which means it receives the most traffic and is responsible for making a strong first impression. The composition and content of the homepage determine whether potential customers stick around long enough to peruse other pages or leave, never to return. Yet many of us waste this precious space on elements we think we need to look professional: a generic heading such as 'Welcome to our website', a few facts about the business and a stock photo or two. But by ticking the perceived boxes of a suitably professional homepage, our business can disappear into marketing mediocrity.

Instead, the homepage of a SSB website needs to be compelling; presenting a snapshot of who we are and what we can do, in a way that grabs and holds the attention of website visitors. The choice, placement and formatting of words on the homepage is pivotal to this, increasing the likelihood of service seekers exploring our website with an engaged, open mind.

Following these three simple rules – along with the steps, tips and techniques outlined in Chapters 8–11 – your website content will speak a language more service seekers will understand, believe and respond to, whether you're briefing a copywriter or writing it yourself.

Learning to apply Secret Service writing principles can feel a little foreign at first – like learning to engage and respond to the love language[11] of a romantic partner – but stick with it. With practice, it will start to flow and become infinitely easier to strike and sustain an emotional connection with potential customers.

Note that, even if you're not planning to write website content yourself, the Secret Service writing principles are still worth learning. With them, you can: 1) keep the individuals tasked with content writing on track, 2) gear your day-to-day, text-based communications to connect, convince and convert, and 3) craft marketing materials that are not only strategic, but full to the brim with a seductive blend of substance and soul.

CHAPTER 5.

PHOTOGRAPHY: PHOTOS TO SWEEP 'EM OFF THEIR FEET

The slickest segue from copywriting to photography is the old saying: 'A picture is worth a thousand words.' As cheesy as it may be, this saying serves a valuable purpose – conveying how powerful images can be as a means to communicate with others.

Before we get carried away though, it's worth clarifying that, when it comes to SSB marketing, words and images are mutually dependent and therefore, equally important. The ability to connect, convince and convert is stunted when words are not complemented by suitable images, and vice versa – images without words are futile. So the words and images we use to represent our business, online or offline, warrant the same high level of consideration.

That said, there is a fundamental difference between how humans process words and how we process images, which makes choosing the right images for our website all the more important.

Processing written words requires certain learned skills, namely reading and language fluency. When reading, our brains are required not only to identify individual characters within hundreds or thousands of groups of characters on a page, but to apply our own logic to derive meaning from them. Reading also takes time, relative to the length of the document or page. The more words there are to process, the more time it takes to read them. Depending on the amount and style of writing, the mental exertion and time investment required can be all too much.

Processing images, on the other hand, is a walk in the park. No particular skills are needed to derive meaning from an image. In an instant, an image can inform, explain, identify and generate powerful conscious and subconscious associations, giving rise to all sorts of assumptions and assimilations unique to each and every viewer.

The most powerful thing images can do is evoke emotion; happiness, sadness, curiosity, repulsion, fear, excitement and everything in between. Although words can do this too, it requires more time, motivation and effort from viewers, through the act of reading, to experience an emotional response of the magnitude of a great image. Such an investment is rare. Bombarded with so many written words each and every day – a high proportion of which are trying to sell something – many worthy words get overlooked or tuned out.

For the purposes of SSB marketing, the difference between words and images can be boiled down to this: processing written words is primarily a left brain (logical) activity, while processing an image is primarily a right brain (emotional or intuitive) activity. Images have the ability to bypass our conscious, rational mind and speak straight to our unconscious; to our 'heart' or 'gut'. In other words, we don't just see a great image, we feel it.

For that reason, images are one of the most important, yet undervalued elements of a skill-or-service provider's website. The right images enable website visitors to feel a connection with us from the moment our website loads. It can instantly differentiate our business from competitors and spark a primal, familial desire to work with us. Without this sense of connectivity, potential customers have no choice but to make a brain-led, logical decision, which – more often than not – results in a decision based on price.

But it's not just any picture that can spark such an influential, emotional response. The power of a picture is entirely variable, depending on its relevance, subject matter, production quality, composition and more. While the right images *are* worth a thousand words (or a thousand customers as the case may be), the images that most of us tend to prioritise in our marketing communications do little to help our cause. Pictures such as logos, graphics and images of a general nature may help draw the eye and establish relevance but they do nothing to meet our potential customers' need for connectivity. The only images that do *that* are photographs... and only certain ones at that.

Unfortunately, the photos that SSB owners and their web designers tend to gravitate toward when seeking to add visual appeal to a website are **stock images.** It's *unfortunate* because stock images can completely undermine an SSB's marketing efforts, with a double whammy of repercussions. Not only can they distort the perception of a business through the eyes of potential customers, they come with an enormous opportunity cost: missing out on the biggest SSB marketing opportunity in the world today.

A Crock of Stock Photography

For those unfamiliar with them, stock images are professional quality photographs and graphics (such as illustrations) made available by photographers and designers for the conditional use of others. They are obtained via online platforms that serve as vaults for millions of image files. Some of these – such as iStock, Shutterstock and Dreamstime – are paid services that charge a fee for the right to use an image, while others – Pexels and Pixabay for example – make images available for free under Creative Commons licensing.

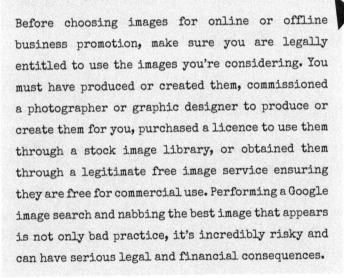

RESPECTING IMAGE RIGHTS

Before choosing images for online or offline business promotion, make sure you are legally entitled to use the images you're considering. You must have produced or created them, commissioned a photographer or graphic designer to produce or create them for you, purchased a licence to use them through a stock image library, or obtained them through a legitimate free image service ensuring they are free for commercial use. Performing a Google image search and nabbing the best image that appears is not only bad practice, it's incredibly risky and can have serious legal and financial consequences.

There are stock images for almost any imaginable subject, from 'asking questions' to 'flying zebras' and everything in between. All it takes to source an image is to choose a reputable service, enter a search term, browse the gallery of results until an image appears that fits the bill, check the pricing and licensing conditions to ensure it's suitable for its intended use and follow the instructions to download the file. Being so quick and easy to source, and cheap in comparison to the services of a professional photographer, it's little wonder stock images are a popular choice for SSB owners and web designers seeking high-quality images to represent a business. Whether it's a shot of a project manager on a construction site, a dripping tap or pool of water for a plumbing service, or a flawless model with long flowing hair for a hairdressing salon... stock images are an SSB owner's marketing dream come true, right? *Wrong.*

The trouble with stock images is that they're generic by nature. Most stock photos – particularly those pertaining to business – are designed to have general relevance and broad appeal to maximise image sales or downloads. Because of this, they have a certain look about them; a look which is difficult to explain in words, but can be spotted a mile off by anyone who's had the experience of trawling through a stock library on a quest to find a suitable image. As Megan Garber of *The Atlantic* magazine observed, 'To see a stock image is, Potter Stewart-style, to *know* you're seeing a stock image.'[12]

Stock photos tend to be highly staged or posed, with any human roles played by anonymous models or actors. They are usually enhanced or embellished with Photoshop effects – edited to within an inch of their life. Some of the 'stockiest' images for commercial use include isolated shots of highly attractive actors posing awkwardly with tools of particular trades, and teams of stone-faced glamour models (selected to ensure a politically correct distribution of gender and ethnicity) stationed strategically around boardroom tables.[13]

Generic stock images of people are detrimental to our marketing efforts in two main ways. Firstly, they are completely inauthentic – misrepresenting who we are and what our business looks and feels like. Although not illegal, visually misrepresenting the owner, management or staff of a business is the equivalent of false advertising. It not only undermines our integrity, inhibits our credibility and diminishes our authority, it can muddy the perception of our business with feelings of detachment or scepticism – deterring customers instead of attracting them.

Secondly, generic stock shots do nothing but conceal our SSB soul with a clumsy corporate mask. They strip us of our humanity, individuality and integrity; the very things we must reveal to generate the marketing momentum we're capable of.

Whether they're of people, places, products, or any other visual subject, stock images are energetically neutral. A stock photo is created independently of the business it represents, which means there's no energetic connection between the two. This matters, because it renders it incapable of evoking the kind of emotional response required to drive leads to an SSB. Even stock images with high contextual relevance (such as photos of a car's engine to represent the services of a mechanic) are energetically neutral. They may logically reinforce the type of service on offer and provide some generic, visual stimulation, but they won't stimulate the brain on a deeper level.

No matter the subject, stock photos waste the opportunity for a website to cultivate a connection with potential customers through the powerful form and function of photography. Featuring stock imagery on an SSB website instead of connective imagery and expecting the site to work as a Lead Machine is like leaving the eggs out of a soufflé and expecting it to rise.

It won't work, because it's missing the key ingredient. Stock imagery is the antithesis of connective marketing and a surefire way to stifle a site's performance.

To be fair, stock photos can be a highly useful resource and do have a place in SSB marketing. For a web designer needing contextually relevant background images, a content writer looking to break up a wall of text in a blog post or an SSB owner preparing a graphic-rich PowerPoint presentation, stock photos can be ideal. If carefully chosen, they can also be good for adding visual context to service pages, such as a picture of a burst pipe on a 'Plumbing Emergencies' page. However, the selected images should never be pictures of people, places or particulars that are noticeably unaffiliated with the business, as they will only detract from its authenticity.

SSB Photography: The Real Deal

With the Secret Service approach to marketing, images worth the proverbial 'thousand words' are the real deal... genuine photos *of* a business, produced exclusively *for* that business.[14] By their very nature, genuine photos are energetically charged with our humanity, integrity and authenticity, giving our marketing communications the ability to spark connectivity in an instant. Switching from generic to genuine imagery has the effect of removing the corporate mask to reveal a charming, trustworthy and seemingly familiar friend; one that potential customers feel drawn to connect – and do business – with. The value of this switch can't be emphasised enough.

The services of a professional photographer may seem like an optional, avoidable expense when all we think our business needs is a website, but high-quality, genuine photography (of a very specific type – revealed shortly) is the most critical of Lead Machine components. For most SSB owners, this requires a big mental shift. It means prioritising the engagement of a photographer *before* seeking the services of a web designer. Whether we're developing a new site or updating an existing one, photography must come first.

Before organising photos for a website, two fields of photography need to be considered: ***product photography*** and ***people photography***. For many of us, these terms conjure mental images of catalogue-ready consumer goods or real-estate-style headshots. As such, both are often dismissed as 'irrelevant' or 'unnecessary' to SSBs but this couldn't be further from the truth. Most skill-or-service providers produce a physical service outcome or 'end result', which can be photographed as a product to contextualise what we sell. Explored later in Chapter 12, product photography (if relevant) is enormously beneficial, providing undeniable evidence of an SSB's capabilities. However, there's a critical component of our market offering that product photography doesn't capture... our connectivity or SSB soul.

People Power

If you have a social media account, you would have likely experienced the power of connective imagery first-hand. It's what causes us to get more 'likes' and comments when we post photos of *ourselves*, *family or friends* than when we post images of nonhuman subjects. That's because photos of us and our 'tribe' provide a window into our world, appealing to the innate social needs and curiosities of our online followers.

Despite a website being a tool for professional connection, the needs of website users are no different to the needs of social media users. Photos of us and our 'business tribe' (staff and customers) are necessary to provide a window into our professional world and appeal to the innate connective needs of potential customers. Photos of products alone can't compete, just as photos of smashed avo on toast are no match for photos of fellow humans on social media. If the subject is not human, it can't fill the need for human connectivity.

As mentioned earlier though, there's a big difference between connective photos of people and the traditional, portrait-oriented headshots we've come to associate with real estate advertising and political campaigns. While traditional headshots are better than no photos at all, they follow a stock-standard, generic formula; the same body angle, the same blank background and the same slightly strained smile. No aspect of this formula is conducive with connectivity.

So what is?

The answer lies in a particular style of photography, used to produce SSB-specific photos as high in quality as stock images... with a couple of crucial, connective twists.

Feel-the-Love Photography

Discovered on my quest to produce SSB sites that actually worked, *feel-the-love photography* is a style of commercial photography that blows stock imagery and the traditional headshot out of the water. With the skill and adaptability of two brilliant photographers – Gianna in Adelaide and Michelle in Sydney – a theory based on nothing but gut-instinct was tried, tested, tweaked and found truer than I could have imagined. Combined with quality copywriting and design, the images we produced had a striking effect. Upon launching a website, leads would often start flowing in – like we'd turned on a tap. What was even more exciting was that these websites seemed to produce reliable and relatively consistent results (stuff that marketers' dreams are made of). Seeing its incredible impact, I made feel-the-love photoshoots a nonnegotiable inclusion of our website packages and the style became a signature of our work.

Coordinating feel-the-love photoshoots was one of the things I enjoyed most about working with the owners of trade service businesses. A common thread emerged between our most successful clients and their resultant photos... a quiet, down-to-earth humility – the kind that only comes with true integrity and mastery of your field. The images had an 'X factor' which attracted potential customers like moths to a flame.

The Feel-the-Love Photoshoot Formula (detailed in Chapter 13) originated from an incredibly simple, yet powerful idea: that potential customers are more likely to engage a skill-or-service provider (or at least, take action towards doing so) if they get the opportunity to *visually validate* them first.

Visual Validation in Days Gone By

A couple of hundred years ago – before the internet, television, email and phones – connecting with potential customers in person was an SSB owner's main means of generating business. If someone needed the services of a blacksmith, for example, they'd visit a local blacksmithery to outline their requirements in person. Before saying a word, however, they would have formed a first impression, based on an unconscious observation geared to answer the question: 'Does he/she look like a good blacksmith?'

Answering this question would require a myriad of micro-judgements, such as:

- Are they dressed like a blacksmith?
- Are they set up with the premises, tools and equipment to serve as a blacksmith?
- Do they look confident as a blacksmith?
- And do they seem approachable?

With a foundation of connectivity established through this visual validation process, the customer would proceed with a verbal enquiry. From that point, as long as the blacksmith was attentive, engaged, capable of meeting the customer's needs and not too overpriced, a deal would be done. By the time price was discussed, a personal connection would usually be established, making it harder for service seekers to walk away on the basis of price. For most, it would have been easier to justify a higher price and proceed with the transaction than endure the inconvenience of having to find an alternative, cheaper provider – so they'd just go ahead.

Amid the industrial revolution and emergence of big business, the crucial role that visual validation played in the acquisition of new customers for SSBs was overlooked. As communication and transportation technologies developed, many of us realised our businesses didn't need to be visible or accessible from the street to survive. At the same time – influenced by the faceless, impersonal nature of corporate enterprise – our marketing efforts became less personal and our humanity became less visible to those seeking our services. In an effort to fit in, we no longer stood out.

Visual Validation in the Modern World

The tendency to 'corporatise' our communications is one of the most easily rectified reasons why SSB owners struggle with the marketing function. To make our communications stronger, all we need to do is give potential customers the opportunity to visually validate us – like they had centuries ago. Unlike days of old, however, this does not require us to work from a street stall or meet every potential customer face-to-face. We just need to be visually accessible on our website through carefully crafted, photographic imagery; images that satisfy our potential customers' urge to verify our humanity, technical aptitude and physical ability to deliver the required service. In other words, we need images that make us look good at what we do.

Achieving this requires a fusion of people and product photography, with an emphasis on one person in particular... us – the owner. It's images of an SSB owner that service seekers are most intrigued and engaged by. We are the pinnacle of authority and accountability in our business and the source of its substance. Without us and our unique soul blend of personality, passion, purpose, physical presence and technical prowess, our business would not exist. Our SSB soul is our greatest marketing asset, which means *we* are our greatest marketing asset and professional photos of ourselves must take pride of place on our website.

When captured and conveyed through professional photography, our SSB soul transmutes into marketing connectivity. Its effect can be likened to celebrity appeal; causing service seekers to feel like they know and trust us already and that making contact with us is the next logical step. Given the importance of service seekers taking action (to come into our awareness as sales leads), this is an incredibly handy benefit.

Equally beneficial is the fact that, by nature, photographs of us and our SSB visually differentiate us from other businesses. No two SSBs or their owners look the same. Given ever-present threats from competition and globalisation, the ability to differentiate ourselves from every other business in the world – through a simple, one-off photoshoot – is an opportunity we'd be crazy to pass up.

It's called *feel-the-love* photography because the aim of the game is to communicate, through photographic images, the passion we have for what we do and who we serve. Upon seeing our photos, potential customers need to quite literally 'feel the love' we have for our work – be it treating patients in a clinic, serving food in a restaurant, laying bricks, fixing cars, cleaning offices, driving tow trucks, consulting with clients, writing reports, taking photos (yep – even photographers need feel-the-love photos), crafting jewellery… whatever the core functions of our business happen to be. Feel-the-love photos provide a visual insight into what working with us and our business family looks like. They are an honest reflection of who we are, what we do and where we work, captured in the best possible light (literally and figuratively).

Trouble 'Picturing' Yourself?

A photo shoot can be a daunting prospect – and that's okay. In truth, few of us are head over heels about being photographed, let alone becoming the face of our marketing communications, but it's something we need to accept and embrace if we want to give our business the best chance of success.

The strongest feelings of resistance about feel-the-love photography tend to arise at the first suggestion of it. When introducing and explaining the concept to groups of SSB owners in training workshops, I noticed some would instantly recoil. It was clear through their body language that they'd dismissed the idea before ever really considering it. In talking to them and reflecting on my own experience, this resistance stemmed from two root causes.

1. **An overactive ego**

   The most common way to dismiss the need for feel-the-love photography is to deem ourselves 'too old', 'too fat', 'too ugly', 'too modest', or too 'something' to be the face of our business. In reaching such a demeaning conclusion, what we're really doing is letting an ego-based fear of judgement (usually the imagined judgement of family and friends) get in the way of doing what's best for our business. It's a self-defeating determination; allowing personal fears and insecurities to take priority over the marketing needs of our business and the connective needs of our potential customers – in turn, limiting our capacity to earn a plentiful living and contribute to the world through service to others.

   While we may not be in our physical prime, nor the most spectacular human specimen, we are exactly who and what our business needs to visually represent it – just as we are. If service seekers responded to superficial perfection, stock photos of airbrushed models would be the ultimate lead driver (which they're not). What they *do* respond to is authenticity – images of us, doing what we do... and loving it. The power of feel-the-love imagery comes not from capturing our physical beauty but from capturing our physical presence as an involved business owner, with a side-serving of personality, purpose, passion and prowess. Rest assured, it's our humanity, authenticity and substance – in conjunction with the technical nuances of the Feel-the-Love Photoshoot Formula outlined in Chapter 13 – that paves the way for visual validation and connectivity, not catwalk-worthy good looks.

It's worthwhile remembering that by going into business in the first place, we chose a different path than most of those around us. We identified an opportunity to do things better or differently within our chosen field of service and seized it. We weren't worried about what people thought of us then and, if we were, we got over it by focusing on the needs of our customers. We believed going into business was in their and our best interests, so we set aside our fears and did it anyway.

A feel-the-love photoshoot is no different. If you're struggling to picture yourself front and centre on your website, it's time to revive the feeling of ambition, confidence and excitement your business was built upon. Once the photoshoot is done, the final images are received and your Lead Machine is working, it will be hard to comprehend a website without feel-the-love photos taking pride of place.

2. **Substandard service**

No SSB runs like clockwork from day one. Some take months to provide a consistently high level of service, while others take years or even decades. The time it takes is largely determined by where a business owner is at in their business journey.

Some of us start out in business by jumping in at the deep end – flapping, floundering and gulping for air until we discover how to tread water, then eventually, how to swim. Others start at the swimming stage, with a wealth of experience in their chosen field (the equivalent of a few swimming lessons) and the ability to deliver high-quality service outcomes (the equivalent of a few laps). But we can only swim so far, without the quantity or quality of our strokes diminishing. At some point, we must figure out how to build a sturdy boat (a viable business model) if we're to survive the stormy seas of business long term.

Where we're at in our business journey impacts our confidence and, in turn, the effectiveness of a feel-the-love photoshoot. If we're at the 'treading water' stage, questioning our ability to deliver a service outcome we're proud of – as I was for many years – the idea of being photographed may feel wrong... and rightly so. We can't expect to 'feel the love' for our business if we're not delivering a calibre of service we're proud of. Nor can we expect a photographer to capture the love we have for our business, or potential customers to be influenced by it, if that love doesn't actually exist.

Faking it 'til you make it only carries us so far. There's a calm, unforced power that comes from having genuine confidence and pride in your business' abilities – a culmination of wisdom, experience and integrity. This develops over time, through mastery of your field; thousands of hours of decision-making and action-taking and resultant highs, lows, successes and failures. It's what feel-the-love photography captures and conveys and what potential customers find most alluring. But it must be genuine. If it's faked, the images won't have the same connective impact.

If you don't feel the love for your business yet, don't force it. Hold off for a few months. Focus on improving your service outcome, customer by customer, or 'stroke by stroke' until you can swim more steadily.[15] As soon as you feel a flicker of confidence, read Chapters 13 and 14, find a feel-the-love photographer and schedule your shoot.

It's worthwhile noting that receiving and viewing the images from a feel-the-love photoshoot can be quite a poignant moment. Something interesting, bordering on transcendental, can happen. Seeing images of ourselves in all our SSB owner glory can fan that little flicker of confidence into a more fervent flame. It can cause us to feel the love for our business more intensely and with more certainty than before... a subtle benefit of implementing the Secret Service Website Formula but one that can further amplify its impact on our business and our life.

While it can feel a little self-indulgent, or even narcissistic, to make ourselves the face of our business' marketing efforts, the opposite is actually true. Putting the connective needs of our potential customers and the marketing needs of our business ahead of our fears and insecurities is chivalrous, generous and courageous. It's not selfish to give website visitors the opportunity to visually validate and sense a connection with us, nor to allow our business to capitalise on our human presence so the marketing function can become easier and less expensive... it's selfish not to.

When we actively and authentically put the needs of potential customers ahead of our own ego, the stormy seas of business start to quell. New opportunities and possibilities emerge, marketing becomes manageable (if not, enjoyable) and we open ourselves up to reaping the immense rewards of marketing connectivity.

Like wearing our heart on our sleeve in pursuit of a romantic partner, a degree of courage and confidence is required to apply the Feel-the-Love Photoshoot Formula – courage to put ourselves out there and confidence that the right people (our ideal customers) will be attracted to us, align with our intention and meet us halfway. It's a tiny risk to our ego, for a potentially enormous reward; a small step out of our comfort zone to a more authentic and abundant career of service.

CHAPTER 6.

THE VIGOUR & VIRTUE OF VIDEO

Compelling copy and feel-the-love photographs are the heart and soul of an SSB site. They are what make the powerful forces of connectivity and visual validation possible; giving us the opportunity to tap into a natural spring of hot leads or be forced to go divining for them elsewhere. As such, copywriting and photography comprise two of the three marketing amplifiers that are essential to the production of a Lead Machine. Along with service-centric web design (the focus of Chapter 7), they are necessary and nonnegotiable, with no exceptions.

The remaining amplifier, videography, is different in that it's entirely optional. Unlike good copy, photos and design, not having a video on our website will not preclude its performance – it might cap it at silver instead of gold-medal-worthy, driving a few less leads per week or month, but it certainly won't knock it out of the race. More often than not, the results obtained through activation of the three essential amplifiers prove sufficient. But for those of us with the desire to put our best marketing foot forward and the budget to go 'all in' with a full quiver of Cupid's arrows, a strategically produced feature video can be an excellent investment.

Video is a powerful addition to a website because it transforms it into an interactive, multi-sensory experience. It adds a dimension to marketing communications that static words, photos and design cannot – one of sound and movement. This is not to suggest that any video is a worthy addition to a website, however. While the right type and style of video can improve the performance of a Lead Machine, the wrong video can stifle it; overshadowing positive first impressions and scaring potential customers away.

Viva La Video: The Online Video Revolution

The opportunity for businesses to connect with potential customers via video is not new but it has never been so accessible to SSBs. From the moment the first television commercials emerged in 1941, TV advertising quickly established a reputation for being the most effective and lucrative form of marketing communication. The combination of *video* as a means to communicate to potential customers and *television* as the medium for that communication, was incredibly powerful. Not surprisingly, it sparked enormous demand from advertisers. But with a finite number of ad slots available on any given channel on any given day, supply was limited. This kept prices at a premium – rendering TV advertising out of reach for the vast majority of businesses.

With the advent of the internet, the game changed. The benefits of video-based communication became available to everyone, including the smallest of SSBs, and users lapped it up. In 2016, video already accounted for 73% of global internet traffic[16] and over a billion hours of YouTube videos were being viewed each day.[17] That's a lot of time, traffic and videos.

It's clear that internet users prefer video content to walls of text. And it makes sense. As explained earlier, reading is cognitively demanding. Watching a video isn't. Video does the mental heavy lifting for us, so we can sit back, relax and absorb the information being presented to us without any real effort.

The human preference for video content, combined with the accessibility of the internet as a platform for sharing and viewing it, has created a perfect storm for video content to thrive. Unlike TV, the internet is globally accessible, has an infinite number of channels and programs and is entirely user driven. Users decide what to watch, when to watch and for how long. Compelled by an insatiable appetite for information and entertainment, we've not only embraced online video, we've come to expect and crave it. It has infinitely expanded our view of the world, giving us instant access to insights and experiences that, not too long ago, would have gone unrecorded and unshared – including those pertaining to goods and services.

Acknowledgement of this reality has seen buzzwords such as *video first content* and *video first marketing* popping up, coined by big business marketers with their finger on the pulse of online behaviour. Corporations such as Facebook are recognising the power and magnitude of video and investing heavily in it as a result; prioritising video above all other forms of communication.

Video marketing is less of a priority for SSBs but the tide is gradually changing. In 2018, the Yellow Social Media Report indicated only 5% of Australian small businesses and 11% of medium businesses used YouTube with similar findings elsewhere.[18] In 2020, the report showed the cumulative total had risen to around 25%.[19] While small business owners are more likely to utilise (or at least dabble in) video marketing, our resistance to YouTube is a concern. It indicates that, in one pivotal way, we are missing the lowest hanging fruit on the video marketing tree.

The term video marketing tends to conjure thoughts of webinars, live video streams on social media and the semi-staged educational videos prevalent on YouTube. These are all forms of *video content marketing* – a subset of *information marketing* that can prove beneficial for SSBs but requires a substantial investment of time and energy to facilitate and sustain.[20] In reality, the ongoing commitment required to reap the rewards of video content marketing is too much for many of us... and that's totally fine. It's not everyone's cup of tea. But electing to avoid video content marketing doesn't mean we should write video off completely.

Video as a Website Enhancer

The alternative to using online video as a marketing *activity* is to use it as a marketing *amplifier* – a means to boost the effectiveness of our marketing efforts through the enhancement of our website. A *website enhancer video* is a one-off, carefully considered, professional production... a far cry from the slap-dash and semi-professional videos associated with video content marketing. To be effective, an enhancer video needs to be geared for connectivity and longevity and be fit to take permanent pride-of-place on our website. A spontaneous, on-the-run recording won't cut it.

The role of an enhancer video is not to drive traffic to a website but to help capitalise on the traffic that's already finding its way there. Through its mere presence, a strong enhancer video has the capacity to increase conversions by transforming a website into a tool for multisensory engagement and next-level connectivity, providing an immersive, yet easily-digestible experience at the click of a play button.

Enhancer videos are not TV-style ads, nor old-school sales videos. Despite fitting the bill as 'one-off, carefully considered, professional productions', TV ads and sales videos tend to have a blatant commercial agenda which – if given pride-of-place on a website – would likely do more harm than good. Unlike the audiences of these other productions, website visitors are under no obligation to be advertised or sold to – they can simply click away. That's why, in the age of online video, brash commercialism and high-pressure sales tactics are out, and connection, education and empowerment are in.

A website enhancer video is a tool for exactly that. It's a means to connect, educate and empower, by providing service seekers with an audiovisual portal into our world; one that allows them to reach their own conclusion about who we are, what we do and our suitability as their service provider. As such, great website enhancer videos are – like feel-the-love photos – carefully planned and produced to connect with website visitors on an emotional level, increasing the likelihood that they'll be logically convinced, then convert into leads... without ramming a sales pitch down their throat.

Enhancer Video Options

For SSBs, three styles of video are worthy of consideration.

1. **Testimonial video** – A video of a customer sharing their experience of finding and transacting with a business. Done well (which doesn't necessarily require professional production, explained later in Chapter 15), video testimonials can provide powerful social proof, giving potential customers the opportunity to see and hear for themselves just how reliable and trustworthy a business is. A series of great testimonial videos on our website not only makes us appear more authentic and believable, it makes our service offering more enticing... inducing the *When Sally Met Harry* effect of 'I'll have what she's having.'

2. **Explainer video** – As the name suggests, an explainer video is used to *explain* how a product, service or process works. It does this in a simple, lighthearted and entertaining way, usually through animation. Explainer videos capture the attention and imagination of viewers by taking them on a short, educational, audiovisual journey. They can be an effective way to make a new or potentially confusing business concept more palatable, which makes them a popular marketing tool for internet marketers and businesses with nontraditional but clearly-defined business models.

3. **Micro-documentary** – A video used to convey the reality, humanity and artistry of a business, in a style similar to a television documentary.

Despite their obvious differences, testimonial videos, explainer videos and micro-documentaries have three things in common: their length, longevity and the need for planning.

The most effective enhancer videos are *short* – between 45 seconds and 3 minutes long, due to the time sensitivity of website users. They're also *designed to stand the test of time*, with content that will stay relevant for years, rather than weeks or months. Lastly, they're *well planned out with a solid structure*. This doesn't mean they should be scripted – in fact, testimonial videos and micro-documentaries usually turn out better if they're not. It simply means there's a plan in place to design, film and edit the required footage – prompting and recording the necessary dialogue and capturing all required shots.

Which Enhancer to Activate?

Of the three types, testimonial videos are the quickest, easiest and cheapest to produce, making them the most accessible. With suitable subjects (customers who are delighted with their service outcome) and a planned approach (outlined in Chapter 15), the production of testimonial videos is relatively foolproof and can add immense value to an SSB site.

Explainer videos are accessible too but they're only relevant when there's a genuine need for explanation. For most SSBs, an explainer video is overkill. Service seekers know roughly how a restaurant, hairdresser or building company works – they don't need cartoon characters to act it out. For innovative businesses with a product or process that warrants explanation, an explainer video can be worthwhile, however, its efficacy hinges on the viability of the underlying business concept and the quality of the script. If the concept and copywriting are on point, an explainer video can be an excellent addition; if they miss the mark, no amount of animated artistry will make up for it.

Generally though, explainer videos aren't the best option for

SSBs because they fail to capitalise on our superpower of connectivity. An explainer video is geared to convince the logical left brain and appease the right; gratifying the inner-child that is the unconscious mind through the use of fun-filled but superficial imagery. While this can evoke a positive response, it's nothing like the invaluable sense of trust, confidence and camaraderie that can be sparked by an unanimated video; one that captures the humanity of a business and provides website visitors with a connective, visually validating experience.

Achieving this requires much the same approach as it does in feel-the-love photography but with video instead of still images. Both require careful planning of people, place and particulars, professional production, a well-coordinated 'shoot' and a focus on the owner to capture the heart and soul of an SSB on film. However, given the added dimensions of video (namely sound and movement), there are extra considerations involved; considerations that are easiest to identify and interpret by thinking of the project not just as the production of a video but as the production of a micro-documentary.

The Feel-the-Love Micro-Documentary

A documentary is 'a nonfictional motion picture intended to document some aspect of reality, primarily for the purposes of instruction, education, or maintaining a historical record.'[21] It's a video-based exploration of a real life subject, often used as a form of journalism, advocacy or self-expression, for the purpose of garnering interest, attention, awareness, understanding or support. Documentaries ooze credibility, authority and expertise and, as such, tend to be perceived as reliable and trustworthy reference materials.

It's this trustworthiness that makes a traditional style documentary the optimum website enhancer video for SSBs, with the exception of its length. Most documentaries produced for TV or online streaming are in the realm of 45 to 90 minutes long. This is perfectly acceptable to Netflix users but not service seekers on a website. To add optimum value to our website, a documentary must provide immediate engagement and be consumable within a matter of minutes. It needs to spark visitors' curiosity, feed their unconscious need for connectivity and visual validation, then leave them wanting more. This is not achieved by presenting a full length feature film explaining the intricacies of our business model or operational processes, but rather by presenting a compelling teaser – a micro-documentary of between 45 and 180 seconds in length.

Unlike a TV ad or sales video, the aim of a micro-documentary is not to sell to viewers, but to immerse them in the reality of our business. This 'reality' is our soul blend of personality, passion, purpose, physical presence and technical prowess. It's *what* we do (the physical skills and processes used to bring service outcomes to fruition), *how* we came to do it (our humble beginnings) and *why*; why we love doing what we do, why our service fills a need or gap in the market, or whatever 'why' stirs the most passion within us. Capturing this in documentary form has a powerful pulling effect, as opposed to the unsolicited push of a TV commercial. It creates a perception that our offering is more than a paid service – it's an admirable feat of human energy and expertise.

The production of a micro-documentary requires us to casually discuss and demonstrate our services on film, with no sales-oriented agenda and no script to read. The aim is for viewers to feel the love we have for the work we do. Not having a sales-focused agenda or script helps facilitate this, unbridling the love in two ways. Firstly, it liberates us to be natural and authentic without the pressure of delivering the perfect pitch. Secondly, it provides an educational, artistic experience for viewers that is far more compelling and infinitely more memorable than a sales pitch; making our services feel like a contribution to our community, rather than a means to meet monthly sales targets.

If a service is not particularly visual or glamorous, it's logical to question its suitability as the subject of a micro-documentary, e.g. 'Who in their right mind would want to watch a micro-documentary of my work as a financial planner or dry cleaner?' This is a valid question, with a two-part answer.

Firstly, beauty and artistry exist in every service, even in the most menial of tasks. Whether it's skimming through a financial report or pretreating stains on a shirt, there are visual intricacies of every job that can make surprisingly interesting viewing when seamlessly captured and cut together as a video. All it takes to isolate and showcase the artistry of these moments is a talented videographer with a keen eye for detail and the right equipment.

Secondly, beauty is in the eye of the beholder. As boring as the provision of a certain service may seem to the masses, to those in the market for it, it can prove fascinating. Service seekers are highly curious and particularly receptive to content presented in an easily-digestible audiovisual format. In service seeking mode, the opportunity for them to watch a video showing a skill-or-service provider in action can be quite irresistible. Many will watch with keen interest, looking for notable points of difference to justify making a decision and taking action. Watching a financial planner or dry cleaner do and discuss their work may sound yawn-worthy, but to a curious service seeker it can be quite enthralling – fast-tracking them to a state of being ready to commit.

Videos in the style of feel-the-love micro-documentaries are, at this point in time, few and far between. That's a good thing. The fact that they're not mainstream is one of the reasons micro-documentaries present such an incredible opportunity for SSBs. There's a point of difference in having a micro-documentary at all... let alone in the irreplicable uniqueness and connectivity of its content.

Videos to View

Referenced below are two brilliant micro-documentaries, both showcasing skill-or-service providers who specialise in sculpture, for ease of comparison.

Figure 5: Illustrated representation of a micro-documentary produced by *Little Story Films* – Nick Warfield, *The Art of What's Left Behind* www.littlestory.com.au/dance-music-art

Figure 6: Illustrated representation of a micro-documentary produced by *Human Postcards* - John George, *It's All About the Carvings* | www.humanpostcards.com/john-george

As these examples demonstrate, a micro-documentary is not something to whip up on a smartphone. To have the desired effect, it should be created with the proficiency and professionalism of a genuine TV production, utilising the services of an experienced filmmaker.

While a micro-documentary may not be the cheapest website enhancer video, it is undoubtedly the most enduring. Done well, feel-the-love micro-documentaries have a plethora of connective and business benefits, which can last for years or even decades. Tapping into these benefits requires working with a filmmaker to create an honest, audiovisual account of us as an expert in our field (the process of which is outlined in Chapter 15). The aim is to produce a video that captures the heart and soul of our business, as if documented for its social and historical significance. Approaching it this way is the key to creating a video that's both beneficial and long-lasting – not only serving the connective needs of our potential customers, but as a momento and proud reminder of the skills we've mastered, the business we've built and the legacy we'll leave behind.

CHAPTER 7.

WEB DESIGN: MORE THAN JUST A PRETTY FACE

If it's not obvious by now, this is not a typical book about web design. There are no screenshots of specky sites to emulate nor strings of programming code to consider, because creativity and technical dexterity are not what we nor our web designers are missing. What's missing is an approach to web design that produces more than just a pretty online face.

There are creatively- and technically-brilliant web designers all over the world, chomping at the bit to materialise our visions of the perfect website. But therein lies the problem. The status quo web design process is such that web designers tend to ask for, accept and execute an SSB client's vision for the look, feel and functionality of their new site, without questioning its capacity to serve as the business' most crucial marketing tool. That means they're unknowingly designing to meet a brief that doesn't take the business' marketing needs into account, thereby producing a site that's likely to disappoint.

Changing the status quo outcome requires changing the status quo process. But to stand a chance of changing such a deeply ingrained, widely accepted practice, we need to go back to basics... what the purpose of website design is and what makes a web design great.

The Role & Responsibility of Web Design

Website design is the field of work relating to the production and maintenance of websites (sets of interlinked pages of online content). It requires a fusion of skills and disciplines, from graphic design and web host management to fluency in various platforms and programming languages, to convert wireframes (graphic design mockups) into fully functioning websites. For organisations with complex website requirements, these skills and disciplines can be divided into two or more roles: web designer, web developer, specialist programmers, database engineers, etc. But for businesses that don't need intricate or groundbreaking functionality (including the vast majority of SSBs), a single web designer is sufficient.

Websites are built for many different reasons – some to serve as libraries or resources, others as platforms for communication, sharing, shopping and more. But websites produced for SSBs have a unique and pivotal purpose... to serve as the hub of a business' marketing activity, geared as a Lead Machine – boosting its chances of survival and growth. That makes designing an SSB site an important role and responsibility. Failing to take it seriously or approach it strategically can have enormous implications, not only for the business as an entity but for the individuals who are supported and sustained by it, and those it exists to serve.

Creating a Lead Machine requires an SSB owner and web designer to be on the same page about the site's purpose as a marketing tool, and to ensure that purpose is prioritised and reaffirmed with every design decision. At least one or the other (the owner or designer) needs SSB-marketing-mindfulness; an understanding of how modern marketing works for SSBs, what opportunities and limitations are in play and how to capitalise on them to produce the most effective site possible.

As a great chef brings various ingredients together to create a meal more delicious than any of those ingredients alone, so too does a great web designer. Instead of cooking ingredients, however, the role and responsibility of an SSB web designer is to bring together high-quality, fit-for-purpose content (copywriting, photos and any videos), then present it in the most user-friendly, psychologically stimulating, goal-conducive way. That may sound obvious but – due to us being over-exposed to the ultra-creative, cutting-edge design of big business and mainstream marketing – it's not standard practice. Instead of prioritising user-friendliness, psychological impact and lead generation in web design, most of us are unconsciously programmed to prioritise creative expression, visual distinctiveness and the opinions of those outside our target market, over all else. In other words, we're hardwired to approach a graphic or web design project like we would a work of art; more of an outlet for creativity and technical ability, than a responsibility to produce a purpose-driven marketing asset.

The Fine Line Between Art & Design

For web designers and SSB owners alike, acknowledging the difference between art and design is a significant step toward the creation of sites that are equipped to serve their intended purpose. This difference is most evident in four subtle but crucial distinctions, outlined below.

1. **Art starts with a blank canvas. Design starts with a brief.**
   Most art projects start out as a mere thought or feeling. They're conceived from the heart, mind and talent of the artist and come to fruition from the inside out. In contrast, design is commissioned for an extrinsic purpose. There's usually a clear brief and a set of prerequisite specifications to abide by, born from the needs of those commissioning the design and, most importantly, those who'll be using or interfacing with it.

2. **Art is interpreted. Design is understood.**
   Art is entirely subjective and open to the interpretation of the individual. Every person who views or experiences a work of art can reach a different conclusion about what the artist is trying to convey. Design, however, should require no interpretation to be understood. Its purpose and message should be intuitively obvious to everyone – to the extent that if it requires any interpretation at all, some say it has failed in its purpose.[22]

3. **Great art sparks debate. Great design sparks action.**
   A work of art is contemplated and evaluated, then shared and debated as a matter of personal opinion. Its 'greatness' is determined by the strength and volume of these opinions over time – which means it's virtually impossible to measure. Whether opinions are good or bad is largely

beside the point. The fact that a work of art receives enough attention to warrant debate is all that really matters.

Great design is easier to determine than great art, as it's more objective and observable. The purpose of a design project is to motivate and facilitate a desired action from the person using or interfacing with it. While the design should be aesthetically pleasing, its fitness-for-purpose and effectiveness – measured by its ability to prompt and produce the intended action – are what count the most. If getting enough opportunities to convert (through visitation or traffic), a design either produces the desired outcome or it doesn't. If it doesn't, it's a poor design.

4. **Art is self-centric. Design is service-centric.**

A work of art is an extension of the artist; motivated by a desire to create something unique as a form of self-expression. Its direction is determined by the artist's intentions, creative preferences and personal style. It is 'self-centric', and so it should be. Design, however, should not.

Great design is about service to others. It comes from a desire to: 1) meet or exceed a brief, in service to those commissioning the design, 2) produce a design with optimum functionality, fitness-for-purpose and ease of use, in service to users of the final product, and 3) motivate as many users as possible to take the desired action, in service to both the commissioning body and users themselves. It's a 'service-centric' endeavour, characterised by empathy, humility and the ability to put others' needs ahead of more self-centric, artistic motivations.

While a neat, four-point comparison of art and design might make their differences sound clearcut, in reality the line between them can be blurry. Sometimes, there are aspects of design in art projects (when an artwork, such as a sculpture, is commissioned by an organisation for a specific purpose) and there's often an artistic component to design (when a project is on track to meet all functional criteria and has some aesthetic 'room to move' – an opportunity to get more artistic without impeding interpretability or effectiveness). That said, when it comes to creating websites for SSBs (and for most other businesses) the line is pretty clearcut.

Where Self-Centric Design Goes Wrong

When the clear waters of SSB web design are muddied by a self-centric agenda (our own, that of a designer or both) it becomes *self-centric web design* and we lose the opportunity to create a Lead Machine. Our website might be one-of-a-kind, visually or technically spectacular and at the cutting-edge of creativity but, if it's not purposefully designed to connect with, convince and convert potential customers, it's almost guaranteed to produce mediocre marketing results. While it might produce the odd enquiry, it'll be a virtual Bermuda Triangle of lost leads.

Unfortunately, the self-centric web design model (explained in Chapter 16) is the status quo and a costly, global epidemic. Not only does it stand in the way of web designers building flourishing freelance businesses, it silently inhibits the success of millions of SSBs across the globe; those whose owners have invested in a website only to find that it's no more effective than a brochure or business card. At a time when SSB web design and marketing should be easier and more cost effective than ever before, the self-centric web design model can make it a real struggle, with significant economic, societal and psychological repercussions.

The mindset of self-centric design is like a default, factory setting. It's something we develop not only by osmosis – through lifelong exposure to big business advertising and mainstream media – but quite overtly, through educational institutions and training programs. The world over, students of design are taught to admire the often cryptic, creative genius of big brands... to seek to emulate their cutting-edge creativity, distinctive design and minimalistic manner, because 'that's what it takes to stand out from competitors'. They absorb all this like a sponge, then unknowingly graduate with the mindset of an artist – ready to put their unique stamp or spin on their clients' marketing communications. A handful get this opportunity through employment at high-end creative agencies. However, many others either choose, or fall into, small business or freelance design work – a path that, when you've never been told that the design needs of SSBs are drastically different to those of the big boys, can be a tumultuous one; laden with all the trappings, trials and tribulations of the 'starving artist' trope.

The Service-Centric Solution

The opposite of self-centric web design and the approach most likely to result in a Lead Machine is *service-centric web design.* Where self-centric designers prioritise cutting-edge creativity or technical wizardry, service-centric designers prioritise the end result or 'greater good' of the project. It's about serving in the best interest of the business concerned, which means serving in the best interest of the business' potential customers (the intended users of the website) to maximise the chances of them responding to a call-to-action.

To those in the know, service-centric web design may sound a lot like user experience (UX) design but that's just one of a myriad of disciplines that fall within it. Among other things, it can encompass:

- **Project management** – Directing a website project, briefing employees and/or third party content creators and managing progress from concept to completion;

- **Business consultancy** – Enquiring, analysing and making suggestions to an SSB owner to improve business performance or profitability;

- **Marketing consultancy** – Enquiring, analysing and making suggestions to improve how the SSB's offering is presented to the market and/or how it is received, perceived and responded to by potential customers;

- **User experience design (UX)** – Envisioning and mapping out the interactions users will have with the website to optimise their experience and the outcome of their visit;

- **User interface design (UI)** – Implementing the UX roadmap with attention to finer details such as fonts and colours to make the site as intuitive and engaging as possible;

- **Graphic design** – Designing graphics to visually represent or enhance the brand or highlight important points or calls-to-action;

- **Web design/development** – Utilising various technologies to action the web design brief, from the design of web page wireframes to the development of a fully functioning site.

... all covered by just one or two individuals.

For anyone who's been employed in one of these roles, the suggestion that one or two people can handle all of them may be difficult to fathom – if not downright insulting. It's only natural to assume each of these disciplines is a field of expertise in its own right, warranting the full focus of one or more highly trained individuals. In the world of big business, this assumption is reasonable but when working with SSBs, it's entirely unrealistic. The vast majority of SSBs don't have the resources to fund multiple experts and, even if they could stretch their budgets further, it would likely be of little use. Each discipline is simply too deep, too narrow and too heavily swayed to fit the needs of big business to be of much practical benefit to SSBs.

For an SSB owner, engaging an individual service-centric web designer is the far superior alternative to an entire team of overqualified corporate experts. All it takes is one person with enough interest, empathy and insight across the above-listed disciplines to change the course of history for a struggling SSB. That person doesn't need to be an expert business consultant, marketer or UX designer. More than anything, they just need the ability to step back from a website project before launching into it; taking the time to see the business for the human enterprise that it is... to consider what it's doing in the world alongside where it wants to be, then – guided by the Secret Service Website Formula – create a website geared to bridge the gap.

As a side note, this is not to say that hiring a service-centric designer is the only way to create a website that works. While outsourcing the role in its entirety is the most streamlined way to develop a Lead Machine, other avenues are available to explore (outlined later, in Chapter 16).

Designer Differences

To comprehend the difference between self-centric and service-centric design, imagine a web design project is a bucket – to be filled to the brim with a designer's attention, effort and expertise. The bucket itself represents the project constraints which, in the case of most SSB web design projects, consists of a budget and a few branding specifications (use of a certain logo, colours, etc).

A *self-centric designer* will approach the project like this...

Figure 7a: Self-centric web design

... while a *service-centric designer* will approach it like this...

Figure 7b: Service-centric web design

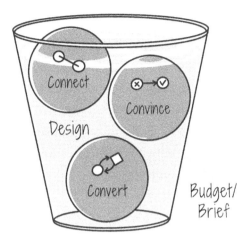

The most obvious difference between the self-centric and service-centric buckets is the latter's focus on elements geared to connect, convince and convert. Design fills up the rest – rather than being the entire focus – flowing in and around the Cs of the C³ Formula to accentuate and support them.

A more subtle difference between the two approaches is that, in service-centric design, it's not just the budget and brand elements that dictate the boundaries of the project but a more comprehensive *design brief.* A great brief (examined in Chapter 16) plays a crucial role in the design of an effective website. It details the purpose, priorities and prerequisites of a site, much like the instructions to a board game.

For web designers, switching from self-centric to service-centric mode requires a mental shift and a new take on the status quo design process (outlined in Chapter 17). In a nutshell, it requires designers to put their consultant and project management hats on – before designing a thing – to determine what content is needed to connect, convince and convert, bring that content into existence, then design a website to maximise connectivity and conversions. A genuine interest in small business and marketing is advantageous to service-centric web design, as is a willingness to be of service to clients, with no underlying artistic agenda. The switch to service-centric design can seem a little daunting at first, but the glowing feedback, organic referrals and feeling of fulfilment that comes from designing websites that actually work quickly outshine any concerns.

Designing for Favourable First Impressions

While a Lead Machine is more than a pretty face, it still has to make a striking first impression. Contrary to popular belief however, a first impression is not determined by the originality or intricacy of the design. Rather, it's determined by:

1. **Red flags** – Visual or functional cues that cause concern, confusion, frustration or overwhelm for visitors, indicating that a website is not designed, built, or maintained in their best interest. If a website returns a security warning, is slow to load, appears contextually irrelevant or has an unfamiliar or messy layout, for example, it will breach basic, unconscious user expectations and raise mental red flags, sabotaging first impressions.

2. **Sensory stimulants** – Unfortunately, the absence of red flags is not enough to make a great first impression. Even if website visitors have no standout concerns, there has to

be something intriguing or impressive enough to get their attention; something that draws the eye and interests them enough to jolt them out of a site-hopping state of indifference to stop for a closer look. For SSBs, the most powerful sensory stimulants are high-quality photos (particularly feel-the-love photos and product shots) and enticing, user-driven headlines. Without sensory stimulants visitors will be underwhelmed, which can be as detrimental as red flags.

Too often, SSB websites are created *with* red flags (poor layouts, loading times, etc) and *without* sensory stimulants (due to the absence of connective imagery and compelling copy), so they're inadvertently geared to make a poor first impression.

With service-centric design and the Secret Service Website Formula, a site that makes a positive first impression is par for the course. When guided by strategy and inspired by SSB soul (captured and conveyed through the marketing amplifiers), a site's visual aesthetics can, quite organically, take shape. As long as the photographs and primary copy (headlines, page names, calls-to-action, etc) are crafted with care and given the prominence they warrant, they'll do the heavy lifting... no cutting-edge design required.

The Need to Take the Lead

Until service-centric design becomes more mainstream, the onus is on us, SSB owners, to take the lead on web design – clearly communicating what we need and expect from our designer upfront. When hiring a web designer, we tend to be too vague and prioritise elements that will have no bearing on our site's marketing performance. This needs to change. Instead of asking for a website, we need to ask for a Lead Machine; an engaging blend of strategy and soul, depicted via a visually striking, user-friendly online interface that's equipped to serve as the hub of our marketing efforts. This is much more than a pretty face, requiring more than pretty design... but it's not rocket science. All it takes is some insight and initiative – on our part, that of our designer or, preferably, both – along with a mutual commitment to create a website that's not only superficially attractive but a magnet for leads and sales.

PART TWO

MAKING THE LOVE: THE MECHANICS OF A LEAD MACHINE

CHAPTER 8.

DIGGING FOR GOLD

Whether you're the one tasked with writing it or a web designer waiting months to receive it, text-based website content can seem like a necessary evil. We all know a website is not a website without words, but only those who've had to write or procure those words know how gruelling a task it can be.

For novices and professionals alike, much of this challenge stems from a misconception that quality website content is something you can write off the cuff. But that's rarely the case. As explained in Chapter 4, compelling copy is a blend of technical copy and sales copy; a fusion of facts and the 'fluffy stuff'. There's more to writing it than stringing decent-sounding sentences together. A foundation of inquiry, research, critical thinking and planning is required to gain a sense of clarity about the business and its marketing direction. Without a clear direction *offline*, we have no hope of writing what's necessary to produce a Lead Machine *online*.

Just as a jeweller needs high-quality gemstones to craft a spectacular piece of jewellery, a copywriter needs high-quality insights to craft compelling copy. Acquiring these insights requires focused effort; doing some basic online research into the industry and competitors, then interviewing the business owner (or ourselves, if writing for our own site) – asking a series of strategically developed questions. Like digging for gold, this process takes extra time but it's critical to identify valuable points of interest, difference and reader resonance – the gemstones of compelling copy.

While writing the content for a Lead Machine requires more than the act of writing, it's not necessary to be a marketing aficionado. In fact, by asking the right questions and really listening to the answers, you'll already be halfway there.

The Gold Digger Content Questionnaire

In 2012, after figuring out the Secret Service Website Formula, niching to trade services and creating set website packages, demand for our services increased dramatically. At that point, I no longer had the time to write client content myself. Through a stroke of luck, I crossed paths with Natasha – a beautiful soul, trained in corporate marketing, with a keen interest in graphic design but an obvious, undeveloped flair for copywriting. Once I explained what a copywriter was and that I thought she had all the hallmarks of a great one, Natasha was as excited to learn copywriting as I was to teach it to her. Things fell into place and she came to work alongside me in my home office.

One of the first steps in equipping Natasha to write compelling copy was to take her through my content questionnaire – the series of questions I'd been using to extract nuggets of copywriting gold from business owners via phone interviews. These questions – since renamed the 'Gold Digger Content Questionnaire' – worked a treat. Among other things, they allowed us to learn first-hand about a business and its stakeholders and seek out marketing angles not being leveraged effectively or at all, from the 'gold' of certain facts, offerings or incentives to strategic marketing 'diamonds'. With the Gold Digger Content Questionnaire, Natasha was equipped to dig for the gold herself – as you now are, with access to it via *www.secretservice.biz/downloads.*

Whether you're looking to work in conjunction with a professional copywriter, or write website content yourself, a content questionnaire such as this is an invaluable resource. It streamlines the creation of high-quality content, exposing deeply buried insights that couldn't have come to light any other way.

A Preliminary Cut & Polish

Once the digging's been done, it's time for some initial cutting and polishing, reflecting on the facts and findings we've collected, to see what we're working with. While some copywriters can get straight down to business, others can't... myself included. I need a couple of days between researching and writing to process the information and allow opportunities, angles and ideas to float to the surface – usually in the middle of a mindless activity like vacuuming.

It's during this time that strategic marketing 'diamonds' can present themselves. These are ideas and opportunities for the business to strengthen its approach to market by changing course in some way – usually niching to a particular target market or specialising in a certain service offering. Diamonds are harder to spot than copywriting gold as – to the untrained eye – they don't look like anything special. But the more digging, cutting and polishing you do, the more your business intuition and marketing-mindedness develop... and the more adept you become at spotting uncut diamonds in the dirt.

NOTE: If working as a service-centric designer or copywriter, it's important to get approval from the business owner before incorporating a diamond idea into the writing of website content. This avoids wasting time and money on a strategic direction that has no interest to the owner.

Writing in Reverse

Once the initial ideas and insights have been crudely cut and polished and any diamond opportunities run past decision-makers, we can get down to the business of writing compelling copy. For this, there's a trick.

As per the Secret Service Website Formula, the words on a Lead Machine (or in any SSB copywriting project) need to be geared to connect with service seekers, convince them and convert them into leads. But although we intend for them to work in that order, it doesn't mean we have to plan and write them that way. In fact, flipping the formula on its head – planning and writing first to convert, then to convince and lastly to connect – can make the copywriting process much easier and more effective. For novices with a technical writing background especially, flipping the C^3 formula and following it with the tips and techniques outlined over the next three chapters can make a world of difference, providing the direction and inspiration necessary to write a website full of truly compelling copy.

So, with a foundation of facts and findings and the C^3 formula flipped, let's start by creating the copy we need to convert website visitors into leads.

CHAPTER 9.

WORDS OF ENCOURAGEMENT: WRITING TO CONVERT

When writing content for a website, the first thing to consider is the site's conversion goal – what action we want visitors to take at the end of their visit. Whether it's submitting an enquiry form, phoning us, visiting us in store or subscribing to an email list, if we're at all unclear about the next step, our visitors will be too, and conversions (aka *leads*) will be few and far between. Not clarifying what potential customers should do next is like sending party invitations without RSVP details; expecting people to respond without stipulating what action they're supposed to take. Whatever the form of communication, if we'd like a response, we need a clear call-to-action.

Of the arsenal of marketing tools and activities available to modern-day SSBs, a website is the most important – requiring carefully considered, well-worded calls-to-action to serve as an effective hub for our other marketing efforts. Strong calls-to-action transform a site from an online brochure to a mechanism for driving leads, by making it easy for service seekers to deter-mine and instantaneously take the next step.

Despite being crucial to performance, calls-to-action are one of the most overlooked written elements of SSB sites. Most of us assume contact details and an enquiry form on a Contact page are all that's needed to generate enquiries from poten-tial customers. But a Contact page – like a business card – is a convenience, *not* a call-to-action geared to drive leads.

While the occasional service seeker may embrace the chal-lenge of scouring a website for a means to get in touch, for most it's too much to expect. A website without a clear call-to-action requires too much initiative and effort from service seekers to act on an impulse to take the next step. It's like opening the front door to a visitor then standing in awkward silence – expecting them to come inside without asking or gesturing them in. The door may be open but without inviting them in, we literally stand in the way of the action we want, keeping them at a phys-ical and emotional distance.

To accommodate the different personalities and preferences of website visitors, we need two types of call-to-action on our website: on-page and off-page.

The On-Page Call-to-Action

An *on-page call-to-action* is geared to capture the details of potential customers on the website itself. It presents visitors with a non-threatening, digital course of action; one that can be taken on the spot, no matter the time of day or night, without having to initiate a verbal conversation or utilise any peripheral resources (phone, email, etc). The aim of the on-page game is to give service seekers an obvious but non-invasive push in the right direction, making the process of expressing interest in our services seem as safe and simple as possible.

While many sophisticated on-page call-to-action mechanisms are available – including 'live chat' and 'automated chat' (chatbot) applications – all a Lead Machine needs is a strategically placed enquiry form with three core components: a 'lure line', some form fields and a button, as shown below.

Figure 8: An enquiry form designed to drive leads

While most of us are familiar with enquiry forms, few realise that a strong lure line, situated above the form fields, goes a long way to determining the quality and quantity of enquiries that flow in through a website.

The All-Important Lure Line

A *lure line* is a concise, carefully worded invitation, stipulating what action we want website visitors to take and what they'll get when they do. It's an opportunity to make the potentially daunting step of initiating contact with us so easy and appealing that disclosing their identity, via the form below it, seems like a no-brainer.

An excellent lure line does three things. It:

1. **Incentivises** – offering visitors something of value in exchange for their contact details;
2. **Reassures** – making it clear that there's no obligation to proceed beyond the initial incentive; and
3. **Motivates** – creating a subtle sense of urgency to act...

... all in one succinct sentence.

The lure line is a crucial component of the on-page call-to-action for a Lead Machine. Without it, there's no apparent reason to take action – no reason to reach out to us there and then – so the majority of potential customers will silently slip away, becoming leads lost to other providers.

Offering an incentive may sound daunting, conjuring images of free ebooks, white papers and other downloadable gifts and rewards. But to set the record straight, not only are download-able incentives unnecessary for the vast majority of SSBs, they can do more harm than good.

The Fatal 'Free Download' Offer

Offering a free download is, in theory, a solid strategy. It starts with the creation of an information product such as an ebook, report, course or video series of direct relevance and interest to a business' target market. Once ready, the product is offered to website visitors in exchange for their contact or subscription details (usually a name and email address).

Free download offers are ideal for *information marketing businesses* (IMBs) selling information products as their primary source of revenue, but for SSBs they're all wrong. A serious service seeker isn't interested in an ebook that will take weeks to read... they're ready to engage a provider now. Any call-to-action that sidetracks that intent is a bad one. It will repel hot leads, muddy your email list with half-hearted subscribers, contribute nothing to sales in the short-medium term (if ever) and, no matter how generous the offer, produce a disappointingly low rate of conversions.

What's more, the decision to offer a free download opens an enormous, time-consuming and often overwhelming can of worms. Producing a quality information product (writing an ebook, for example) takes a substantial amount of time to plan, write and design properly... and it doesn't stop there. To stand a chance of converting subscribers into qualified leads and sales, a series of strategic emails and offers is needed, which can take as much planning and preparation as the download itself, as well as causing the line between SSB and IMB to become blurred – sparking a confusing business identity crisis.

Luckily for us, there is a far less time-intensive, obstacle-ridden alternative.

The 'Stepping Stone to Service' Offer

For SSBs, the strongest incentive to use for an on-page call-to-action is hidden in plain sight... something most of us provide as a matter of course but overlook the value of to those seeking our services. This strong incentive is merely the free quote, consultation or other preliminary aspect of our sales process we undertake free of charge and obligation, before a prospect proceeds with a service transaction. A 'free quote' may sound a bit cliché, but when worded in a clear, concise and conversational way (as in the examples below), it becomes a compelling call-to-action to website visitors; a 'stepping stone' toward the engagement of our services and bait for us to reel in juicy leads.

Example Lure Lines for Stepping Stone Offers

- 'Request a Free, Same-Day Quick Quote'
- 'Request a Free, In-Home Consultation & Quote'
- 'Request an Obligation-Free, 30 Minute Consultation'
- 'Come & Try Before you Buy... Request a Free Trial Session Now'
- 'Planning a Function? Request our Function Pack Now'
- 'Considering a Procedure? Request an Obligation-Free Consultation Now'

Crafting a Compelling Lure Line

Several copywriting tactics are used in the lure line examples above, which set them apart from typical phrases found above enquiry forms on SSB sites.

1. **Calling it a request:** 'Request' is an influential word, signifying upfront that website visitors will be eligible to receive something if they take the specified action. Calls-to-action framed as requests tend to be more effective than those that aren't. They leave the popular 'Contact Us', 'Get in Touch' or 'Enquire Now' calls-to-action in the dust.

2. **Reducing perceived risk:** Terms such as 'free', 'complimentary', 'obligation-free' and 'risk-free' help

minimise the perceived risk of responding to a call-to-action, increasing the likelihood of visitors responding favourably.

3. **Saying when:** As simple as it is, tacking the word 'now' (or the less potent word 'today') on the end of a call-to-action can help subvert procrastination by subtly encouraging an immediate response.

4. **Getting rhetorical:** The use of a rhetorical question such as 'Planning a Function?' at the beginning of a call-to-action can boost engagement by resonating with visitors it's applicable to, compelling them to read on. Beyond that, it gets potential customers in the habit of saying 'yes' to us... an old sales strategy worth bearing in mind.

5. **Capitalising first letters:** The use of upper case letters at the beginning of the words in a lure line (other than joining words like 'a', 'to', 'the' etc) is important. It provides the best of both alphabetical worlds – commanding more attention than lower case lettering but making it easier to read and process than 'all caps'.

With these five tactics taken into account, a lure line crafted around a stepping stone offer presents the most clear, direct path for website visitors to step toward the engagement of our services... essential to the creation of a Lead Machine.

Benefits of a Stepping Stone Call-to-Action

Calling website visitors to action with a stepping stone to service offer provides a real world incentive with high perceived value. Not only does it offer something physical (a quote or consultation), it gives service seekers the ability to check a task off their personal 'to do' list, by taking an action step toward the engagement of a provider. This provides an immediate sense of accomplishment... more valuable than any free download.

Stepping stone calls-to-action are equally as beneficial for SSB owners. Beyond encouraging conversions, they sort serious buyers from those with ulterior motives – such as curious competitors and students seeking information for school assignments – who would be lured by a free information product but not a free quote or consultation.

Stepping stone offers also allow us to collect more detailed information from website visitors. Online etiquette dictates that we shouldn't expect more than a name and email address from visitors responding to a free download offer but stepping stone offers are different. Given the real world nature of a stepping stone offer, it's logical that more details would be needed for it to be provided. As such, it's perfectly acceptable to ask for:

- Name
- Email
- Phone
- Town/suburb
- Enquiry/details

This information is far more useful than a name and email address alone. Instead of receiving a mere subscription, we receive an actionable, contextual lead. This serves as an invitation for us to make contact with the prospect. It also gives us the ability to personalise and customise our communications from that point, maximising the chances of converting the lead into a sale.

... All this, with a fraction of the time and effort required to create, implement and follow-up on a free download offer.

For these reasons and more, a stepping stone to service offer is the smartest on-page call-to-action for SSBs. Luckily for us, it's also the simplest – with a snippet of compelling copy and a basic, five-field enquiry form on every page all that's needed for a website to be functionally equipped to serve as a Lead Machine.

The Off-Page Call-to-Action

Off-page calls-to-action encourage visitors to take actions away from a website, such as phoning a business, visiting brick-and-mortar premises, or sending an email – the first two of which are well-founded. The latter we can scrap.

Email Out, Contact Form In

Email is often listed on SSB sites and marketing communications as a means for service seekers to make contact. But encouraging email with a call-to-action, or even the inclusion of an email address on the Contact page, is a bad idea. For one, it can attract the attention of time-wasters – those who engage in back-and-forth communications with no genuine intention of engaging our services. Not only that, making an email address visible on a website makes it more vulnerable to spammers fishing for email addresses to add to spamming databases. This increases the likelihood of our email accounts being bombarded with junk mail, while making them more susceptible to security violations.

The preferable on-page alternative to listing an email address is a simple enquiry form on the Contact page. This requires similar fields to that of the on-page call-to-action but without a stepping stone lure line. To keep it open to visitors with non-sales enquiries, it can simply read, 'Got a question or general enquiry? Complete the form below.'

As with any website form, a Contact form can be set to send to a designated email address. Set up like this, submitted enquiries will land in our inbox as if sent by email but, because the address is hidden in the form's backend settings, it won't be at the mercy of time-wasters or spammers.

The Phone Call-to-Action

The phone is a pivotal tool for SSBs, providing the quickest, most direct way for potential customers to make an enquiry or booking. Many service seekers – particularly repeat customers – prefer the speed and directness of a phone call, rather than waiting around for a response to an online enquiry. Our website needs to support that preference.

Encouraging website visitors to call us is as easy as featuring our phone number at least twice on every page – once quite prominently and the other more subtly. There are three main opportunities for this: in the header, in the footer and in 'summary sentences' (explained shortly).

Common phone calls-to-action include:

- Phone 7654 3210 (the word phone may be substituted with a telephone icon)
- Phone Us Now 7654 3210
- Call Now 7654 3210
- Free Call 1800 765 432

...or variations thereof.

It's important to note that the type of phone number we promote in our marketing communications (be it a mobile, landline, voip, toll free, etc) can say a lot about our business, making it more or less likely for potential customers to take action. To check if your phone number is helping or hindering your marketing efforts, refer to Chapter 12 of *Secret Service Marketing*.

The Place Call-to-Action

A place call-to-action is applicable to SSBs delivering services to customers at a fixed location or brick-and-mortar premises. It's particularly imperative to those that appreciate walk-in enquiries or patronage, such as cafés and salons.

For these 'walk-in friendly' businesses, the place call-to-action must also appear at least twice on every webpage: above the phone call-to-action in the header, in the footer and/or in a 'feature strip' beneath the main content section (demonstrated in Chapter 18).

Place calls-to-action can include:
- 'Visit us at [address]'
- 'Visit us in store at [address]'
- 'Find us at [address]'
- 'Located at [address]'

...or similar. This is all it takes to communicate that a business has a physical location and that walk-ins are welcome.

For those of us who have a business premises (such as an office) but don't want to encourage unannounced walk-in visitors, a place call-to-action should be avoided. Instead, a physical address on the Contact page, accompanied by the words 'By appointment only' is the best bet. This allows the business to benefit from the authenticity and groundedness of a physical address, without encouraging unwanted foot-traffic.

The Summary Sentence

Most SSB site owners leave visitors hanging at the end of a page – to our own detriment. Abandoning visitors after the body content of a page, abandons them at a pivotal point in the user experience – when they're deciding whether to take action, navigate to another page or leave the site altogether. Leaving them to their own devices at this point is not only neglectful, it's dangerous. Just like a cracked bucket leaks water, a Lead Machine without a *summary sentence* at the bottom of each page loses leads, missing an important opportunity to call service seekers to action.

All that's needed to rectify this is a single sentence on each page, stationed beneath the body content and formatted as a sub-heading so it stands out. The aim of this sentence is to bridge the gap between the subject or focus of the page and the two primary calls-to-action, making it clear what visitors' options are for taking action.

Figure 9: Body content with a summary sentence (indicated with a star)

A summary sentence is similar in composition to a lure line, with three pivotal differences. Firstly, as its name suggests, the sentence *summarises* the main off-page and on-page calls-to-action, condensing the visitor's next step down to a choice of two alternatives, presented as an 'either/or' scenario. This preserves the sense of choice experienced at the end of a page but narrows down the options; helping to prevent visitors' minds from wandering to the option of exiting the site.

Secondly, a summary sentence can be substantially longer than a lure line. It can take up to three lines, at the full width of the body content above it, without requiring capitalisation of the first letter in each word. This gives us more room to write a compelling call-to-action.

Lastly, summary sentences change from one page to the next. For the sentence to serve its purpose of bridging the gap between a page of content and our calls-to-action, it needs to make reference to the subject matter of that particular page. No two summary sentences should be exactly the same because no two pages of content are exactly the same.

Calls-to-Action: The Key to Conversions

When planning, writing for and designing a Lead Machine, calls-to-action take top priority. If on-page and off-page calls-to-action are determined first, all content can be written and the site designed around them, for maximum emphasis and optimum performance.

It's important to note that although both types of call-to-action are crucial elements of a Lead Machine, off-page calls-to-action (phone and place) should not detract from the on-page call-to-action. The main purpose of a Lead Machine is to drive online leads. The on-page call-to-action is the mechanism that facilitates that. This makes it the most important functional element of the entire site – worthy of serious copywriting consideration.

CHAPTER 10.

WORDS OF AFFIRMATION: WRITING TO CONVINCE

*** WARNING! DETAIL AHEAD ***

Chapters 10–18 contain detailed instructions that may be overwhelming at first. If you get bogged down in them, switch to skim reading and return to each section as it becomes applicable.

Once we're clear about our website's conversion goals and corresponding calls-to-action, it's time to work out how we're going to convince visitors to take action.

To *convince* is to cause others to believe in the truth of something. In Secret Service Marketing, these 'others' are our potential customers and the 'truth' is that we are the best service provider to meet their needs – to the extent they'd feel silly to go elsewhere. Convincing potential customers that we're the best choice requires more than connection or charisma, it requires the preparation and presentation of a compelling case: a strong argument with solid evidence and clear, concise delivery.

Like a lawyer preparing a case to prove his/her client's innocence, convincing copy needs to be written in full view of the marketing facts and possibilities. Only after careful consideration and preparation can we expect to present a convincing case; emphasising facts that support our cause and, if necessary, addressing or overcoming those that don't.

While *images* on our website are our primary means to *connect, words* are our primary means to *convince*. It's by doing both – connecting through imagery *and* convincing through words – that we give ourselves the best possible chance to convert. As Joseph Sugarman wrote: 'You sell on emotion but you justify a purchase with logic'.[23] This is exactly what an SSB website needs to do. On a well-tuned Lead Machine, the connective nature of the imagery combined with the convincing nature of the copy create a 'perfect storm' scenario to convert website visitors into leads. The images spark an emotional right-brain response (a subtle sense of liking who/what they see), which makes the logical left brain more receptive to reading and processing the copy. If the copy isn't convincing enough, the C^3 process will likely stop short of a conversion. If it is, it'll pave the way for visitors to transition from liking us to trusting us enough to take action. This is an important distinction, best summarised by Zig Ziglar:

> 'If people *like* you, they'll listen to you.
> But if they *trust* you, they'll do business with you.'[24]

Third Party Proof

The quickest way for SSB owners to build the trust of service seekers is to provide ***third party proof*** of our ability to walk the talk. Sometimes called *social proof*, third party proof demonstrates to potential customers that a business is trusted by third party entities (past customers, organisations, etc), by offering evidence of affiliation, association or our ability to deliver what we promise.

High-quality third party proof provides a service seeker with invaluable insight that can make or break an initial connection – much like meeting the family and friends of a romantic partner. Endorsements from third parties bring a powerful sense of relatability, perspective, substance and certainty to a blossoming relationship. They provide a mental injection of credibility and validation; compounding the initial feeling of connection and making potential customers more likely to believe they've found 'the one'.

Most of us have received some form of endorsement but, like an ace up our sleeve that never makes it to the table, it can be of no benefit if hidden away. For maximum impact, our endorsements need to be considered strategically and displayed proudly, with evidence of them (third party proof) adorning our website like badges of honour.

Five types of third party proof are of most relevance to SSBs. Some of these take more time and effort to earn, collect or display than others but they tend to be the ones most worth pursuing – providing compelling, irrefutable evidence of a business' capabilities and standards. Their presence can significantly reduce the perceived risk of our service, increase trust and serve as powerful points of difference – driving many more conversions. So as you read through them, take particular note of those that seem the most daunting or challenging... they're probably the ones you stand to benefit from the most.

1. Accolades

An *accolade* is an award, grant or other official acknowledgement bestowed upon a business (or an individual within it) by a reputable outside body, such as a business group, industry association or government department. Examples include 'Small Business of the Year', 'Award for Excellence', 'Business Person of the Year', or a federally funded research and development grant.

Accolades are arguably the most powerful form of third party proof for SSBs. Winning or earning an accolade demonstrates a degree of superiority over competing businesses, as recognised by an objective panel of business or industry experts. An accolade is indisputable, which makes it extremely helpful in building the trust of potential customers. It verifies our expertise and value, resulting in more leads from service seekers who are excited and determined to work with us, no matter the cost.

That said, accolades rarely come easy. It takes time and energy to seek out awards and opportunities of relevance, then follow the strict and often long-winded criteria to enter the race. Some SSB owners may see this as a waste of time and energy but it's an excellent investment with a relatively high probability of success. In local business and industry awards particularly, there are often less applicants than you'd expect, giving any business with the foresight, focus and tenacity to enter, a real chance of winning.

Win or lose, throwing a hat into the ring of accolades can be hugely beneficial, even if it's only from a planning or networking perspective. It's an excellent opportunity to review where your business is at and where it's going, make new business and industry contacts and identify areas for improvement to raise your chances of scooping the pool next time around.

If and when you do win, the effects of receiving an award, grant or acknowledgment can be quite staggering. Depending on the profile and prominence of the accolade, it can boost leads and sales for several years... but *only* if capitalised on via marketing.

In terms of copywriting, capitalising on an award or other accolade doesn't take much. All that's needed is a clear, concise statement of fact, such as 'WINNER Best Restaurant Award – Small Business Awards for Excellence 2023' – preferably in the form of an official 'winner' logo, obtained from the awarding body. Not only will an official logo feature the details of the award, it will contain certain visual elements (fonts, graphics, etc) to verify its credibility.

Once an official 'winner' logo has been received, there's no room for humility. Only by making it publicly visible can it stand a chance of having the desired effect. That means embracing it as an extra element of your business' branding; featuring it online, offline, in-store, on signage, in email signatures and everywhere in between, for a good two to three years.

If it's worded well and an official logo adopted as a temporary addition to the brand, an accolade will generally speak for itself. However, phrases such as 'award-winning' or 'South Australia's best...' (as applicable) can be slipped into the business' website content and other marketing communications to further leverage the accolade and give the copy extra *oomf*.

Note that, even after a major win, it's good to continue applying for awards or other accolades. Every time we receive an accolade, we communicate to past and potential customers that our business is still relevant, desirable and reliable. It forces a refresh of market perception. Continuing to apply for accolades and winning the occasional one, helps prevent us from slipping into 'has-been' or 'one-hit-wonder' territory; keeping our business a strong and steadfast presence in the minds of prospective customers.

2. Accreditations

An *accreditation* is an endorsement earned through training, an approval process or other merit-based system. It can take the form of a qualification, training or compliance certification, membership, registration, clearance or status, issued by a suitably authorised body – such as an educational institution, registered training organisation (RTO), industry association or government department.

Evidence of an accreditation on a service provider's website can play a minor or major role in the attraction of new customers, depending whether it is a 'foundational' or 'elective' accreditation.

Foundational accreditations are those we attain to become legitimate service providers in our chosen field, such as tertiary qualifications for doctors and lawyers or licensing for builders. The vast majority of service seekers will assume we're qualified to deliver the services we're offering, so foundational accreditations don't carry much marketing weight. While listing or briefly mentioning them is worthwhile – providing subtle reassurance that we're above board – making a big deal about them won't drive more leads.

Elective accreditations, on the other hand, are optional (or perceived to be) which means they pack more of a marketing punch. Elective accreditations include compliance certifications, special statuses and titles, memberships, police clearances and more; those that we seek, earn and acquire in addition to our foundational credentials. Incorporated into our marketing communications, an elective accreditation can be a valuable asset, creating a notable point of difference between our business and others.

The key to getting the most out of accreditations is to accentuate the electives and understate the foundational. Emphasising an elective accreditation can only have a positive effect (neutral at worst). Emphasising a foundational accreditation – such as a medical degree – can have an adverse effect, calling into question our post-educational experience and accomplishments. The simple inclusion of post nominals or a builders licence number after the full name of the owner on the About page is adequate reference to a foundational accreditation, while elective accreditations are worthy of more attention.

Membership of an applicable industry body (the Master Builders Association, for example) is one of the most worthwhile accreditations an SSB can attain. The benefits of industry association membership often include industry-specific support, advice, training opportunities, discounted services and more but the greatest benefit is the marketable point of difference the accreditation itself provides. Due to the often stringent membership criteria and code of conduct, association membership helps 'sort the wheat from the chaff' of providers in an industry. It creates a distinction between *us* (accredited providers) and *them* (non-accredited providers) which bolsters our marketing efforts.

This distinction can be made through words, images or, preferably, a blend of both. Examples of words written to promote elective accreditations are:

- 'Member of Master Builders Association NSW since 1998'
- 'Fully Police Checked and Cleared'
- 'Approved Installer of Samsung Energy Storage Systems'

To be conveyed most effectively on a website, a single accreditation would be the focus of a banner or feature strip, with a line of copy (as per the examples above) accompanied by relevant imagery and – most importantly – any official accreditation insignia. Organisations that grant elective accreditations typically issue logos for use in conjunction with a business' branding, just as award bodies issue logos to award winners. Including these logos (be them membership logos, certification seals, badges, etc) in all business and marketing communications is key to capitalising on them, as they contain visual cues that help leverage the professionalism and trust of the accrediting body.

3. Affiliations

For the purposes of marketing, **affiliations** are relationships with reputable businesses or brands that make us look good by association.

For SSBs, the most common affiliations are *supplier* affiliations. These stem from sourcing products to sell, install and/or maintain for customers, then developing preferences for certain suppliers (businesses or brands) over others. An IT consultant specialising in particular brands of hardware or software, or an air conditioner mechanic who sells and instals certain brands of air conditioner, are prime examples.

Customer affiliations are also common, stemming from the delivery of services to business customers. Customer affiliations are most relevant to SSBs in business-to-business (B2B) fields of service, such as web design or consultancy, but they can also be relevant to those with a predominantly consumer market – a masseuse with corporate clients who engage him/her to provide on-site staff massages, for example.

Although supplier and customer affiliations are common among SSBs, many of us miss the opportunity to use them to strengthen our marketing communications. Affiliations are a powerful form of third party proof. Incorporating them into our marketing allows us to leverage the awareness, salience, strength and trust of the affiliated entities to be more appealing to service seekers. It can also help us differentiate ourselves from competitors by being perceived as a specialist provider of/to the affiliated brands or businesses.

On a website, affiliations have the most impact when presented visually on a banner or feature strip, with a short, snappy heading. A line such as 'We supply, install and repair...' or 'Our clients include...' followed by the logos of affiliated brands or businesses is ideal. In this format, the logos of affiliated brands or businesses – included with their permission of course – speak volumes. They serve as powerful endorsements, boosting our business' credibility and enhancing the perception of its capabilities.

It's important to resist the urge to link through to the websites of affiliated entities. Linking to other sites is a surefire way to distract website visitors, lose their attention and – in many cases – lead them to a list of alternative service providers. Not linking to third party sites allows us to keep visitors on our site, maximising the chances of us reaping the benefits of our affiliations.

4. Appearances

An *appearance* is a favourable mention, review, interview or article about us or our business in the media. It can be on mainstream media (television, radio or print), on a reputable online site or service (such as a news feed, high profile blog or podcast) or social media – shared by another business, organisation or influential person (known as an 'influencer'). Appearances build instant trust and rapport because it's perceived that – to have been featured by the media body or content creator – our business must have earned its stripes.

In the past, a media appearance by an SSB would typically result in an immediate but impermanent upswing in sales, which would wear off after a couple of weeks. These days it's different. Thanks to the internet, we have the opportunity to extend the initial impact and residual reach of our media appearances in several ways – the most enduring of which is to simply feature them on our website. When stationed online, even the most fleeting appearance can serve as a powerful and permanent endorsement and have a long-lasting effect on an SSB's bottom line.

There are two main ways to make the most of a media appearance via a website:

1. **Repeat the performance** – Securing a digital copy of the appearance (be it a video, audio or image file) to permanently station on your website is key to capitalising on it. For screen or audio appearances, this means finding out in advance if the media body will make it available, or if you'll need to record it independently. For written articles published online or offline, getting a digital copy is usually as easy as screen-shotting or scanning it, then

tidying it up – cropping and brightening the image using photo editing software.

The final file (proof of the appearance) can be embedded on the About page or – if you have multiple media appearances – on an 'In the Media' page. A banner or feature strip can then be designed for the homepage, announcing and linking through to the appearance/s. For example, 'Did you catch us on *Channel 7*'s *Today Tonight*? Watch the replay now...' Note that any reference to the date of publication is avoided, for the sake of longevity.

2. **Milk your media profile** – The main reason media appearances make such effective third party proof is the high regard for, recognition of and reliance on the media by the general public. This can be used to your advantage by featuring the logos of the media channels, programs or publications your business has appeared on, under a heading such as 'As seen on...' or 'As featured by'. Summarising your media appearances in this way can have a surprisingly positive influence on the perception of the business by website visitors.

5. Attestments

Attestments are the fifth and final type of endorsement. They've been left until last for a reason... to give them the attention necessary – from a collection and copywriting standpoint – to realise their potential as the single-most influential form of third party proof.

For our purposes, an attestment is the endorsement of a business by a customer – be it a verbal or written compliment, statement, review, or a more comprehensive testimonial or case study. As much as our (or our copywriter's) words are important, there's nothing quite as powerful as the words of satisfied customers, simply because they're more impartial. What past customers say about us and our business is easier to believe than what we say (with obvious bias) about ourselves.

The inclusion of a few glowing attestments on an SSB site can have a host of benefits. Attestments provide evidence of specific capabilities and outcomes, which help us drive more leads and pave the way to bigger and better projects (if applicable). They're also a means for service seekers to relate to others' situations and experiences, including their demographics, needs and feelings. For serious service seekers, the triumphant tales of relatable individuals who've walked the path they want (but are hesitant) to tread can be extremely compelling and highly influential. They validate the suitability and credibility of our business, making other claims and promises on our website all the more believable.

The more attestments we have, the better. A decent compilation of attestments demonstrates that we're not only capable of following through on our marketing promises, but that we do so consistently. It legitimises us as a reliable operator. As such, it pays to view the collection of attestments as an essential, ongoing marketing task; a small but regular investment of time, with no risk or financial outlay yet the capacity for an enormous return.

The collection of attestments is an opportunity every SSB owner can embrace but few do, for three reasons:

1. The feedback we receive from customers usually comes in the form of casual, unprompted remarks, delivered face-to-face or by email, so we don't think we can use them for marketing purposes (if we think to use them at all);

2. We forget to ask for feedback, or are too embarrassed to broach the subject; or

3. We ask, but end up with feedback that isn't as glowing as we'd anticipated.

But it's easy to turn that around.

Turning Unsolicited Feedback Into an Amazing Attestment

Unsolicited (unprompted) feedback from customers is the most genuine, heartfelt and natural attestment possible and, as such, can make for outstanding third party proof. The trouble is, it's usually communicated privately – in person, by phone or written message. Most of us would assume we can't use private comments to endorse our business publicly – and that's correct. It's not good practice to make private comments public without the permission of the person who made them, but one quick question can change that.

Upon receipt of positive feedback from a customer, all that needs to be said is 'I'm delighted to hear that. Thank you for taking the time to let me know. Would you mind if I shared that feedback with others via our website?' This one simple question is key to turning private, off-the-cuff feedback into future leads and sales. Asked courteously and with appreciation for the kind comment, the vast majority of customers, if not all, will be happy to oblige.

Asking for Attestments

Obtaining a customer testimonial at the end of a successful job or project gives us the ability to capitalise on that work for years to come. Too often though, we miss the window of opportunity to ask, or blow the opportunity to get the best possible testimonial by asking at the wrong time or in the wrong way.

The best time to ask for a testimonial is the point at which customers have the strongest feelings about the service outcome. For hospitality, beauty and other low-risk services that provide short-term outcomes, this is immediately after the service has been delivered – before customers forget the little details that made their experience positive. For higher risk services with lasting outcomes – such as construction, cosmetic dentistry or certain business-to-business services – it can be better to wait a few months until the benefits of the service transaction have been realised before asking for feedback. Determining whether to ask upfront or bide your time is key to attaining the deepest, most impressive and engaging testimonials.

Unfortunately though, asking at the right time doesn't guarantee a great response – we can still blow it by not asking the right way. Many of us find asking for a testimonial awkward, or that the question generates feedback that seems generic, forced or insincere... not at all reflective of the delight the customer displayed upon delivery of the service. However, worded differently, it's possible to avoid the awkwardness and solicit far stronger testimonials; ones that serve as valuable marketing assets long into the future.

One of the most important things to know before asking for a testimonial is *not* to call it that. There's a sense of cheesiness and inauthenticity associated with the word 'testimonial' which is best avoided upfront. More importantly however, the word and common phrasing of the question 'Can you please provide a testimonial?' is simply not specific enough – it doesn't prompt customers to reflect back on their experience with us in a deep way.

A second crucial point to note is that high-quality, detailed testimonials don't come from asking one question... they come from asking several, starting with:

- *'Jenny, now that we've finished your project, would you mind quickly helping me out by answering a couple of questions about your experience?'*

Most people derive a sense of satisfaction from helping those they've established a relationship with, so it's unlikely for such a request to be rejected.

After getting permission to proceed – and ideally, to record the conversation on a smartphone or tablet (or at least take notes) – it's a matter of asking pre-prepared, open-ended questions geared to extract meaningful answers. Following is a series of questions I've found to work particularly well. Of course, not all questions suit all businesses or all customers – they can be customised as necessary.

- *'How did you hear about me/us?' or if already known, clarify with 'So you heard about us though [name of person, media body, etc], is that right?'*

This question helps cast the customer's mind back in time.

- *'Before you hired me/us, what was your biggest fear or concern about choosing a [builder/accountant/designer/masseuse]?'*
- *'And I guess you realised you had nothing to worry about! So what was your experience instead?'*

These questions are designed to extract a 'story' from the customer, from fear and concern at the prospect of engaging a service provider, to complete satisfaction. This approach creates more than a testimonial; it creates a relatable, transformational story – a written 'before and after' capable of striking a chord with service seekers who have similar needs, fears and inse-curities as the attesting customer. Upon reading it, they'll feel a sense of assurance that they've come to the right place and confidence that they'll have an equally satisfying experience.

The next question to ask is:

- *'What did/do you enjoy/appreciate/like most about [the experience or outcome delivered – e.g. having your wedding reception at our venue, your new kitchen, your new website] and why?'*

This question may need tweaking, depending on its relevance. For plumbers or financial planners, there'll likely be less emotion to tap into – asking what they appreciate about their new pipe-work won't have the same effect. An alternative question for less tangible or repair-oriented businesses is 'What did/do you appreciate most about our service?'

Either way, this question guides the customer to link a posi-tive emotion to a specific aspect of the end result. They might say 'I really appreciated the attention to detail – the room looked spectacular and felt so warm and inviting' or 'I really love the layout of the kitchen – it's so functional and easy to cook in.'

A good question to wrap things up is:

- *'If you were to recommend me/us to a friend or colleague in a casual conversation, what do you think you'd say?'*

This question helps extract a naturally enthusiastic and persua-sive response.

Lastly, in order to use the collected information for marketing purposes, we need to request permission to do so, as follows:

- *'That's it! That was fantastic. Thank you so much. Would it be okay if we summarise what you've said into a snippet of client feedback to feature in our marketing materials? We can email it through for your approval first, if you like?'*

Once permission is granted, it's a matter of selecting the best, most relatable or influential parts from each answer and melding it together into a cohesive paragraph, trying to retain the customer's voice and vocabulary. Done well, the result will be an engaging, honest and authorised attestment that serves as a powerful convincement statement – or **convincer** for short – as in the example below.

'When I first contacted Laura, I had a website which looked nice but hardly anyone had found or contacted us through it. I was also stuck paying a monthly fee for it, which really bugged me. I decided to invest in a Cyberstart SmartStart website and I'm so happy I did. Almost immediately, we started getting quote requests from people who had never heard of us, who found our website via Google. I would tell anyone in trade services (besides my competitors!!) to trust Laura 100%. She really knows her stuff, is always there when we need her and is genuinely committed to the success of our business.'

Although this may seem long, it's worthwhile producing (and getting approval to use) a comprehensive testimonial, as it's more flexible. It can be used in full when applicable, in a sales presentation for example, or in part, extracting punchy snippets for use online or in a flyer.

Preparing and Presenting Attestments

Attestments are such effective third party proof for SSBs that they warrant a dedicated page at the top tier of a website's main menu. To avoid the negative associations with the word *testimonials*, it's better to name this page *Customer [or Client] Feedback*.

When preparing the content for the Customer Feedback page, there are a few things to bear in mind to maximise its impact.

- **Keep it real** – Ensure attestments are genuine and authorised to avoid the many ramifications of fabricating them.
- **Change it up** – Display attestments one by one down the page, alternating between short snippets of feedback and longer testimonials for the visual and mental stimulation of the reader. It also pays to: 1) alternate between two different sizes or styles of text, 2) highlight with colour or bold text the most important words or phrases in each attestment, and 3) leave an adequate break between each one. Incorporating some video testimonials (from Chapter 6) will further enhance the page, giving it an extra, immersive dimension.
- **Use "quotation marks"** – Quotation marks at the beginning and end of an attestment are a subtle but crucially important indicator that the words are spoken by a third party. They can shift a potential customer's vibration of thought, from 'I'm being *sold* to' to 'I'm being *told* something by a third party... this, I can trust'.
- **Identify the attester** – Underneath each one, listing certain details about the person who provided the attestment gives them a more relatable sense of identity. These details can include:
    - The attester's **name** (preferably first and last, e.g. 'Jamie Peters' or an initialled variation such as 'J. Peters' or 'Jamie P.' if they prefer);
    - Their **age** or other personal detail (only if relevant to the service);
    - The name of the **business** they represent (B2B services only);

- The **suburb/town** they reside or operate;
- Their **state** or **country** of residence;
- The **service rendered** (e.g. kitchen design and replacement, wedding function, bookkeeping services);
- The **date** the attestment was received;
- A **photo** of the attester and/or the completed project to feature alongside the testimonial. This makes the world of difference as it grounds the attestment in visual reality.

Added to an attestment, these extra details paint a picture of the attester, adding believability, credibility and relatability in spades.

Collecting & Publishing Third Party Proof

No matter the type, third party proof rarely appears out of thin air. Like any website content, the *5As* revealed above need to be deliberately cultivated. Whether its writing award submissions in the quest for *accolades,* working to attain or retain *accreditations,* seeking out *affiliations,* lining up *appearances* or asking customers for *attestments*, the attainment of high-quality third party proof requires proactive effort on an ongoing basis.

To give the collection of third party proof the attention it deserves, it helps to put prompts and procedures in place. This starts by identifying which of the 5As are most applicable to our business, then working backwards to determine the steps or systems required to attain them. For example, cultivating accolades might involve creating a list of relevant awards, anticipating the time required to develop submissions, then allocating blocks of time in our calendar to ensure they're submitted by their due dates. Collecting attestments might involve determining what, how and when customers need to be prompted to provide feedback, then distilling this information into a 'feedback collection procedure' to be actioned by certain members of staff.

Once we have third party proof, we need to publish it on our website. Extra prompts or procedures may be required for this – to refine, format and upload content, for example. Publishing third party proof goes hand in hand with collecting it. Without making it publicly accessible, there's no point having it.

Proof Positive

Third party proof is not only integral to an effective Lead Machine, it can be integral to business survival and growth due to its ability to subvert scepticism. Most service seekers know not to get too excited by a business' marketing claims and promises, because they know businesses are biassed. Third party proof neutralises this scepticism by connecting service seekers with the determinations, opinions and insights of more objective parties. It allows them to evaluate a business from a different, more believable (and often more favourable) perspective. This gives the business a distinct marketing advantage.

Displaying adequate third party proof is even more crucial for businesses delivering residential or high-risk services. Marketing a service that has the capacity to make potential customers feel vulnerable (physically, mentally or financially) without providing proof that those vulnerabilities won't be exploited, can cause the service offering to be dismissed for not feeling 'right' or 'safe'. Providing third party proof is the quickest, most effective way to reassure service seekers that the offering is legitimate and that they'll be in safe hands, so they feel comfortable responding to a call-to-action.

No matter what service we provide, third party proof is key to compelling, convincing copy. Prioritising its collection and display is not only one of the cheapest, most rewarding marketing tasks we can undertake, it's one of the best things we can do for our website and for our business' future.

Logic Levers

The second copywriting convincer is the *logic lever*. Logic levers are saleable statements of fact that resonate with the logical left brain to spark, strengthen or substantiate a service seeker's desire to engage us. They work by creating a logical point of difference between our service offering and that of competitors. When presented along with third party proof, cleverly crafted logic levers can leave website visitors with the feeling that they'd be silly to continue the search for a service provider elsewhere.

The four primary logic levers available to SSBs are:

- **The service specialty statement** – A slogan, subline, catchcry or claim, carefully crafted to position a business as the leader or expert in a particular facet of service or niche market, e.g. 'The Small Block Building Specialists' or 'The No-Meat Magicians: The First Choice in Catering for Vegan and Vegetarian Events'. Promoting a particular area of expertise, let alone niching to a small, specific market, can feel irrational and uncomfortable but done right it can be one of the most fulfilling, lucrative and business-sustaining moves an SSB owner can make.[25]

Sometimes, for businesses whose operations are restricted to a particular geographic area, all it takes to create a service specialty is a little local knowledge. Making mention of a distinctive feature or characteristic of the area or its residents (such as the climate, a common problem or design style) and the business' specialisation in that distinction, can be a surprisingly lucrative marketing angle, e.g. 'The Tudor Transformation Team: Specialists in Tudor Home Restoration'.

- **The numerical evidence statement** – A statement of fact grounded by an amount, percentage or other numerical indicator, which gives context to a service offering or outcome. A numerical evidence statement can be a highly effective way to justify the need for, or value of, a service. For example:
  - 'Outstanding customer payments affect the mental health of 79% of small business owners.'[26] (Debt collector)
  - 'In a survey of last year's clients, 95% reported that our service had paid for itself through the generation of extra sales, in three months or less.' (Web designer)
  - 'On average, the final sale price of our clients' homes is $30,000 higher than the original market estimate, far exceeding the cost of our services.' (Home stylist)
  - '$1100 of energy can be saved every year, by switching from electric to [alternative system]. That means, within just 2–3 years, your new system will have paid for itself.' (Plumber)

A numerical evidence statement can be shortened to a bold claim for use in a banner or headline. For example, 'Want a website that pays for itself in three months? Click here to find out how...' or 'Want to boost the value of your home by $30,000? Here's how...'. This would link through to (or precede) a page of content that substantiates the claim, including facts, findings, calculations or case studies and the details of what's required to achieve the claimed result.

Numerical evidence statements can be built on a foundation of intrinsic or extrinsic research. Intrinsic research is specific to a business. It can include accessing customer data, undertaking questionnaires or surveys, preparing case studies, generating internal reports and more. Extrinsic research is more general in nature, specific to an industry, target market or larger population. It can include online research, accessing the findings of independent bodies (such as the ABS in Australia) or approaching applicable groups or associations for statistics and other numerical insights.

Intrinsic and extrinsic research are both invaluable. One little fact or finding can completely change the feel and focus of your copy; allowing you to articulate and substantiate customer needs, expectations or outcomes in a logical, impactful way.

- **The security statement** – A security statement is a guarantee, warranty, assurance or promise to deliver a certain outcome for customers. At a minimum, every business is required to guarantee their products or services to comply with national consumer law.

In Australia for example, a consumer has the legal right to expect that a product or service they purchase will function as promised and serve their required purpose. If it doesn't, they have the right to request remediating action – be it a repair, replacement or refund.

While we're all legally obliged to uphold basic consumer protection laws, few capitalise on this obligation for marketing purposes. Simply stating what you'll do if customers aren't happy with your service can be a highly effective logic lever. For example:

- '100% Hair Repair Guarantee – If you're not satisfied with your cut or colour, we'll fix it free of charge.'
- 'Risk-Free Design Guarantee – If you're not completely satisfied with the drafting of your design, we'll keep working until you are.'

A step beyond what's required under consumer protection law, a *warranty* is a non-compulsory guarantee that takes our promise of remediative action further. Warranties assure the quality of products, parts and/or workmanship for a set period of time – anywhere from three months to a lifetime. Once offered to a customer, it becomes a legally enforceable term of the transaction agreement, which must be upheld. While a long warranty period can be an enticing logic lever for some service providers (builders, for example) it can also open a legal and operational can of worms. It's a good idea to seek advice before implementing and marketing a warranty, to ensure the offer isn't going to be more trouble than it's worth.

Price guarantees are another temptation for SSBs but they're not recommended. Price-match guarantees (such as 'Receive a cheaper quote and we'll match it') or price-beat guarantees ('Find a better price and we'll beat it by 10%') should be left to big businesses. For SSBs, price guarantees are not a sustainable approach to marketing. They eat into profits, encourage potential customers to waste the time of businesses they have no intention of transacting with and promote unhealthy, price-based competition – all of which are avoidable by following the Secret Service methodology.

For SSBs, the most powerful guarantees are *gallant guarantees* – those that take courage to implement. A gallant guarantee promises financial compensation or another tangible benefit to customers, in the event a certain outcome is not achieved. Examples include 'No win, no fee' offers by legal practices, 'Installation within three days, or receive $500 cash' or 'Wait no longer than one hour, or receive a $30 gift voucher'. The power of a gallant guarantee lies in the fact that there's a clear advantage to the customer, and disadvantage to the business, of the stated outcome not being achieved. The higher the value of the outcome (winning the legal case, installation within three days, etc) and the promised compensation (fee remission, cash or voucher) the more persuasive the guarantee. It demonstrates a level of confidence, experience and accountability that can be extremely appealing to service seekers. That said, gallant guarantees are not recommended for SSB owners who lack the confidence or experience to deliver on the stated promise the vast majority of the time.

Whether it's promoting a basic consumer guarantee, warranty or gallant guarantee, a solid security statement can be extremely convincing. It can significantly reduce the perceived risk of a service, increasing the proportion of service seekers who choose to transact with you. A security statement can also be a great way to differentiate your business from others in the market – many of which may provide similar guarantees but fail to actively promote them. As an added bonus, a security statement can also keep you accountable and motivated; an incentive to consistently produce high-quality outcomes, and work as efficiently and effectively as possible.

- **The sale sweetener** – Sale sweeteners are statements geared to encourage potential customers to proceed with a purchase in a timely manner, by offering a tangible bonus, incentive or monetary saving, subject to certain conditions or constraints. Examples include: 'Free landscaping packages valued at $4,500 for the first 10 customers', 'Bonus style cut with every colour treatment, for a limited time only', 'Complimentary car wash for first time customers… just use the words *Free Wash* when booking your service' or 'Redeem this coupon for 20% off your first booking'.

  Incorporating at least one condition or constraint into a sale sweetener is important, as it gives the offer a sense of exclusivity and urgency. The most effective conditions are usually 'limited time only' offers, limited quantity offers and redemption deals requiring customers to redeem a code or coupon to take advantage of an offer.

Monetary sale sweeteners such as dollar or percentage discounts are best avoided due to the impact they have on SSB profit margins. If you're determined to offer a monetary sweetener, be sure to: 1) crunch the numbers first to check the deal's financial viability, and 2) check the fine print thoroughly to ensure no loopholes can be exploited.

Whether it's a service specialty, numerical evidence or security statement, sale sweetener or combination thereof, logic levers warrant prominent positioning on our website. They are best displayed in banners or feature strips on the homepage, then expanded on or reinforced in the site's body content.

Unleashing the Full Force of Convincement Statements

No matter how well-written the copy, the full effect of third party proof and logic lever statements can't be achieved without making them visually stimulating. They need imagery – be it graphics, photos, logos or a combination thereof – to spark interest and reinforce the meaning of the words (explored with diagrams in Chapter 18). Visual components, such as a photo of a customer next to a testimonial or eye-catching insignia alongside a statement of guarantee, make reading, interpreting and accepting claims, proof and promises easier and more interesting, therefore more likely. Strong visuals bring out the meaning and power of strong copy, like a magician making the invisible appear. *Visuals* equal *visibility*.

Designing in coherence with strategically crafted snippets of copy is essential to create a Lead Machine. That means a business' third party proof and logic levers (as well as its calls-to-action, from Chapter 9) must be attained and/or written prior to its website being designed. Only if they're part of the original brief, can a website designer factor them into the design – allocating enough time, energy and page space to unleash their lead-driving potential.

Emotional Intelligence

The third and final convincer is *emotional intelligence*. This is about using words to tap into service seekers' emotions – increasing the likelihood of them taking action. The aim is to: 1) *stimulate* any pre-existing and/or desired feelings about the service, 2) *resonate* with those emotions, so service seekers feel validated and understood, and 3) convince them, with logic, that we can help *alleviate* the bad emotions and *effectuate* the good.

In essence, the use of emotional intelligence in copywriting plays on service seekers' emotions to influence a desired response. That may sound manipulative... and in the wrong hands, it can be. It's the intent, honesty and capacity to deliver underlying our written words that separates artful persuasion from heinous manipulation. Big businesses selling unhealthy foods and beverages under the corny guise of happiness, joy and social success are the ultimate manipulators – fuelling corporate growth at the expense of human health. They have no real choice, as there's no other basis on which to build a human connection. Fortunately for SSBs, we do, so we don't need to rely on emotional intelligence in the same way.

What SSBs need emotional intelligence for, is to bridge the gap between our target market's needs or wants and our business' ability to satisfy them. We do this by tapping into the main drivers of our target market's behaviour – *pain* and *pleasure*. This takes empathy... the ability to figuratively slip ourselves into the shoes of an ideal customer to experience life from their perspective or, in other words, to feel what they feel. Once we've determined the pain and pleasure points pertaining to our services, we can use clever copywriting to join the dots between them and the solution or outcome we offer.

Pain Points

Pain points are emotional hooks that highlight concerns, frustrations or challenges experienced by those considering the engagement of our services. A strong pain point, articulated clearly and prominently, will resonate with those who are experiencing it, giving them hope that their pain can be relieved.

There are three types of pain:

- **Active distress** – An active pain, challenge or symptom, causing suffering or distress to the point of desiring (and often, actively seeking) relief. For example, Googling 'trouble conceiving naturally', 'toothache', 'anxious pet dog', 'burst hot water unit' or in a business context, 'how to reduce Eftpos fees' is indicative of active distress.

  SSB websites typically focus on the service solutions available to customers, not the pains those solutions alleviate. By failing to explore active distress pain points, we miss a vital opportunity to convince website visitors that our service is: 1) relevant to them, and 2) a means to end their suffering. In turn, we miss the opportunity to send an enticing message of understanding, hope and urgency.

  A strong active distress pain point – experienced or witnessed firsthand – can cultivate more than compelling copy, it can transform your business. As I did with the *Busy/Slow Cycle*, identifying and articulating the pain point of a niche market[27] is one of the most productive forms of business planning a struggling SSB owner can undertake, particularly when you make it your mission to discover the underlying cause of the pain and develop an accessible cure.

- **Old wound** – An old wound is a recollection or memory of having been 'burned', let down or disappointed in the past, having engaged a business to meet a particular need. An old wound can be formed as a result of one painful experience – such as spending thousands of dollars on a website that didn't work – or when a series of minor frustrations culminate in an unhelpful, negative belief, e.g. 'tradies never arrive on time'.

  Old wounds often surface as feelings of scepticism or mistrust toward a whole industry or profession, with lawyers being a classic example. Unless we address any relevant industry-wide generalisations in our copy (if we genuinely buck the trend, that is), they can sabotage our marketing efforts, offsetting the effect of third party proof and logic levers, and making it much harder to convince potential customers to take action.

  Good copywriting diffuses the emotion associated with old wounds, allowing our key convincers to have their desired effect. It openly and directly addresses service seekers' old wounds, empathising with those who've been hurt, then explaining why and how we're different to other providers and what that means for them. Done well, this transforms the underlying emotion from one that has a negative influence over buyer behaviour to one that has a positive influence. It's not enough to just say the right thing, however. We've got to back it up – reinforcing our words with operational policies and procedures to ensure we can deliver on every marketing promise we make.

- **Fear-of-future** – A fear-of-future pain is a concern about something happening in the future, as a consequence of not proceeding with a service transaction. Fear-of-future pains are not usually top-of-mind for service seekers. They tend to exist more unconsciously. However, clever copywriting can expose and fuel them, helping to present a logical case for potential customers to take action.

  The most applicable fear-of-future triggers for SSBs are:

  - **The consequences of not proceeding with a service** – e.g. emphasising the emotional and financial ramifications of not engaging the services of a marriage counsellor, or taking out a certain insurance policy.

  - **The risks of engaging an alternative service provider** – e.g. risks of experiencing sloppy workmanship or poor communication (consistent with commonly held beliefs about an industry), wasting time and money, or being the object of social ridicule or condemnation.

Exploring fear-of-future pain points sets the stage for explaining that 'this pain and suffering can be avoided by simply choosing us… so act now', giving them an instant means to relieve the emotional pressure.

If this sounds manipulative… it is. It's also quite a predictable technique which savvy service seekers see straight through. For these reasons, it should only ever be used to expose legitimate threats, backed by strong evidence or examples.

Pain points are an important consideration when writing page content for Lead Machines. They aren't usually something to emphasise via banners or feature strips but they do play an important part in developing engaging, keyword-rich headings and body content and generating more traffic via search engines.

Crafting convincing pain point copy involves exploring the physical and emotional implications and intricacies of the pain, without getting caught up in the semantics of the solution. If offering a counselling service for the treatment of workplace anxiety, for example, the copy should focus on the pain of the problem more so than the methods used to treat it. Once the pain has been explored, the service can be briefly introduced, then a strikingly different, pain-free scenario presented – reinforced with customer testimonials. The contrast between the existing painful reality and the potential pain-free reality paints a powerful picture, which too much focus on the specifics of the solution can detract from.

A final thing to consider when writing about pain points is the number of negative and positive inferences. When tapping into service seekers' pain and problems, it's easy to get carried away with words such as 'no', 'not', 'don't', 'never', 'hard', 'difficult', 'bad', etc. However, too many negative inferences can taint the energy of a website, putting visitors off. While pain point copy can paint a bleak picture, it should always be balanced out with hopeful, positive insights – ensuring that the site remains, overall, resoundingly positive.

Pleasure Points

The second foundation for emotionally intelligent copy, and the antithesis of pain, is pleasure. *Pleasure points* work through positive enticement – positioning a service as a means to attain or experience a positive outcome or feeling, such as a sense of joy, relaxation, personal satisfaction, strength, success, approval, attractiveness or other desirable social construct. The aim is to increase the appeal and value of a service by communicating that it's more than a transaction... it's an investment that will make service seekers' lives better in some way.

Most pleasure points tend to be forward-facing – promising an outcome or experience in the future, as a result of engaging in a transaction, e.g, 'Staying in one of our glass glamping suites, you'll fall asleep under the stars and wake up surrounded by nature, all in 5-star luxury'. Rearward-facing pleasure points are also possible, with angles such as 'recreate the moment', 'reclaim your youth', or 'rekindle the spark'. Either way, the idea is to paint an idealistic picture of the outcome or experience available, grounded by key facts.

Writing about pleasure points alone is not enough to convince website visitors to take action. However, in conjunction with strong imagery and third party proof it can be highly effective, particularly in industries such as hospitality, personal wellness and experiential services.

Features & Benefits

The third and most important basis for emotionally intelligent website copy are features and benefits.

Features are typical characteristics, qualities or important parts of something. For a tangible product, they're usually presented as a dot-point list of physical, functional or measurable characteristics that give potential customers the opportunity to assess the product's suitability and weigh it up against comparable alternatives. For skill-or-service businesses, preparing a list of features can be harder to wrap your head around, but it's no less important.

For us, features are notable attributes (qualitative or quantitative) about our business and the services we offer; things we know are important or special, that can help differentiate us from competitors. For example:

- Certified technicians
- Non-toxic chemicals
- State-of-the-art job management software
- Locally sourced ingredients
- In-house baking
- Multiple function areas
- Average two-day turnaround
- Full service agency

But features only have meaning and value when they're put into context. As SSB owners, we have a body of operational insights that enable us to innately recognise the benefits of our business' features. To those without these insights, including most of our potential customers, features have no real meaning, which means they're not very convincing.

To transform a feature into a statement with meaning and value, we need to unpack its *benefits.* That means spelling out exactly *what the feature means for customers*. Luckily, a little copywriting hack makes this easy.

All it takes to extract the benefits of a feature are the words 'which means', 'what that means is' , or 'so'. For example:

'We use state-of-the-art job management software, which means you'll know – down to a 20 minute window – when we'll be arriving... no more waiting around for hours or rescheduling your entire day to accommodate tardy tradespeople.'

Differentiating between features and benefits can be confusing but, with the 'which means' technique, the difference suddenly becomes clear. A feature is a fact about the business or service. Benefits are what make that feature 'beneficial' to potential customers... how it makes their life easier or better. Features and benefits often overlap with pain and pleasure points, so if you've got third party proof and logic levers underway, and are ready to write convincing body content, start with features, unpack the benefits and you'll be well on your way to writing emotionally intelligent copy.

CHAPTER 11.
WORDS OF LOVE: WRITING TO CONNECT

Written words are vital to convince and convert website visitors, but they also play a role in connecting with them. Together with photography, copywriting enables us to spark a connection with visitors in the first few moments of landing on our site. It then gives us the opportunity to forge an even deeper connection, turning a positive first impression into a more solid, lasting one. Deepening the connection is important because – no matter how solid our convincement or conversion tactics are – if visitors don't feel a strong enough connection with us, they'll leave.

Connective website content is easiest to write after planning and writing conversion goals, calls-to-action and convincement statements (or *convincers* – as introduced in Chapter 10). Only then can we craft cohesive, goal-oriented copy in full view of what we're working with, what we have to offer and what we're aiming to achieve; weaving the calls-to-action and convincers through our writing, in a connective way.

Writing to connect is less about *what* we write and more about *how* we write. The style, tone, personality, framing and formatting of our copy all matters – determining if our words will catch the eye and contribute to a positive right brain response, or if they won't. It's not just the main blocks of content that need to be connective either – it's every word on every page that plays a part in the user experience, starting at the very top... the words that comprise the navigation menu.

The Power of Page Names

The names we give the various pages of our website are more important than most of us realise. Due to their prominent position, page names are often the first words on a website to be read and interpreted and, as such, can have major implications for connectivity. Page names serve as both signposts and labels – guiding website visitors to the information they seek and shaping their perceptions about the extent and suitability of our services. They can draw potential customers in or push them away, so it's crucial to give them the consideration they deserve.

When planning a website and considering page names, there are several common practices to abide by and some to avoid, as outlined below.

- **Home, About and Contact** – Home, About and Contact pages have a well-worn place online and deservedly so. Found on most websites, they're not only familiar, they've come to be expected, so it's never advisable to remove or rename them.

    About and Contact pages started out as About Us and Contact Us but have been condensed over time. It's better to leave off the 'Us' as it's outdated and takes up valuable room in the navigation bar which can be put to better use.

- **Services** – Many SSB owners lump all their services onto a single Services page but that's not ideal. For one, it can make us look like a 'jack of all trades, master of none', which doesn't help our marketing cause. Beyond that, it's detrimental to SEO; limiting our ability to be found through service-specific searches on Google and other search engines.

  Instead of one combined Services page, it's far better to have separate pages for each service or customer base, titled accordingly. This helps site visitors quickly deduce what we do, while enabling our website to perform better in search engines. The names of each service page must be as easy to comprehend and visualise as possible. 'Piano Lessons' is better than 'Keyboard Tuition' for example, and 'Home Extensions' and 'Commercial Fitouts' are better than a hybrid 'Building' page. Unless it evokes a clear image of the service on offer, it's not the best name for a service page.

  If there are less than three service pages, they can be included at the top tier of the navigation menu for quick and easy access. If there's more than three, they can be accessed via a drop-down menu under 'Services' or preferably 'What we do'.

- **Gallery** – For those of us who produce a visible end result – be it restored kitchens, clean carpets, corporate functions, installed solar panels or any other outcome that can be captured on camera – a photographic portfolio page is essential. Upon landing on a website, the Gallery page (which can be called Portfolio, View Our Work or other term if preferred) is often the first page service seekers navigate to, as it provides immediate visual validation. Users tend to trust what they *see* more than what they read so, given the opportunity, they'll view and assess a gallery of images before investing time in a site's written content. That makes a Gallery page vital. Galleries do more than showcase our capabilities; they increase the chances of our compelling copy being read.

- **Blog** – On an SSB website, a Blog (short for Weblog) is a page on which excerpts of articles or 'blog posts' are listed in chronological order from newest to oldest. Clicking an excerpt opens the full post, where website visitors can read the article in its entirety, make a comment (if allowed by the site owner) and share it with others by email, social media, etc if they choose to.

  Blogging is not necessary for a Lead Machine to work but it can be a highly beneficial 'extra-curricular' marketing activity, as explored in Chapter 4 of *The Modern Marketing Arsenal*. Blog posts are a means to relay more in-depth information about micro-topics – such as individual active distress pain points – without weighing down the site's main pages. Blog content is also excellent for improving SEO – helping the site rank better for related queries in search engines.

- **Links** – It can be tempting to minimise the amount of content on a website by including a page of links to the sites of suppliers or other organisations, but outbound links are terrible for an SSB site. The aim of the game is to keep visitors on your website for as long as possible or until they respond to a call-to-action. Outbound links do nothing but shoot them off to another site, where they'll likely stumble across another link... straight into the arms of a competitor.

Many website owners believe outbound links help websites rank better in search engines, however this is a fallacy. It's *inbound* links (links to your website listed on other sites) that can help your SEO. Outbound links do nothing but help the business being linked to, so scrap the Links page and make room in your menu for a page with more substance.

- **The 'scary' stuff** – A website's main navigation menu shouldn't include pages that don't support its marketing cause. Although they might be required, pages of fine print such as Terms of Use and Privacy detract from the positivity of a website. Including them in the main menu would only work against us, scaring potential customers away. Instead, any potentially off-putting pages are best included in the footer menu – where they're readily available but will only be accessed by hyper-vigilant visitors.

- **Pricing** – One of the many decisions SSB owners face when preparing website content is whether to list prices. The answer is... it depends.

  For most, the answer is no. Price is the holy grail of information sought by service seekers, and a main driver of buyer behaviour. If we make our pricing accessible online, we lose the opportunity to use it to incentivise our on-page call-to-action as a 'stepping stone to service' offer (explained in Chapter 9). That means we lose the opportunity to drive leads and, in turn, convert leads into sales through the connective power of real-time conversation.

What's more, revealing prices on a website makes us more likely to be judged and dismissed on the basis of price. When prices are available online, carefully crafted content, convincers and calls-to-action can be overlooked. This puts us in a vulnerable position. Without having the opportunity to connect, convince and convert through our site's content, we are at risk of being judged on the basis of price alone and – if we're not perceived as 'cheap' enough – coming off second best when inevitably compared to our competitors.

While not listing prices on an SSB site is ideal, it's not a hard and fast rule. For some businesses with competitive prices it can be beneficial to include them – especially if accompanied by an on-page call-to-action form and a casually worded disclaimer stating that prices may vary depending on certain listed factors so 'please complete the form above for a free, fixed price quote'.

Other SSBs are obligated to list their prices. In the hospitality industry for example, service seekers expect to be able to access menus online. If not provided, they're likely to move on to the sites of more transparent providers.

When including prices, there are a couple of points to note. Firstly, it's better to call a pricing page Menus, Packages or Specials than to use the word 'prices', as it puts the emphasis on what customers get, rather than what it will cost them. Secondly, just because you decide to list prices on your website, doesn't mean the price of every service needs to be included. If it suits your business model, have your cake and eat it too; listing prices for low-risk services, while dangling the prices of higher risk services as a carrot to drive leads. For a restaurant, this would mean making meal and beverage menus available online but offering function pricing in an alternative format (a function package, or free consultation and quote) which needs to be requested via an on-page enquiry form. This can strike a great balance – instantly gratifying lower-end customers, while driving leads from higher-end prospects.

Body Content: From Bland to Disneyland

As our visitors' eyes move below the main menu, they tend to scan the page looking for a point of interest to land on. For most SSB sites, the main body of a webpage is the bland bit; a slab of paragraphs with no visual allure or linguistic pizazz. Given that visual interest and engaging language are two of the main determinants of how connective our content is, that's a worry.

As introduced in Chapter 2, connectivity is a fundamental human need stemming from deep in the *unconscious mind,* which has the attention span of a seven-year old child. If our website content is perceived by a visitors' childlike unconscious mind as bland or boring, it will be near impossible to satisfy their need for connectivity. If it's perceived as interesting and exciting, it will work in our favour – cultivating a connective experience. As such, the aim of the game is to write and format content to please a service seeker's inner child... taking them from 'bland' to a proverbial 'Disneyland'. To help with this, 10 connective content writing hacks are outlined below.

1. Raise Your Business' Voice

Uniquely, copywriting for SSB sites requires a blend of three voices or narratives – first person plural, second person and third person. In practice, this means:

1. Using collective first person terms such as 'we', 'us' and 'our' when referring to the business;
2. Using second person terms such as 'you' and 'your' when referring to website visitors/service seekers; and
3. Using third person terms including people's names and pronouns such as 'he', 'she', 'him' or 'her' when referring to the business owner or individual staff.

It can take time to adjust to this approach, particularly when used to a more detached, technical style of writing, but developing it (or outsourcing the responsibility to a professional copywriter) is invaluable. When combined, these three narratives create a voice that speaks from the business as a collective entity to website visitors as individuals, while positioning the business owner as a figure of authority. It is a potent blend, imparting a sense of expertise, professionalism and trustworthiness while invoking a feeling of inclusion, involvement and assumed agreement from potential customers.

To conscientious sole traders, writing 'we' and 'us' when we're really an 'I' and 'me' can feel a little like false advertising – let alone referring to ourselves in the third person. However, this narrative is well and truly warranted. Even the smallest of businesses require a minimum of two entities to operate: the business and its owner. This makes it entirely appropriate to write in a plural first person narrative with second and third person references for others and ourselves. It may seem somewhat schizophrenic but it's actually just writing from the perspective of the business; as if the business entity itself could talk.

There's one circumstance in which the singular first person voice ('I', 'me', 'my') is more appropriate than the business' voice – when we're quoting someone's written or spoken words. The prime use of first person quotations is for testimonials; providing a means to convey the voice of happy customers in our marketing communications (covered in Chapter 10). But quotations can also serve another handy purpose – a means to convey our own voice (or that of key staff or stakeholders) in a direct, credible way. Whether it's a statement about the main benefits or outcomes of our services, what sets our business apart, or something a little more personal (what drives us to do what we do), presenting a thought or fact as a quotation changes the way it's perceived and therefore how we as the owner are perceived. The statement becomes more objective and we become a believable voice of authority and reason.

All that's needed to transform an otherwise inappropriate segment of singular first person text into a quotation is formatting. When quotation marks (often called inverted commas or speech marks) and the name of the quoted individual are added, the statement can become an impactful piece of third party proof. Whether it's positioned as a 'blockquote' between paragraphs or showcased in a banner or feature strip, a quotation can add another dimension to written website content and be an excellent way to spark a connection with website visitors.

2. Mind Your WEs & YOUs

Many of us use the first person plurals 'we' and 'our' quite naturally when writing website content but don't feel as confident when it comes to using 'you' and 'your'. To avoid these second person terms, many of us refer to our target market or potential customers as 'our customers' or 'our clients'. This is counterproductive however, as it creates a tone that ignores and excludes those we most need to include and impress – our potential customers.

For potential customers taking the time to read our content, repeated use of 'we' and 'our' and avoidance of 'you' and 'your' is equivalent to a one-sided conversation... 'We do this', 'We were established in', 'We provide', 'We offer', 'Our aim', 'Our customers'. Not only is this inconsiderate, it's bland, boring and borderline narcissistic. Needless to say, it's a writing habit to break.

All it takes to break the curse of one-sided copy is a single trick. While writing, strive to offset every use of the word 'we' or 'our' with 'you' or 'your' – so there's a relatively equal balance of both. Doing this, the finished piece will be far more inclusive and engaging – not only because it will refer to the reader more often, but because the needs and perceptions of potential customers will have had to remain top of mind the entire time. The more mindful we are while writing – even if just to strike a healthy balance of WEs and YOUs – the more considered, connective and compelling our content will be.

3. Get Hooked on Headings

Well-crafted page headings are a powerful addition to any SSB site. An engaging heading creates an organic, alluring segue into a page's body content, like the headline of a newspaper article. It draws the eye, summarises the content beneath it in a concise, clever way and helps transition visitors into reading mode.

To serve this important purpose, formatting is crucial. Headings should be formatted in a substantially larger font than the paragraph text and in a bright colour which complements the design and branding. Font selection is also important. Headings should be easy to read and require no extra effort to decipher, so cursive or other decorative fonts are best avoided.

All text-heavy pages of a website stand to benefit from the inclusion of a strong heading. On the homepage, a heading should clearly summarise what the business does and for whom (including the region it operates if limited to a specific area) as not to keep visitors guessing. On inner pages (excluding low-text pages such as Gallery and Contact), the aim of a heading is to hook visitors into reading the entire page. To do this, each heading must be specific to the subject matter of that page, e.g. a heading that reads 'To repair or NOT to repair? That is the question...' on a 'Repair or Replace?' page of a hot water plumbing website.

4. Keep it Simple, Stupid

Oscar Wilde once said: 'Oh don't use big words. They mean so little.' This is good to bear in mind when writing website content. We are not writing an academic essay, nor trying to impress industry peers with our use of high-tech jargon. We are writing to engage and sell. This calls for a conversational tone and commonly recognised words and phrases (aka *layman's terms*). If we don't keep our content simple, chances are, we'll overwhelm potential customers and make engaging with our business seem all too hard.

5. Yay for Clichés

Clichés, colloquialisms and common sayings cop a lot of slack among professional writers but they're an undeniably powerful copywriting tool. A cliché – used straight or with the twist of a play on words – can help convey a complex or boring concept in a conversational and highly relatable way. There is a sense of familiarity in clichés and colloquialisms that aligns perfectly with the SSB need to evoke a sense of familial connection through our marketing messages.

As a connoisseur of clichés and colloquialisms myself, there are hundreds of examples throughout the *Secret Service Business Series.* But for good measure (yep... that's one too), here are a few more: 'faster than a speeding bullet', 'straight from the horse's mouth', 'more than you bargained for', 'icing on the cake', 'the road to recovery', 'spring in your step', 'the early bird catches the worm', 'it goes without saying', 'get the juices flowing'. The options are endless.

6. Embrace Imagery

One of the reasons clichés are so effective is that they're often metaphorical; giving a concept context by representing it with something easy to visualise, e.g. 'throw a spanner in the works' or 'sleep like a baby'. Using a metaphor is a powerful copywriting technique – not just for crafting snappy one-liners, but for crafting paragraphs of compelling body content. By interweaving reality with imagery, a boring or confusing concept can transform into a riveting, yet logical explanation.

Like clichés, imagery is rife throughout my writing. *The Secret Service Website Formula* is riddled with romantic imagery, and

Secret Service Marketing regularly references action heroes and missions, not because I'm a sucker for romance or action adventure movies but because they make potentially boring topics easier to digest... and hopefully, more entertaining.

7. Repetition, Rhyme and Rhythm

Injecting personality, playfulness or pizazz into our writing takes an awareness of its 'musicality' – particularly its sense of melody and rhythm.

Melody is achieved through word selection and poetic techniques such as alliteration (repeating a letter or sound, as in 'sailing the stormy seas of small business') and rhyme (as with 'seal the deal' or 'from go to woah'). Words that flow well together – along with the occasional poetic flourish – make content easy and interesting to read, therefore more likely to be read and acted upon.

Poetic techniques need to be used with discretion, however. If writing to promote something serious or emotionally triggering, such as mental health, funeral or legal services, a sense of playfulness could come across as crass or inconsiderate. This needs to be considered before getting creatively carried away.

Rhythm is more of a writing mindset than a technique. It's as vital a consideration when writing copy as when composing music – both need a sense of rhythm to get and hold audience interest. Word selection, grammar, the use of patterns, phrasing and sentence structure all contribute to the rhythm of our copy. They give us the power to create a feeling of ebb and flow – propelling the reader through to a harmonious finish (a compelling call-to-action).

Writing with rhythm is not a clear-cut concept. There's no framework to follow like there is when composing blues music, for example. The ultimate test of copywriting rhythm is simply how it sounds when read aloud; does it roll off the tongue effortlessly, compelling you to keep reading, or is it stilted, clumsy or confusing? Until it sounds effortless and engaging when read out loud, it likely needs more work. In body content, this often involves variegating the length of sentences. Using a variety of sentence lengths – from short, snappy ones to long, lyrical ones – creates a sense of tension and release, which is more interesting and enjoyable to read.

8. Exclamation Temptation

A surefire way to spot an amateur copywriter is the overuse of exclamation marks – on headings! And subheadings!! And every other sentence!!!

Exclamation marks undermine the professionalism, integrity and believability of our writing, which is why good copywriters use them sparingly. They know that a well-constructed point proves much stronger when concluded with a simple full stop.

Punctuation marks to explore instead of the exclamation mark are the ellipses (...) and the question mark (?). Ellipses have various uses in technical writing but in copywriting they're used to create a sense of anticipation or intrigue – often midway through a sentence... or at the end of a heading. Question marks are handy in headings too, allowing us to appeal to potential customers through the use of rhetorical questions, e.g. 'Got pest problems at your place?' Used responsibly (no more than about twice per page), ellipses and rhetorical questions can make website content far more engaging.

9. Break the Rules

Many of us find copywriting difficult because we're held hostage by the rules and rhetoric of technical writing. The proper use of words, grammar, sentences and paragraphs is burned into our brains. We accept it without question, assuming that any deviation from it will result in us being judged as unintelligent or unprofessional – so we stick to the status quo.

But we can't write compelling copy without breaking a few technical writing rules. Three of the rules I consistently break when writing website content, and their copywriting replacements, are outlined below:

Technical writing rule	Copywriting rule to replace it with
Paragraphs must contain two or more sentences.	Paragraphs can be as short as you like, down to a single word. If a sentence or phrase creates more visual and mental impact as its own paragraph, go with it.
Sentences and paragraphs must never begin with joining words like 'and', 'but' or 'so'.	Not only is it okay to start sentences and paragraphs with joining words, it's a highly effective copywriting practice. A joining word creates a casual bridge between two sentences or paragraphs, propelling readers forward when they may otherwise stop.
Avoid conversational contractions such as 'we're', 'they're' and 'you're'.	Copy should be as palatable and conversational as possible. The more fluidly your words flow together, the easier they are to read and interpret. So if a sentence flows better with the contraction 'we'll' instead of 'we will'... write it like that. If a heading is more relatable with the phrase 'Go get 'em' instead of 'Go get them'... write it that way. As long as appropriate grammar is used to indicate the contraction is intentional (typically an inverted comma in lieu of removed letters), you'll have the desired effect while keeping grammar-savvy readers satisfied.

10. Have Fun with Formatting

As connective as a page of content may be, if it looks boring it won't be read. It's got to look the part to play the part.

As visitors' unconscious minds are akin to seven-year old children, the visual formatting of our content needs to stimulate young brains. Paragraph upon paragraph of small, grey text won't cut it. To *stimulate* rather than *intimidate*, walls of text must be broken down and spiced up. There are several ways to do this.

- **Subheadings** – In conjunction with a big, bold heading on each page, medium-sized subheadings, wherever relevant, make a long page of content more palatable by breaking it down into smaller, manageable portions. They also make it easier for visitors to find or return to information of relevance to them; a small consideration which can make a big difference to the user experience.

- **Short paragraphs** – On a website, paragraphs of approximately three to four lines are ideal. Long paragraphs are intimidating and can impede readability, so it's best to break them down into smaller ones.

- **Dot point and numbered lists** – Bulleted and numbered lists are commonplace in copywriting... and for good reason. Not only do they provide visual respite from a page of paragraphs, they also give us the opportunity to communicate more with fewer words, giving our body content greater impact.

  To take advantage of this opportunity, each and every listed point needs to be considered as carefully as if it were a heading. It's also worth noting that:

- Readers tend to gravitate to the *first, second, last* and *second-to-last* dot points, so they need to be the strongest;
- Lists with an odd number of listed points (such as three or five) tend to prove more effective than those with an even number;
- Short, punchy lists are more powerful than long, exhaustive ones;
- It's best to avoid full stops in a bulleted or numbered list, opting for commas or no punctuation at all;
- 'And more...' makes an enticing final point for a list of inclusions, features or benefits.

- **Text style** – Most websites have a pre-set stylesheet that determines the style or appearance of headings (h1), subheadings (usually h2 to h5), body or 'paragraph' text (p), list points (li) and more. The careful selection of these styles – in terms of font type, size and colour – makes all the difference to the appeal and readability of website content.

    Two fonts and two colours (in addition to black) are needed to format the body text on a Lead Machine. A basic, easy to read font is required for paragraphs, and a more distinctive (but still legible) font for headings. Variations of both – in terms of size, colour, boldness and italics – can then be applied for subheadings, blockquotes, captions, etc. There's never any reason to use more than three types of font on a website, and overtly fancy fonts should be avoided, for the sake of user experience.

As mentioned earlier, page headings are more effective when strikingly large in size. A large heading draws the eye, creating a seamless segue from first seeing a page to reading it and responding to the call-to-action.

- **Emphasis** – Text styling is key to differentiating between headings, subheadings and paragraphs in body content but for SSB sites it has an extra application – emphasising important words and phrases. Used strategically, **bold**, *italic*, coloured and highlighted text draws visitors' eyes through the content, boosting their comprehension of key points, while adding visual interest to the page (stimulating the childlike right brain). This makes it easier to read and understand.[28]

The value of emphasising text – particularly through the use of colour and highlighting – can be difficult for web designers to accept. Many designers find text inconvenient as it is; something to divert attention away from, not accentuate. But adding visual interest to text contributes to a website that works... and at the end of the day, that's what matters.

Pages that Must Engage

To create a Lead Machine, the connectivity of two particular pages is paramount. The Home and About pages are crucial, not only because they're highly frequented but because they're our main opportunity to blow our own horn. If written without considering service seekers' connective needs, however, all we'll blow is our chances.

Hitting a Home Run

The homepage is the most visited page on a website, therefore the single-most important page of the entire site. If we want above-average performance from our website, we need an above-average homepage.

'Home runs' aren't scored with a mere bunt of the ball though. Certain written elements are needed to help move visitors from base to base as swiftly as possible.

- **Heading** – Of all pages, the homepage needs the strongest, most well-considered heading. Ideally, it should summarise three business-critical details:
  1) what the business does, 2) who for, and 3) where it operates, in a clear, concise and suitably engaging way.
- **Body copy** – The body copy of a homepage is best kept short. All we want to do is elaborate on the heading – clarifying what we do, why we do it and how it benefits customers – then leave readers wanting more. This can be done in three to four small paragraphs. Any less and we miss connective and SEO opportunities. Any more and we risk our website being dismissed as too boring or long-winded to bother with. Three to four short paragraphs strikes the ideal blend of sufficiency and substance.
- **On-page call-to-action** – As explained in Chapter 9, an on-page call-to-action is critical to the creation of a Lead Machine. Comprising a lure line, enquiry form and Submit button, it is key to the site's performance so it must take pride of place on the homepage (as well as most other pages).

- **Summary sentence** – Also explained in Chapter 9, a sentence beneath the body copy, formatted as a subheading (larger, bolder, coloured, etc) is an important inclusion on any text-based page of content, including the homepage. The summary sentence on a homepage is slightly different to that on other pages though, as it can be geared towards encouraging visitors to explore more of the site, rather than taking immediate action.

As well as these, a minimum of three of the following elements, displayed in a more visual format, should be featured on the homepage:

- **Third party proof** – Accolades, accreditations, affiliations, appearances or attestments, displayed via banners or feature strips.
- **Logic lever** – A service specialty, numerical evidence, security or sale sweetener statement, displayed via a banner or feature strip.
- **Owner introduction** – A feature strip entitled 'Meet the Owner...' or similar, which concisely introduces the owner and links through to the About page via a 'Read more...' button.
- **Service snapshot** – A feature strip entitled 'What We Do...' or similar, with a scrolling gallery of labelled images, each one clearly stating the service on offer and linking through to a relevant subpage for more information.

To hit a home run, the words on the homepage must cover all bases... they must connect, convince and convert. Calls-to-action and key convincers need to take pride of place, and every word within and beyond them considered for its ability to connect. That means prioritising quality over quantity – spending time and money where necessary to get the homepage right. How compelling a homepage is, largely determines the effectiveness of the business' other marketing efforts, so it's worth the time and effort to smash it out of the park.

An Above-Average About Page

The About page is the greatest opportunity for an SSB to reveal its soul. It's a chance for us to convey who we are as people, recount our business journey and outline our achievements without risk of seeming brash or boastful. Yet most of us fail to take advantage of it.

An About page can include:

- A brief rundown of where and how you developed your expertise, gained experience and mastered your craft, prior to starting a business.
- The pain points or market trends you noticed that inspired you to start the business.
- When and why you chose to hone in on a particular niche market or field of service.
- Your business mission.
- Your accomplishments and accolades.
- Why your service is different or better than other available alternatives.

To create an emotional connection with potential customers, the About page needs to go beyond mundane or superficial facts. It needs to tell a story of how the business came to be and evolve over time – who brought it into existence, when, how, why, for whom and to what end. It should be an honest, humble, human tale – written with passion and personality – with key dates and names woven into it for context and legitimacy. Written well (remembering to refer to yourself in the third person, unless writing in the format of a letter, within quotation marks), the About page can be one of the most powerful means to cultivate an emotional connection with potential customers. Intertwining key facts with connective copy can make a striking impression – subtly framing yourself as the hero or heroine of your field or industry.

Practical Magic

If writing feels hard, takes a long time, or isn't effective the first time around, it's logical to question your writing abilities. But rest assured, most of us are capable of writing compelling copy. As author William Zinsser wrote:

> 'Writing is thinking on paper, or talking to someone on paper. If you can think clearly, or if you can talk to someone about the things you know and care about, you can write.'[29]

But that doesn't mean it's easy. Zinsser also said:

> 'Writing is hard work. A clear sentence is no accident. Very few sentences come out right the first time, or even the third time. Remember this in moments of despair. If you find that writing is hard, it's because it is hard. It's one of the hardest things that people do.'

So, if writing is frustrating, it doesn't mean you're not cut out for it. It means you care about what you're writing... and that's the best possible basis for crafting compelling, connective copy.

If a particular headline, word or sentence has you stumped, the key to pushing through is getting out of your own head. This can mean taking time out or – if you know what you're trying to say but can't find the words to say it – seeking online inspiration.

When writing, I keep four extra browser tabs open at all times for this very purpose, for instant access to the following resources:

- **Thesaurus** (e.g. *www.thesaurus.com*) – to find a better word or expression for one I have in mind, including those starting with a specific letter (to create alliteration).
- **Dictionary** (e.g. *www.dictionary.com*) – to check the suitability or spelling of words.
- **Rhyming dictionary** (e.g. *www.rhymezone.com*) – to find a suitable rhyming word.
- **Cliché finders** (e.g. *www.westegg.com/cliche* or *www.rhymezone.com*) – to find clichés or colloquialisms containing a certain word.

Most recently, I've added a tab to my copywriting reference hub: the artificial intelligence (AI) text generation chatbot, ChatGPT (*https://chat.openai.com*). While I'm never satisfied with the text produced by chatbots and typically rewrite 80% of it, ChatGPT, Google Bard or Bing Chat can save hours of time and frustration by kickstarting 'blank slate' writing projects. Instead of staring at an empty page, suddenly I've got a clear structure for the body of text I need and, within it, a few standout phrases to massage into high-quality, authentic copy.

Together, these tools are my copywriting magic kit. Over the years, they've expedited and enhanced my copywriting efforts, expanded my vocabulary and developed my writing intuition, allowing me to perform increasingly captivating writing acts... as they can for anyone with an interest in marketing. Used regularly and in conjunction with the tricks and techniques presented over the last few chapters, they'll help unleash your copywriting prowess too – and you'll find that the magic of connecting, convincing and converting becomes more practical, more natural and a whole lot more fun.

CHAPTER 12.

GETTING LOUD & PROUD WITH PRODUCT SHOTS

If forced to choose, most of us would associate ***product photography*** with retail goods, not service outcomes, which makes sense. In an age of digital consumerism, we rely heavily on images of mass-produced retail goods to buy them sight unseen. But product shots are no less relevant for skill-or-service businesses. When featured in SSB marketing communications, a striking product shot can have a powerful cut-through effect

– cultivating positive feelings about a business and a spark of desire to engage its services.

Three forms of product photography are most relevant to SSBs: *retail product*, *end result* and *visual signature*. Depending on the business model at play, photos from at least one of these categories can be critical; setting clear customer expectations, contributing to a sense of professionalism and, most importantly, demonstrating what we're capable of.

Retail Product Photography

Many of us stock small retail products as a sideline or supporting act to our business' main event... and wisely so. Developing or on-selling retail products (a range of hair care products at a salon, for example) can be a great way to build or capitalise on a strong brand while generating a stream of income that's not reliant on physical labour.

To build momentum with retail products – especially online – catalogue-worthy photos are vital. For third-party products, this can be as easy as requesting product shots from a supplier or distributor. For products developed in-house, a professional photo shoot is a must. It takes a surprising amount of time, equipment and knowledge to produce the simplest of product shots, so an experienced retail product photographer is worth their weight in gold.

IMPORTANT!
Although the photos in this chapter are printed in greyscale, full colour photos are critical to Secret Service success. A bonus file containing colour versions of these images is available to download from *www.secretservice.biz/downloads.*

Photos 1 & 2: Retail product shots – Handmade botanical products and perfumes by Cherie Em *www.cherie-em.com* | Photography by Drawcard Photo *photo.drawcard.com.au*

Photo 3: Retail product shot – Unclad wines by Ivybrook Farm *www.ivybrook.com.au* | Photography by Drawcard Photo *photo.drawcard.com.au*

Photo 4: Retail product shot – Handmade earrings by minski++
www.instagram.com/minskiplusplus | Photography by Drawcard Photo
photo.drawcard.com.au

Photo 5: Retail product shot – Element Grey benchtop (as backdrop)
by Stone Ambassador *www.stoneambassador.com.au* | Photography
by Drawcard Photo *photo.drawcard.com.au*

The biggest decision to make before choosing a retail product photographer is the desired image background. Retail product shots can be isolated with a white or coloured background, staged with a plain or patterned background, or given greater context through an on-location shoot. This all depends on how and where the images will be used and the mood you want to create – natural, clinical, homely, luxurious... The possibilities are endless. To narrow things down, it can be useful to explore the sites of retailers whose brand identity you admire to see the approach they've taken, then look for a photographer with a similar style of photos in their portfolio.

End Result Photography

Whether we sell retail products or not, what most of us *do* have to photograph is a combination of *end results* and *visual signatures* unique to our skill-or-service offering.

An **end result** is the outcome we provide to a customer. This outcome can be visible – therefore, photographable – or not, depending on the nature of our business.

For those of us with a visible end result, it's vital to display photos of past skill-or-service outcomes on our website. Whether we work in construction, crash repairs, cosmetic dentistry, dog grooming, food services or any other service involving *creation* (the production of something from scratch) or *transformation* (improving or overhauling something that previously existed), high-quality end result photographs are critical. They speak a thousand words by giving context to our market offering – conveying the type and calibre of work we're capable of and providing undeniable proof of our ability to get the job done.

Photos 6 & 7: End result shots – Kitchen benchtops and splashbacks by Stone Ambassador *www.stoneambassador.com.au* | Photography by Drawcard Photo *photo.drawcard.com.au*

For those of us with a skill-or-service outcome that's invisible or not visually appealing, end result photography is not always possible or practical. Advisers, consultants and technicians in many fields of service face this dilemma. For some (accountants, for example), end result photography is legitimately irrelevant. For others however, a little open mindedness and foresight is all it takes to create, and capitalise on, valuable photo opportunities. A plumber's services may not produce visually appealing outcomes all the time but, occasionally – upon the installation of a new toilet, set of taps, bathroom vanity or laundry tub for example – a brilliant 'before and after' photo opportunity arises. No matter how rare or fleeting such opportunities may be, capturing them on camera and displaying the resultant images on a website can be surprisingly powerful. It showcases our technical proficiencies, memorialises our work and attracts more of the same kind of work by default.

Photos 8a & 8b: Before and after shots – Benchtop makeover with DIY photography

Visual Signature Photography

Visual signatures are the aesthetic or tactile elements of the customer service experience – the funky wallpaper or centrepiece, a steaming cup of tea and stack of books on a waiting room table, an important piece of technical equipment, a sign-written vehicle, a laptop branded with our business' logo – anything that visually or experientially sets our skill-or-service offerings apart from those of our competitors. These seemingly insignificant sensory details, provided for the attention, appreciation or enjoyment of customers, are an integral part of our offering that, when captured on camera, can play an integral role in our marketing communications. Photographed well, they not only establish authenticity and uniqueness, they help build a sense of connection and anticipation – allowing service seekers to imagine what it would look and feel like to engage our services.

Photo 9: Visual signature shot – Four-legged friend at DoubleGlazed
www.doubleglazed.com | Photography by Drawcard Photo
photo.drawcard.com.au

Photo 10: Visual signature shot – Signage at Ivybrook Farm, Thomas Road,
Maslin Beach *www.ivybrook.com.au* | Photography by Drawcard Photo
photo.drawcard.com.au

Photo 11: Visual signature shot – Signage at Unley Park Dental Clinic
www.unleyparkdental.com.au | Photography by Drawcard Photo
photo.drawcard.com.au

Note however, the words *photographed well*.

To add value to our website, visual signature shots must be of excellent quality. When constructed, captured and edited with photographic artistry, visual signature shots make a significant contribution to the market perception of a business – proving that it physically exists and implying that it is run with high standards and attention to detail. Poorly constructed, low-quality images can have the exact opposite effect... doing more harm than good. For this reason, visual signature shots must be professionally produced or not used at all. While there's a place for amateur photos in the online marketing of many SSBs, visual signature and feel-the-love photos are not it. These are the domain of a specific type of professional photographer, revealed in Chapter 14. For now though, let's focus on photos we can safely snap ourselves.

DIY End Result Photos

Amateur or DIY photography is most useful for creating an ever-expanding archive of end result shots. Photographing the outcomes we achieve for customers is not only a handy skill to develop but an invaluable marketing task. While it's not advisable to use DIY photos as hero shots (those prominently displayed as website banners or feature images) they're ideal for photo galleries, blog posts and social media activity – where it's not always the professionalism of a photo that matters, but the legitimacy and operational momentum it conveys.

Luckily for us, DIY photography is easier, quicker and less expensive than ever before, thanks to the emergence of smartphones. Doing it ourselves no longer requires purchasing nor lugging around a big, expensive camera. With a smartphone and mini tripod, some basic tips and tricks and a bit of practice, we have all we need to capture respectable end result shots. At worst, photos taken on a smartphone are better than no photos at all – providing simple, visual proof of our capacity to deliver. At best, they can become an intrinsic aspect of our online presence – embraced, enjoyed or even eagerly anticipated by our online audience.

However, like any tool, a camera (smartphone or standalone) is only as good as the hand that wields it. Without an applied awareness of the basic principles of photography, amateur shots can appear slapdash or sloppy, and imply the same about the business they're representing.

3 Steps to Stronger Shots

Progressing from slapdash to advanced-amateur status in photography can be accelerated with the following three steps:

1. **Get Googling** – Thousands of websites offer free photography tips; more and more of which focus on smartphone photography. Googling 'How to take product shots on a smartphone', for example, taps into scores of handy insights – from the bare basics to backdrop hacks and clip-on camera lenses. To avoid overwhelm, start simple and slow. Commit to making the most of your device as it is, resisting any urge to buy special apps, gadgets or gizmos. In the world of photography, a bit of insight, exploration and experimentation goes a long way.

2. **See the light** – Lighting is one of the most critical and conscious considerations in photography, even for seasoned pros. Good lighting boosts our chances of taking a great shot, while poor lighting hinders them. A pivotal step towards the production of better photos is to start noticing the sources of light in your shooting environments, then researching and experimenting to capitalise on or enhance them.

   Most cameras, including those in smartphones, work best in strong, natural light. The closer to daylight, the sharper the image produced. If the subject (person or thing to be photographed) can be transported outside, the colour and clarity of the resultant image is usually far better. If it can't be moved outside, peripheral lighting equipment such as a specialist flash kit, lightbox or set of standing softboxes may be required to take well-lit shots.

When photographing outside, bear in mind that daylight doesn't mean direct sunlight. With the full glare of the sun comes issues such as overexposure and shadowing, which can be difficult for a professional photographer to navigate, let alone a novice. To save time and frustration, shoot on a cloudy day or in a solid shadow cast by a building or tree.

3. **Look on the bright (and straight) side** – Many of us overlook the role of editing in DIY photography, to the detriment of our shots. In settling for raw, untouched images, we forgo one of the greatest benefits of digital photography: the ability to enhance our images before releasing them into the public domain, where they will represent our business for better or worse, for years to come.

Often, cringe-worthy product shots can be easily, yet dramatically improved by tweaking their brightness and straightness. Using the 'brightness and contrast' and 'rotation' options in a basic image-editing program, it's usually possible to transform average images from unappealing and unprofessional to acceptable – or even quite striking. Brightening a photo and rotating it by a few degrees if it's off-kilter can make an enormous difference – shifting the focus from the poor quality of the image to the high-quality of the product or service outcome depicted within it. While it won't have the artistry and appeal of a professional shot, it will be acceptable in an online gallery... contributing to the perception of the business, rather than detracting from it.

Photos 12a & 12b: DIY end result shot before and after editing –
Chair reupholstery project

Becoming a reasonable photographer takes effort. Without consciously striving to improve – through research, trial and error – most of us would continue to click haphazardly and the quality of our shots would plateau. That's fine for personal photography but, for commercial photography, there's too much at stake. If our business produces a visible end result, we have a responsibility to generate high-quality product shots; we either learn, practise and improve our photography skills **or** commit to invest more money, more often, in the services of a professional photographer.

Going Pro

Whether we're snapping product shots ourselves or not, it's important to invest in professional product photography occasionally – even if it's only once every couple of years. Professional photography showcases a business' capabilities in the most pristine, professional and visually appealing light. It literally freeze-frames our skill-or-service outcomes at their freshest, finest and most influential – fit to feature in banners, brochures, ads and elsewhere.

A commercial photographer with expertise in an applicable field – whether it's the photography of buildings, food or drinks, or custom jewellery – is the secret to brilliant product shots. Photographing certain product categories is an artform in itself. Building interiors are an entirely different kettle of fish to wine bottles, for example. Hiring a photographer with relevant skills, experience and equipment can make all the difference to the integrity and impact of the final images.

How often to engage a product photographer depends on your business type and model. For an architect or builder with a small number of high-end projects, commissioning a photographer to shoot each service outcome (new build) may be feasible; for hairdressers, carpet cleaners or restaurants – businesses with a comparatively high customer turnover and low customer spend – it wouldn't be... but that doesn't mean it should be ruled out. For these businesses, hiring a professional photographer just once per year to capture two to three specially selected skill-or-service outcomes (hairstyles, cleaned carpets, plated meals, etc) is an excellent, budget friendly alternative. One quick shoot per year can be all it takes to produce a growing archive of 'wow-worthy' end result images.

Even if there's only a few to begin with, displaying professional product shots on a website takes the believability of an SSB's marketing claims and the perception of its technical capabilities to another level. It immortalises our work, giving us the ability to capitalise on it for years or (in the case of a large-scale design or building project) decades after completion – as a portfolio piece, a talking point and a catalyst for securing bigger, better projects. So it's time to shift our thinking. Professional product photography is no longer something we can dismiss as unnecessary, extravagant or relevant only to retail businesses. In fact, for those of us with a visual end result, no other marketing investment provides such incredible value, certainty or prolonged benefit, with the exception of one...

CHAPTER 13.

THE FEEL-THE-LOVE PHOTOSHOOT FORMULA

As important as product shots are, there's more to SSB photography than material objects. Capturing the humanity of a skill-or-service business in still images is key to marketing it – providing the most direct means to satisfy service seekers' intrinsic need for connectivity.

Connective needs derive from the right brain, which is highly visual and wired for human connection. Connective images of people (feel-the-love photos) work on both fronts, via the eyes and 'heart'. That means they can have a deep and profound effect on skill-or-service buying behaviour.

As introduced in Chapter 5 however, the need for connectivity isn't satisfied by any old headshot. Images of the people who underpin an SSB – carefully constructed and captured to convey who they are and what they do – are crucial. Attaining these takes more than snapping a few stilted headshots... it takes a fully-fledged photoshoot.

The 3Ps of a Feel-the-Love Photoshoot

To produce suitably connective feel-the-love photos, three aspects of a photoshoot require consideration and planning.

1. People ('Who')

The first thing to consider when planning a photoshoot is who to feature in the photos.

In case it hasn't been emphasised enough, the most important person to be photographed for inclusion on an SSB website is the business' owner. It's as vital for an SSB owner to appear on his or her website as it is for the lead actor in a movie to appear in the movie's trailer. Both serve as human lures, enticing potential customers to the main event.

There's no substitute for the owner's photographic presence on an SSB website without limiting the site's connectivity. As SSB owners, we are as integral to our business' marketing efforts as we were to its operational efforts on the first day of trade; grounding it with our physical presence and technical prowess.

But it's not all about us. Having key staff members, if applicable, and a couple of customers (actual or acting) available to roleplay typical service scenarios is ideal. Staff and customers add another dimension to SSB images, making it easier for service seekers to visualise engaging with our business and responding to a call-to-action.

Beyond this 'business family' of key staff and token customers, a professional shot of us (the owner) with actual family members or a beloved pet is worth considering for inclusion on the About page. Being seen with loved ones can be very endearing; subtly communicating that a) we're capable of connection with others, and b) there's more to our life than business, which can attract more business by default.

Having all staff present for a series of full group shots is good but not critical, so there's no need to panic if it's too hard to coordinate. Typical group shots contribute little to connectivity and can have a short lifespan – becoming obsolete if a staff member leaves on bad terms, for example. It's far better to have connective shots of two or three key staff than group shots of everyone.

2. Place ('Where')

The second consideration for a feel-the-love photoshoot is its location. The optimum place is an active worksite or two – a premises, workplace, construction site or combination thereof – wherever it is that we physically interact with clients and/or make our magic happen. This sets the scene to capture us and our team doing what we do day-to-day, which is essential for service seekers' to visually validate our service offering.

Anonymous locations are best avoided, in favour of those with a genuine association to the business. For example, conducting the shoot at a local park would only be relevant if we designed the park's playground or we maintain its gardens. A contextually relevant background is critical to a connective image, due to its added depth of meaning and capacity to resonate with potential customers on multiple levels. In other words, choosing a meaningful operational location goes a long way to producing images that are worth a thousand words.

For businesses with foot traffic, a feel-the-love photoshoot is best scheduled and conducted before or after hours. In a café or restaurant, for example, a consistently quiet period of the day or an hour or two before doors open to the public is ideal.

This avoids the added pressure of a live working environment, which can stifle the calm, warm atmosphere required for a successful shoot.

3. Particulars ('What')

The third and final consideration – one that can undermine the entire shoot if not taken seriously – is the finer detail, or particulars. These are the activities and accessories (specific to the service on offer) featured within feel-the-love photos; things the owner, staff and customers are doing, experiencing, wearing, holding or using, which visually validate them as the 'real deal'.

Activities are the essential, sometimes menial tasks we undertake to satisfy the needs of our customers. An activity could be cutting hair, using a jackhammer, looking at building plans, consulting with a patient, plumbing a sink, grooming a dog, sketching a design, serving a drink, running a workshop... whatever we do operationally – day-to-day, job-to-job or project-to-project – to meet and exceed customer expectations. Some of these activities may seem too insignificant to bother capturing on camera, let alone incorporating into our marketing materials but just because they're insignificant to us doesn't mean they're insignificant to our potential customers. Quite the opposite... they provide the visual validation that's unconsciously required to justify the engagement of our services. As such, they're invaluable to our marketing efforts.

Accessories are physical items involved in, or produced as a result of, our operational activities. There are two types of accessory, corresponding with the two types of product shot outlined earlier: end results and visual signatures. An ***end result*** is the final product or visible outcome of a service, such as meals and drinks in a restaurant, handcrafted jewellery or a newly installed kitchen. ***Visual signatures*** are items and elements that represent our service offering, are required to deliver it or are unique to our business – helping to distinguish it from others in the market. These can include fixtures, fittings, furnishings or other decor, tools and equipment, vehicles, building frontages and streetscapes, signs, menus, plans, folders, uniforms, safety gear and more; anything that proves our business physically exists, is suitably equipped to operate and provides an appropriate atmosphere.

It's essential to factor accessories into a feel-the-love photoshoot because they give our activities and resultant images authenticity and context. Accessories are required for almost every imaginable activity. A chef cooking a meal in a café kitchen for example, requires several accessories: a uniform, lit stove-top burner, frying pan and ingredients, to name a few. These accessories need to be anticipated and prepared in advance for a feel-the-love photoshoot to be as successful as possible.

Consideration of the particulars is one of the main things that sets feel-the-love photography apart from standard commercial photography. The right activities and accessories bring the people and place elements of a photoshoot together to create highly engaging ***service scenarios*** (roleplays of relevant, easily recognisable work tasks). Photos of service scenarios are infinitely more powerful than traditional head or group shots as they provide immediate, indisputable proof of our business' fitness for purpose – visually validating our service offering. What's more, they tell a compelling, visual story and convey a sense of human activity and energy, which – unlike generic images – spark the connectivity required to consistently drive leads.

Feeling the Love... From Behind the Lens

There are certain nuances to the feel-the-love photoshoot formula that a photographer needs to know to produce connective images. Without this insight, photographers can gravitate to settings and styles that might be fine for traditional headshots or product photography but useless for driving online leads to an SSB. So let's look behind the lens, starting with a basic but crucial consideration – image orientation.

Orientation

For the purpose of website design, landscape-oriented (short and wide) photos are more useful than portrait-oriented (tall and thin) photos. Landscape-oriented images are more conducive to being cropped into **banners** – eye-catching feature areas that span the width of a webpage. Banners are the most striking way to display connective imagery on an SSB site, so ensuring photos are planned and shot to fit them is vital. As a rough guide, at least 90% of photos generated from a feel-the-love photoshoot should be landscape-oriented.

Figure 10: The ideal orientation of shots taken on a feel-the-love photoshoot

90%
Landscape orientation

10%
Portrait orientation

Composition

Various shot lengths and styles are necessary to produce a comprehensive range of feel-the-love photos. The ideal proportion of shot lengths in the final suite of images is:

Figure 11: The ideal length of shots taken on a feel-the-love photoshoot

LONG SHOTS (10%)

Long shots are those taken from as far back as necessary to capture the entirety of a subject, such as the full form of a person (head to toe). Landscape-oriented long shots make highly effective and versatile banner images, as they are easy to crop to the required size and shape without losing the context of the image.

While converting long shots to banner images is easy, the process of capturing them in the first place can be challenging, if not impossible. There needs to be quite a distance between a camera and a standing human subject to fit them in a landscape-oriented frame; a distance that's implausible in a lot of service scenarios due to the confined nature of most SSB premises. Unfortunately, if a building's walls get in the way, there's not a whole lot that can be done about it (except perhaps shooting through a window).

However, there's always scope for long shots outdoors. If an SSB's services are delivered outside (landscape gardening, al fresco dining, etc), then long shots of service scenarios captured outdoors are a must. And even if they're not, outdoor long shots can be used to put a modern spin on the traditional group shot. When a photographer is not limited by four walls, unique and engaging group shots can be composed, such as the one below. Whether it's a group of staff leaning, sitting or standing with applicable accessories (in this case, glasses of wine) outside their business' premises, on an active worksite or among a lineup of branded business vehicles, some of the most connective long shots can be those captured outdoors.

Photo 13: Long shot – The Ivybrook Farm family *www.ivybrook.com.au*
Photography by Drawcard Photo *photo.drawcard.com.au*

IMPORTANT!
Although the photos in this chapter are printed in greyscale,
full colour photos are critical to Secret Service success.
A bonus file containing colour versions of these images is
available to download from *www.secretservice.biz/downloads*

MEDIUM SHOTS (70%)

Medium shots are taken closer to a human subject than long shots – usually incorporating the head and torso and cutting off at the waist or legs. Medium shots are more conducive to a feel-the-love photoshoot than long shots, requiring less distance between the camera and the subject. But their practicality is not the reason why medium shots should comprise 70% of feel-the-love images... It's because they are the most effective.

High quality medium shots infuse an SSB site with context and connectivity – critical to the creation of a Lead Machine. They have the capacity to strike an optimum balance of people, place and particulars; far enough back for the background of a service scenario to contribute to the context and validity of an image but close enough for the foreground to depict intricate connective details, such as facial expressions and energetic exchanges.

Three particular types of medium shot need to be composed and captured at a feel-the-love photoshoot: ***candid action shots, semi-paused smiling shots*** and ***authority shots.***

Candid Action Shots

Candid action shots are those of an SSB owner or staff member who is immersed in a service scenario. Whether they're rewiring a switchboard, chopping ingredients or serving a customer, they are focused intently on the task at hand, as if a photographer wasn't there. The aim is to capture the person absorbed in a moment of active service, not looking at the camera.

Although they're not always the most connective, candid action shots have a host of other benefits. For one, they provide pure visual validation – showing the owner or staff with their nose to the grindstone. They also play a pivotal part in the shooting process – helping the individuals being photographed relax into their role. Lastly, as the only type of medium shot that doesn't feature someone looking at the camera, they add variety to the mix of final images – preventing shots from losing their impact by looking too similar.

Photo 14: Candid action shot – DoubleGlazed *www.doubleglazed.com*
Photography by Drawcard Photo *photo.drawcard.com.au*

Photo 15: Candid action shot – Ivybrook Farm, Thomas Road, Maslin Beach
www.ivybrook.com.au | Photography by Drawcard Photo
photo.drawcard.com.au

Photo 16: Candid action shot – minski++ *www.instagram.com/minskiplusplus*
Photography by Drawcard Photo *photo.drawcard.com.au*

Photo 17: Candid action shot – SA Irrigation & Landscaping
www.sairrigation.com.au | Photography by Drawcard Photo
photo.drawcard.com.au

Photo 18: Candid action shot – Unley Park Dental Clinic
www.unleyparkdental.com.au | Photography by Drawcard Photo
photo.drawcard.com.au

Photo 19: Candid action shot – Tiling Services Australia *www.tilingsa.com.au*
Photography by Drawcard Photo *photo.drawcard.com.au*

Semi-paused Smiling Shots

The semi-paused smiling shot is the same as a candid action shot but with a crucial distinction... a smile, directed at the camera (and therefore, at viewers of the image) by the owner or featured staff member. To capture a semi-paused smiling shot, the service scenario is literally paused, mid-task, and the owner or staff member ('server', for ease of reference) prompted to turn and smile warmly at the camera. Semi-paused smiling shots are arguably the most important of all feel-the-love images because they provide connectivity and visual validation all-in-one.

Photo 20: Semi-paused smiling shot – Beggs Building
www.beggsbuilding.com.au | Photography by Michelle Ridland

Photo 21: Semi-paused smiling shot – Beveridge Constructions
www.beveridgeconstructions.com.au | Photography by Michelle Ridland

Photo 22: Semi-paused smiling shot – minski++
www.instagram.com/minskiplusplus | Photography by Drawcard Photo
photo.drawcard.com.au

Photo 23: Semi-paused smiling shot – Need Trade Services
www.needtradeservices.com.au | Photography by Drawcard Photo
photo.drawcard.com.au

Photo 24: Semi-paused smiling shot – SA Irrigation & Landscaping
www.sairrigation.com.au | Photography by Drawcard Photo
photo.drawcard.com.au

Photo 25: Semi-paused smiling shot – Tiling Services Australia
www.tilingsa.com.au | Photography by Drawcard Photo *photo.drawcard.com.au*

For semi-paused smiling shots to be as effective as possible, there are three rules to follow:

1. **The solo smiler rule** – Only one server in each service scenario (the owner or a single staff member) should be prompted to smile at the camera at any one time. If everyone in a service scenario smiles at the camera at once, the images can seem too staged and lose their connective charm.

2. **The candid customer rule** – Service scenarios are meant to highlight the physical presence, personality, passion and prowess of the server, *not* the person being served. If customers are to participate in a service scenario, they should be directed to focus on playing their role candidly *without* looking at the camera. Customers can contribute enormously to a service scenario but if they look directly at the camera it will detract from the scene, diluting the connective impact of the image.

As callous as it may sound, it can help to think of customers as merely props or placeholders. Like any other accessory, customers are there to enhance the visual interest, authenticity and believability of service scenarios, not to play a starring role. Thinking of customers as human props instead of models helps ensure their presence adds value to the final photos, rather than undermining them.

3. **The senior smiler rule** – When shooting a service scenario of two or more servers, the owner or most senior staff member in the frame should be the designated 'smiler'. All others should work happily around them, ignoring the camera. Depending on the size of the business, this tends to limit the smiling 'stars' of the photoshoot to between one and three senior individuals – those with the most expertise, authority and accountability.

   Without this rule, staff members can be starred for the wrong reasons, such as youthful exuberance or good looks. This can dilute the connective power of the images; wasting the opportunity to capture the mastery and maturity of senior staff.

   An SSB's most senior authority and greatest marketing asset is its owner. The final photos need to reflect this, in both quantity and quality. As the owner, there should be more photos of us – smiling warmly at the camera – than any other person. For this to happen, we must embrace the role of 'senior smiler' in every service scenario applicable to our areas of expertise. Unless a business has no other staff, the owner doesn't need to be in every shot of every service scenario but the more shots they feature in (with and without other staff), the more connective the final suite of images will be.

Authority Shots

Authority shots are geared to emphasise the authority and approachability of the owner. The aim is to capture their professional identity in such a way that it's obvious they're the leader and driving force of the business.

Composition-wise, an authority shot is an offshoot of the other medium shots, taken after a service scenario has been completed. It requires stripping the scenario back to basics; just the place, the owner (or owners, if more than one) and minimal particulars – no activities or foreground accessories – just something to sit or lean on, if desired. An authority shot is a simple still shot of the owner, sitting or standing in a comfortable position, smiling warmly while looking directly at the camera.

Photo 26: Authority shot – Beveridge Constructions
www.beveridgeconstructions.com.au | Photography by Michelle Ridland

Photo 27: Authority shot – A Rare Notion *www.ararenotion.com.au*
Photography by Drawcard Photo *photo.drawcard.com.au*

Photo 28: Authority shot – SA Irrigation & Landscaping
www.sairrigation.com.au | Photography by Drawcard Photo
photo.drawcard.com.au

Photo 29: Authority shot – Tiling Services Australia *www.tilingsa.com.au*
Photography by Drawcard Photo *photo.drawcard.com.au*

Photo 30: Authority shot – Unley Park Dental Clinic
www.unleyparkdental.com.au | Photography by Drawcard Photo
photo.drawcard.com.au

Photo 31: Authority shot – Guess who | Photography by Drawcard Photo
photo.drawcard.com.au

Authority shots are more posed than candid action and semi-paused smiling shots but should still look relaxed and natural. A prime example would be a builder standing in front of a worksite with arms crossed, or leaning against the open door of a work ute.

To be suitable for an authority shot, the owner's stance should feel comfortable, look natural and have no negative associations. While it could be argued that the crossing of arms is inappropriate for a commercial photoshoot, it can look authentic and endearing if the subject's field of expertise requires physical exertion (building, fitness training or sculpting, for example). For more professional, white collar services (like psychology, consulting or accounting), standing with arms crossed can appear guarded or untrustworthy, just as having hands in pockets can give the perception of detachment or laziness. Considering how authority shots may be perceived is important to ensure they don't accidentally impede connectivity.

CLOSE-UPS & EXTREME CLOSE-UPS (20%)

The remaining 20% of photos are reserved for **close-ups** of human interactions with accessories (hands using a tool, for example) and **extreme close-ups** of accessories themselves (the visual signature product shots introduced in Chapter 12). Close-up shots add variety and artistic appeal to the subpages of a website; providing a reprieve from medium shots so they don't start to lose their connective impact.

Photo 32: Close-up shot – Inside Out Makeovers & Maintenance
www.insideoutmakeovers.com.au | Photography by Drawcard Photo
photo.drawcard.com.au

Photo 33: Close-up shot – Inside Out Makeovers & Maintenance
www.insideoutmakeovers.com.au | Photography by Drawcard Photo
photo.drawcard.com.au

Photo 34: Close-up shot – minski++ *www.instagram.com/minskiplusplus*
Photography by Drawcard Photo *photo.drawcard.com.au*

Photo 35: Close-up shot – Need Trade Services *www.needtradeservices.com.au*
Photography by Drawcard Photo *photo.drawcard.com.au*

Photo 36: Close-up shot – SA Irrigation & Landscaping
www.sairrigation.com.au | Photography by Drawcard Photo
photo.drawcard.com.au

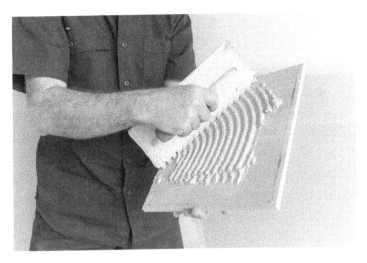

Photo 37: Close-up shot – Tiling Services Australia *www.tilingsa.com.au*
Photography by Drawcard Photo *photo.drawcard.com.au*

With an assortment of lengths and styles of shot, the images produced through a feel-the-love photoshoot should be distinctly different but united in look and feel.

Shoot Direction

One of the main factors determining the success of a feel-the-love photoshoot is the photographer's ability to direct people and proceedings. Only the photographer can see the people, place and particulars as they appear through the camera lens, so only the photographer has the power to oversee and influence them for the business' greater good.

The individuals participating in feel-the-love photoshoots are generally not experienced models. Business owners may be confident and in control, day-to-day, but that doesn't mean we're confident in front of a camera, or that we're equipped to control the proceedings of a photoshoot. Like any other amateur model, we need clear direction from the photographer to: 1) put our best face forward, and 2) move swiftly from one service scenario to the next – ensuring we end up with an ample assortment of high-quality images.

Without the photographer taking charge, we can inadvertently sabotage ourselves; hiding modestly in the background, encouraging others to take our place at the centre stage of a service scenario or avoiding the camera altogether. These tactics may seem funny at the time but, left unchecked by the photographer, they can undermine the entire Secret Service Website Formula, making them less amusing in the long run. Engaging a photographer with strong leadership and people skills (and a solid understanding of the purpose of the shoot) mitigates this risk. The right photographer brings a sense of confidence, direction and momentum to a shoot, boosting productivity and energising those involved, resulting in a strong set of final images.

Directing a feel-the-love photoshoot requires a fusion of technical- and self-confidence, humility and social finesse. It takes a certain level of technical experience and creative foresight to confidently take control, keep people on track and produce an adequate assortment of high-quality images. It takes humility to act and serve in the best interest of a business, and empathy and social diplomacy to bring out the best in the individuals involved. There's always something to do: prompting participants to stand or move in different ways, to change accessories or activities, relate to each other more warmly, smile, look focused, behave more naturally (by asking the right questions, telling jokes, suggesting exercises, etc)... all the while identifying image opportunities, considering the intricacies of lighting, composition etc, ensuring enough images of key individuals and service scenarios are attained, maintaining a calm, confident and encouraging demeanour and physically taking photos. Feel-the-love photography is the ultimate in multitasking; a role that might sound difficult to fill but, when you know what kind of photographer to hire (revealed in the next chapter), it becomes infinitely easier.

CHAPTER 14.

10 STEPS TO A PHOTOSHOOT THAT'S FAST, FUN & FLATTERING

The old saying 'failing to plan is planning to fail' definitely applies when it comes to a photoshoot. The worst way to approach it is to say 'we'll work it out on the day'. While you might end up with a couple of decent shots, it'll be a far cry from what could have been achieved with a bit of forward planning.

With that in mind, there are 10 steps to plan, prepare for and execute a first class feel-the-love photoshoot.

1. Select Strong Service Scenarios

It pays to start with the end in mind; brainstorming a list of three to five operational activities that will make strong, photographable service scenarios. The most connective scenarios involve:

1. The **production** of an end result (a chef preparing meals, a barista making coffee, a builder using a power tool, an architect drafting a building, a mechanic fixing a car, etc).

2. The **delivery** of an end result to a customer (meals or drinks being served, an architect showing a client the plans for their dream home, a mechanic handing keys back to a vehicle owner, etc).

3. The **experience or enjoyment** of a service or end result through images of happy interactions between the business owner or staff and customers.

For each service scenario, map out who will be in the frame (the *people*), where it will be staged (the *place*) and what will be happening or featured in the shot (activities and accessories comprising the *particulars*).

A detailed list of service scenarios is vital to guide a shoot's proceedings and ensure the photographer has a range of photo opportunities to capture. It serves as a clear, organised yet flexible brief – paving the way for the photographer to do their best work in alignment with the business' needs and expectations. A list of three to five service scenarios provides enough scope for a dynamic, productive shoot, without stifling the photographer's creativity or intuition.

Not all feel-the-love photos need to be of service scenarios but most will stem from them. Opportunities for other shots – extreme close-ups of accessories or visual signatures, for example – tend to present themselves as the shoot unfolds, or they can be left until the end.

2. Perform a Sitemap/Scenario Cross-Check

A photoshoot is a rare event for most SSBs, so we need to make the most of it – ensuring we get enough images to adorn our website. Nothing's more annoying than realising, after the event, that the opportunity to get professional images of certain service scenarios has been missed. This can be avoided by cross-checking the list of intended service scenarios with the website's proposed sitemap (outline of required pages) in advance – making sure there's at least one applicable banner image planned for every page. If a particular page doesn't have an applicable planned image, there's an *image gap* to address. Most image gaps can be filled by adding certain service scenarios or product shots to the photoshoot schedule.

Figure 12: Example of a hand-written sitemap / service scenario cross-check

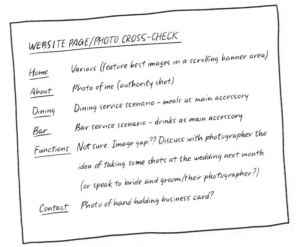

3. Find a Photographer

Commercial photos of any variety are best obtained by hiring a professional, but feel-the-love photos even more so. Beyond their fancy cameras, technical knowledge, peripheral equipment and editing applications, feel-the-love photographers have something special. They have the empathy, artistic insight, eye for detail and split-second timing required to capture the humanity of an SSB and produce an impressive collection of images, crafted for connectivity.

There's an enormous difference between a feel-the-love photographer and a typical commercial photographer – the type most business owners would instinctively think to hire. Unless we only sell physical products, or are prepared to hire two separate photographers (one for products and one for people), engaging a traditional commercial photographer can be a major mistake. That's because most are trained to capture the surface of physical things – usually very still, lifeless things or unemotive human models. To produce a Lead Machine, we need to capture more than what people look like... we need to capture the essence of who they are. This requires a photographer who doesn't specialise in photographing 'things' but one who specialises in photographing people.

I learned this the hard way, after hiring a respected commercial photographer to do a shoot for an interstate client. Upon receiving the final images, I was incredibly disappointed and it suddenly dawned on me... I'd hired the wrong guy. As crazy as it sounded, I didn't need a commercial photographer. I needed a wedding photographer.

Experienced wedding and/or family photographers have the ability to notice, and capture on camera, fleeting human moments and the feelings behind them. They are masters at transmuting people's actions, interactions, emotions, characteristics and personalities into images that tell a unique and engaging visual story – all under the immense pressure of a once in a lifetime event. Like a ninja, a good wedding photographer skillfully integrates into the environment of each shoot, capturing split-second moments of joy, love and connection – many of which are so organic and all-consuming that the subjects don't even realise they're being photographed.

Great wedding photographers not only *capture* naturally occurring moments, they can successfully *manufacture* them. Calmly and confidently, they guide, relax and relate with the individuals they're photographing; coaching them to exude natural, connective warmth on cue. This is no mean feat, requiring finely tuned technical and social skills, along with plenty of patience. The ability to manufacture moments *with* feeling *through* feeling, enables them to bring out the best in their human subjects and capture that 'best' on camera.

This fusion of skills and attributes makes wedding photographers perfectly suited to the role and responsibilities of a feel-the-love photographer. They're primed to help present an SSB as a soulful human enterprise by capturing its people, places and particulars in their best, most connective light.

4. Phone the Photographer

After identifying a local wedding/family photographer, the next step is to phone them, explain what's required, request a quote and, if happy to proceed, book a shoot. Explaining what a feel-the-love photoshoot is – with reference to this book – and discussing service scenarios (people, places and particulars) is important from the get-go, setting expectations and boosting the chances of the final photos fitting the bill. Ideally, the photographer will help fine-tune the details; suggesting the best time of day to shoot in certain locations, etc.

5. Rally the Troops

If any staff, customers or family members are to participate in the shoot, they need to be aware of its purpose and importance, as well as what's required of them: where they need to be, when to be there and what they need to do to prepare and participate effectively. There are four steps to this:

1. **Clear your calendars** – As soon as the shoot is booked, make it official by entering it in calendars, diaries and/ or scheduling systems. It needs to be clear that no other appointments are to be scheduled during that block of time.

2. **Source a model release form** – Model release forms are documents signed on the day of the shoot by participants or 'models' (staff, customers and others to be photographed). These release the participants' legal rights to the images, so they can be used in marketing communications with no legal ramifications.

   Some photographers can supply a model release form upon request. If not, one can be sourced online and, ideally, looked over by a lawyer. Getting model release forms completed and signed on the day then filing them away for safe-keeping is a bit like a free insurance policy, geared to protect your photographic investment.

3. **Set expectations** – The next step is to provide written instructions to participants, outlining what's expected of them on the day. To assist with this, a draft document titled *Website Photoshoot – Staff Email* is available to download from *www.secretservice.biz/downloads.*

4. **Hold the tone** – The attitude staff bring to a feel-the-love photoshoot is largely determined by that of their leader.

It's important to remain upbeat and enthusiastic about the shoot from the moment it's scheduled, and to talk about it regularly in the lead-up, so the significance of the shoot isn't lost or overlooked.

6. Prepare the Particulars

In the weeks leading up to the shoot, it's crucial to check the accessories required to execute the planned service scenarios. Will they be available and accessible for use on the day of the shoot? Are they clean and in good working order? And, thinking outside the box, are there any opportunities to brand certain accessories with the business' logo or colours?

Capturing brand elements in feel-the-love photos – be it a logo on a shirt or a feature wall in a key colour – makes a big difference to the authenticity and visual impact of a website. The best and easiest way to do this is to wear branded uniforms for the shoot or, at least, matching shirts or aprons. A bit of consideration about what each person will be wearing can have an enormous impact on the final images – sparking visual interest through colour repetition, reinforcing the brand and verifying that the people and scenarios depicted in the images are the real deal.

Safety gear and high value assets, like vehicles or technical equipment, provide extra opportunities for brand placement. A sticker, printed in-house, is all that's needed to add a logo to a hard hat, for example, while some inexpensive adhesive signage is enough to transform a plain vehicle into a branded asset, suddenly worthy of being featured in photographs. Small amounts of suitably coloured paint or decor can also be used to inject brand colours into the working environment, thereby sneaking them into the images. This can make a striking difference to the overall impact of a website.

We only get one chance to make a first impression. The images captured in a feel-the-love photoshoot go a long way to determining the outcome of that chance – whether service seekers will be attracted or repelled in the first instance. Cultivating opportunities for visual branding helps make the most of it, by creating more authentic, engaging and enticing imagery.

Anticipating and alleviating threats to the first impression is just as important. Unironed shirts won't necessarily be noticed on the day, for example, but they'll stick out like a sore thumb in photos. The more opportunities and threats are anticipated, acted on or addressed ahead of time, the better the final images will be – hence the need to set clear expectations of staff, prepare accessories in advance and, importantly, tidy up.

7. Tidy the Shoot Locations

While a certain amount of 'stuff' can contribute to the authenticity of an active work environment, there's a big difference between stuff and mess. Rubbish and excess clutter will detract from the people, place and particulars in a photo, reducing its impact. There's only so much that can be removed or repaired during editing without distorting the image, so it's not wise to rely on the magic of Photoshop to remove unwanted clutter or unsightly features.

Instead, check the shoot locations in advance. Remove any rubbish and store any old or unused furniture (spare chairs, etc) out of sight. Clear floors and benchtops of clutter, other than the accessories to be used in service scenarios. Dispose of all rubbish and do a thorough clean – wiping down benches, cleaning floors, windows and mirrors. Temporarily remove any printed signs, posters and point of sale materials and move bins out of sight to help the area feel cleaner and larger. This may seem like overkill but, trust me, the benefit of a thorough pre-shoot tidy up will become clear upon receiving the final images.

8. Get Made Up

Most of us aren't professionally photographed every day, so it's the perfect opportunity for a makeover. Whether it's engaging the services of a personal stylist to help identify or develop a signature style, buying/borrowing items of clothing or jewellery, or scheduling a hair or makeup appointment, the rule is this: Anything that helps you align who you feel you are on the *inside,* at your most confident, with the image of yourself that you present on the *outside* is a worthy investment.

Here's why...

The closer we come to aligning our inner sense of self with our projected outer self, the more at home we tend to feel in our own skin and in front of a camera. We feel calmer, more confident and, in turn, appear more authentic, powerful and attractive to others.

For SSB owners, aligning our inner and outer selves means letting our honest preferences relating to image and style float to the surface. A feel-the-love photoshoot is the perfect opportunity to explore your professional self image; determining what makes you feel the most comfortable and confident. Makeup, no makeup or a bit of lippy? Uniform, dress, suit, or jacket and jeans? Sophisticated, edgy or retro? Warm or cool colours? And so on. There's no right or wrong answer – only what feels right while being occupationally appropriate. A 'power outfit' and professional hair and makeup session – if that feels right – is not about putting on a mask for the camera. It's about removing any veils of insecurity that may otherwise inhibit you, so you can present yourself at your professional best.

Actualising your personal image preferences is key to being captured on camera in your most powerful energetic state. For those of us who are a little camera shy, getting 'done up' can provide an enormous confidence boost, bringing out our performance persona and helping us appear more relaxed and natural in front of the lens.

Seeking to present yourself at your professional best for a commercial photoshoot may feel self indulgent but, of all the days of your career, that's the day for it. The calm, confident persona presented on that one day will be captured and capitalised on for as long as the photos are accessible online. That makes getting done up, in whatever way feels authentic, a lucrative, long-term investment. It's a step of the process to embrace and enjoy, guilt-free; one that helps ensure the final photos become an income-inducing asset that are utilised proudly for years to come.

9. The Final Formalities

Other than getting dressed and done up on the day of the shoot, there are a couple of last minute tasks to check off before handing the reins of control over to the photographer. One is to double-check the places and particulars; hiding any residual clutter and rounding up the required accessories, ready to move as seamlessly as possible from one service scenario to the next. The other is to get model release forms signed as participants arrive for the shoot and collect them in a folder to file in a safe place. Once that's done, there's one last step...

10. Relax

As soon as the photographer arrives, the organisation of the shoot is complete and it's time to slip into another role... star of the show. Relax, embrace and enjoy it, trusting the photographer to guide you through the process and you'll be surprised how happy you are with the final shots.

CHAPTER 15.

LA VIDÉO DE L'AMOUR

While it may not be pivotal to the creation of a Lead Machine, videography and the Secret Service Website Formula are a match made in heaven. Videography has the unique ability to bring sights and sounds together to create a highly connective, somewhat immersive experience. This makes it a powerful addition to any SSB website project.

As introduced in Chapter 6, three types of website enhancer video can be well worth featuring on the main, more static pages of an SSB site: *testimonial videos,* an *explainer video* or a *micro-documentary.* Although these may have sounded quite self-explanatory when presented earlier, there are nuances to each that can make or break the impression they leave on potential customers. Without an awareness of these nuances prior to production, time and money can be wasted, and the opportunity to boost visitor engagement and conversions can be lost. So let's take a look at the technical subtleties of each.

Testimonial Videos

Testimonials recorded on video can be highly beneficial to a business' marketing efforts but – as with other enhancer videos – they can do more harm than good if poorly planned and executed. Putting a customer on the spot, with no prior notice or predetermined questions, is a surefire way to capture a lacklustre testimony. It will be bland, bleak and devoid of the little details that make testimonials believable, resulting in an underwhelming or even off-putting video... a far cry from the powerful piece of social proof it could have been with a more considered approach.

All it takes to produce a great testimonial video is clear direction. This is easiest to achieve by adopting an interview structure: question, answer, question, answer, etc. Posing a series of predetermined questions helps focus a customer's attention on specific aspects of the service and outcome, rather than setting them up to provide a wishy-washy, token response. It guides their thoughts, feelings and resultant verbal spiel, leading to a series of higher quality, more comprehensive insights. Cut together with some basic editing – omitting the original questions – these responses can be brought together to create a seamless and engaging video.

The questions to ask to obtain a video testimonial are no different to those for a written one. All that's needed is a concise set of three or four questions, designed to extract a story from the customer – from initial fears to post-service delight. For a list of suggested questions, refer back to 'Asking for Attestments' in Chapter 10.

A testimonial video is best kept short (from 20–60 seconds) and need only be a medium shot of a single person talking. For added effect, it can be spliced with close-up shots and/or video footage or photos of the end result. That's about as complicated as it gets.

The technical simplicity of testimonial videos means hiring a videographer to produce them can be feasible. Professionally produced videos, complete with high end lighting, sound, composition and editing, contribute a great deal to the perception of a business, through the implication of high standards and attention to detail. Getting a set of three or four testimonial videos professionally produced is the most cost effective way to tap into these benefits. It is less involved than the production of an explainer video or micro-documentary, therefore less expensive – particularly if scheduling several customers to be filmed over the course of a morning or afternoon, at a single location (avoiding multiple recording sessions). It's the best way to reap the rewards of professional video, on a tight budget.

While getting testimonial videos produced professionally is a worthy consideration, it's not the only option. Thanks to smartphone video technology, recording them in-house is quicker and easier than ever before. With a smartphone, a predetermined list of interview questions and a happy customer, testimonial videos can be captured whenever and wherever convenient, with no out-of-pocket expense.

6 Tips for Recording Testimonial Videos on a Smartphone

To get the most out of a smartphone as a means to record testimonial videos, there are six things to consider before hitting 'Record':

- **Sound quality** – The sound in a testimonial video should be good enough not to draw attention to itself. If the video is too soft or muffled, for example, it's likely to be perceived as annoying and unprofessional, causing viewers to give up and click away.

   For testimonial videos, or any recording of someone talking, the voice should be crisp, clear and not impeded by ambient noise. To achieve this, a phone-compatible lapel microphone (also called a lavalier microphone) is usually necessary. A lapel mic, clipped to the clothing of the speaker, dramatically improves the quality of a smartphone recording and, in turn, the professionalism of the final production.

- **Lighting** – While sound quality is by far the most important element of a DIY testimonial video, good lighting goes a long way too. As with photography, being mindful of the strength or absence of light in the shooting environment greatly enhances the quality of a smartphone video production.

- **Background** – Just like with a feel-the-love photoshoot, giving some thought to the background of a testimonial video (what's in the shot, behind the customer) can make a big difference to the end result. Recording a testimonial in situ, with the customer's home, workplace or other relevant location in the background is ideal. This gives the testimonial an added sense of authenticity and context;

making it (and corresponding marketing communications) all the more believable.

- **Stable footage** – Aside from poor sound and lighting, nothing screams 'amateur' more than a shaky picture; when the footage jolts or jiggles about, due to the recording device being held by hand. To avoid the distraction or disorientation this can cause to viewers, the video should only ever pan (move) with a purpose or stay still.

A stable picture is achieved by keeping the recording device in a fixed position – usually with the help of a tripod. A full-size tripod (with a smartphone adapter attachment) is preferable as it's easy to manoeuvre to the desired height and angle. However, a mini tripod perched on a shelf or ladder can do the trick too.

Note that zooming in or out while recording is as amateur as poor sound quality or a shaky picture. The recorded zoom is an outdated practice; abandoned by professional video producers in favour of 'fixed focal length' filming. Zooming creates an unnatural, awkward effect, which draws attention away from the subject to the movement itself, so it should be avoided at all costs.

Although less visually offensive, using a smartphone's zoom function to hone in on a subject *before* pressing 'Record' isn't ideal either. Due to the digital zoom technology used in smartphones (as opposed to the optical zoom in higher end, standalone cameras), it's better to move the phone to the required distance than to zoom into it. By moving the phone, the video will appear sharper, therefore more professional.

- **Proximity** – For a testimonial video, a medium shot of the customer's head and torso – recorded at eye-level from a distance of approximately one metre – is ideal. This creates a comfortable sense of 'personal space' for viewers, similar to that of a face-to-face conversation... not too close to feel encroached upon and not too distant to miss subtle facial expressions.

- **Post-production** – What happens with a testimonial video after recording it can make all the difference between an average production and great one. Post-production edits can include cutting out interview questions and awkward silences, adding overlaid text titles and captions, inserting photos of the service outcome or adding background music. A couple of tactical tweaks – actioned with basic video editing software – can enhance the video significantly, improving its ability to engage and influence website visitors.

   If post-production sounds all too technical, consider outsourcing it. Video editing is an ideal project to outsource via an online freelancing service such as Fiverr or Upwork. A crystal clear project brief and the time to sort through a deluge of quotes from offshore applicants is all that's needed to get an initial video editing project underway. This process becomes much quicker once you've found a freelancer you're happy with. Simply return to the same person with each new video, inviting them to quote on the project exclusively. Before long, they'll know exactly what you require and expect; making light work of post-production.

The Explainer Video

The second type of website enhancer video – *applicable only for SSBs with a non-traditional business model* – is an explainer video. Explainer videos are fun, informative videos that are usually one to three minutes long. They can increase engagement and website conversion rates when used by the right business for the right reason – usually to explain an innovative solution to a problem.

A good explainer video is geared to be fun and easy to watch through a combination of sound, movement and storytelling. A voiceover typically does the 'explaining' while text and pictures focus the viewers attention, draw the eye and visually reinforce the spoken message.

The most effective explainer videos tell a story rather than merely stating facts. This is commonly achieved through narrated animation – a cartoon featuring a fictional character who represents the business' ideal customer. The character is introduced (e.g. 'This is Julie'), then their journey followed from pre-purchase problem to post-purchase satisfaction, emphasising the emotions they felt along the way.

Depending how they're produced, explainer videos can be expensive. High-end, custom animation by an experienced agency can cost thousands of dollars per minute of animation, rendering it out of reach for most. Plenty of budget friendly alternatives are available though. For those with the time and motivation, explainer videos can be generated for minimal cost using online video production platforms like Animaker or Powtoon. Another option is to post a job on Fiverr or Upwork; finding and hiring someone to create a video to meet a clear brief.

But before getting carried away with colours and cartoon

characters, the most important aspects of an explainer video are its script and voiceover. If the script is sloppy and the voiceover computer-generated or read in a foreign accent (not native to the country in which the business is located), it won't matter how good the video looks, it will drive website visitors away. For this reason, it's worth engaging a copywriter to craft a compelling script and a local voiceover artist to read it. An experienced copywriter will write from a viewer friendly marketing perspective instead of a boring, technical one – distilling the problem, solution and selling points into a clear, concise and consistently engaging narrative. In doing so, they'll lay the foundations for a successful explainer video, reducing the risk of the production turning out to be a waste of time and money.

The Feel-the-Love Micro-Documentary

While explainer videos can be beneficial for those with non-traditional business models, for most SSBs a micro-documentary is the far superior choice. The soul and sensorial reality of a service-based endeavour can't be captured or conveyed with a cartoon. An animated explainer is devoid of a human presence, which means it's ill-equipped to satisfy the connective needs of service seekers. A micro-documentary is exactly the opposite; primed to capture the reality, humanity and artistry of an SSB for maximum connectivity.

As with feel-the-love photos, producing a feel-the-love video requires careful consideration and planning. There are many aspects to filming and editing a micro-documentary that can't be left to chance, starting with its scenes.

Clips & Components of a Micro-Documentary

Part of what makes a traditional television documentary informative, interesting and engaging is the selection of scenes and collation of clips, edited together in a sensical way. No one scene lingers for long. It changes every few seconds – often alternating from someone speaking, to a series of clips evidencing a spoken point, then back again. This creates a sense of momentum which carries viewers through to the film's end.

A feel-the-love micro-documentary is no different in that it needs a progression of clips and components to keep viewers engaged. Unlike a traditional documentary, however, the components of a micro-documentary must do more than maintain interest and momentum. They must evoke a sense of connectivity and offer the utmost in visual validation... to the extent that viewers feel more compelled to take action at the end of the video, than they did at the start. To give ourselves the best chance of achieving this, there are seven main clips or components to consider.

1. Candid Action Footage

Like candid action shots in a feel-the-love photoshoot, candid action footage shows us (the SSB owner) going about our work as if the camera wasn't there. This is best captured through staged service scenarios, filmed from one or more perspectives (distances and angles), from long shots to extreme close-ups. Shooting from more than one perspective is worthwhile, as it paves the way for a more dynamic, engaging micro-documentary that immerses viewers in our working world – the epitome of visual validation.

An artistic take on candid action footage can be achieved through time-lapse photography. A time-lapse segment consists of hundreds or thousands of individual images of a process or event, captured sequentially at set time intervals. When cut together and played as a video, this creates the effect of compressing time or fast-forwarding. As a segment of a micro-documentary, time-lapse is not only entertaining for viewers, it can boost the perceived value of our services – allowing us to demonstrate a slow and intricate production process in a short period of time.

2. Owner Interview Footage

Most documentaries of human subjects feature interviews with experts, and for good reason. Logical and emotional insights are more meaningful and believable when delivered 'straight from the horse's mouth' by those with an intimate knowledge and first-hand experience of the subject.

In an SSB, the expert is us – the owner. Our business would not exist or, in most cases, function without us. This makes us the expert by default – pivotal to the production of a successful micro-documentary. Our physical, intellectual, emotional and verbal input is as essential to the success of the final video as it is to the success of our business; to reap the potential benefits, we must be prepared to go all-in. For a micro-documentary, this means being interviewed on camera.

Besides the words that are spoken, the one thing that sets owner interview footage apart from more agenda-driven videos (e.g. sales videos) is where the attention of the interviewee is directed. Instead of talking down the barrel of the camera, the interviewee's eyes and attention are directed toward the camera operator or interviewer positioned just off-screen. This is a subtle but important distinction. It helps create a video that's more editorial in nature, rather than an overtly commercial plug.

Directing our attention to a camera person or interviewer doesn't mean staring point-blank at them. It means communicating with them naturally, as if in a heartfelt conversation with them alone. Human communication is more than words; it's our body language, mannerisms, tone of voice and more. Engaging in a one-on-one conversation with a physical person located just off-camera draws these out of us more effectively than the unnatural scenario of speaking to a piece of equipment. It helps us communicate at our most natural, memorable and endearing. And for viewers to 'feel the love' we have for our business, that's exactly what we need.

Another subtle but important consideration for owner interview footage is the background of the shot. Just as it is in a feel-the-love photoshoot or testimonial video, the background is a prime opportunity to add depth of meaning and visual interest to interview footage. Instead of a blank wall, which provides no additional stimulation or context, it's preferable to film an owner interview against the backdrop of a business' daily operations. This generates more engaging, connective footage, primed for visual validation.

As any documentary-maker or journalist will attest, the key to great interview footage is a series of well-prepared, open-ended questions. How questions are posed can make all the difference to the responses given – not only in terms of the language we use but the tone, manner and general enthusiasm we have for what we're saying. For this reason, it's a good idea to seek input from the videographer or a copywriter when writing interview questions for a micro-documentary, ensuring they are geared to extract the most engaging responses.

When preparing for the owner interview, note that:

- Only a few interview questions are needed. Given the length of a micro-documentary, three or four are all it takes.

- All questions should be edited out of the video at the post-production stage (as suggested for testimonial videos). The purpose of set questions is to guide proceedings and prompt verbal responses to attain quality footage. Including them only wastes viewers' time and stands in the way of a seamless, engaging narrative, so it's better to cut them out.

- Interviewees can prepare in different ways, from writing a full script of responses to 'winging it' on the day, but striking the middle ground between these two extremes tends to produce the best result. Writing a script (with the intention of learning it by rote or reading word for word) can impede performance – coming across as boring or inauthentic. Not preparing at all can be even worse – resulting in a shallow or insecure performance that fails to resonate with viewers.

  The key to avoiding these extremes is to find a happy medium between 'overthinking' and 'underthinking' the interview. This can be found by carefully considering the most compelling aspects of your work and story, mulling the questions over in your mind and practising responding to them with heart and feeling. This lays the foundations for a compelling blend of casual but considered interview footage.

3. Owner Commentary

If the thought of being interviewed on camera is stomach-churning, there is an alternative... writing and recording a scripted, audio-only commentary, which is added to the video as a voiceover in post-production. As long as it's done well, this can result in an equally compelling production.

If not a confident script writer, it can be worthwhile seeking the help of a copywriter to craft a compelling commentary. To ensure the copywriter is clear about the purpose of the project, start by providing an example (such as the *It's All About the Carvings* micro-documentary shared earlier and below). Then, work closely with them to craft a script to the required length with an authentic voice and tone. Once written, refined and rehearsed, it can be recorded on the day of filming or in a studio, as determined by the filmmaker.

4. End Result Footage

End result footage is the video equivalent of product photography. It's a scene (or multiple scenes) depicting the end result or outcome of a service transaction. Ideally, it would be captured in situ and/or with the customer who purchased it. Optimum end result footage of a set of custom-made sails for a boat, for example, would be filmed at sea, complete with the boat owner raising/admiring their purchase.

5. Authority Shot Footage

An authority shot in micro-documentary terms is almost exactly the same as in a feel-the-love photoshoot. It's footage of the SSB owner in a confident stance, in their work environment, smiling warmly and directly at the camera.

A single authority shot at the very end of the film has a striking impact. As the only scene to feature a person looking squarely at the camera, it has the ability to cut to the connective heart of viewers, leaving them with a long-lasting, mental imprint of the face of the SSB owner, which embodies the sentiment of the film. This lingering imprint can draw visitors back to the website with the intention of taking action, long after their first visit.

6. Background Music (or not)

Background music is worth considering for enhancer videos of all types. It can help set a tone and bring multiple clips together into a cohesive production. That said, it's entirely optional. Sometimes, the purity of the spoken word, without music, can be more powerful. Alternatively, there may be ambient sounds involved in the delivery of a service (as there is in *It's All About the Carvings*), which can be recorded and utilised throughout the video for maximum sensory immersion.

If opting to include music in any commercial video, note that a paid licence from an authorised body (such as the Australian Performing Rights Association) may be required. To avoid copyright infringements or other nasty surprises, be sure to speak to your videographer about musical options and associated costs.

7. Call-to-Action (or not)

Whether or not to include a call-to-action on the closing screen of a micro-documentary is debatable. Many marketers would say it's a no brainer... that every opportunity should be taken to call potential customers to action – especially an online video. But as a Secret Service Marketer, I disagree. In my opinion, a micro-documentary is stronger without a call-to-action.

It should be agenda-free from start to finish and leave viewers wanting more; looking around the page for what to do next. An on-page call-to-action, stationed to the right or just below the embedded video, can then capitalise on this curiosity without tarnishing the benevolent nature of the video.

With these newfound insights, it's worthwhile rewatching the micro-documentary examples provided in Chapter 6 (pages 92 & 93). *The Art of What's Left Behind* features prime examples of time-lapse photography, interview footage and background music, while *It's All About the Carvings* makes brilliant use of owner commentary and ambient sounds. Both videos use candid action footage, with authority shots at the end for a strong, clear and connective finish.

To Film or Not to Film...

Amid the agenda-driven noise of online marketing, an unexpected dose of romanticism is a powerful thing. While feel-the-love photos deliver this hit quite sufficiently, a micro-documentary emphasising the human heart and soul of a business – the mastery of the work, the practical but often raw beauty of the work environment and the primacy and individuality of the owner – takes it to a whole other level.

A feel-the-love micro-documentary doesn't come cheap or without effort though. So, if you're looking to reap the rewards of an enhancer video with minimal expense or input, put the idea of a micro-documentary on the backburner and fire up a few testimonial videos instead. But if money's no object, or you're lucky enough to have an aspiring videographer in your entrepreneurial circle, plan and produce the best micro-documentary you can muster and prepare to reap the romantic rewards.

CHAPTER 16.

FIRST STEPS TO A STRONG SITE

Just as there are many ways to find 'the one' in a romantic sense – from online dating to a serendipitous encounter – there are many ways to land your dream designer or website. But rather than rattling off the options, let's approach them as a series of questions; the four questions you'll likely ask yourself when embarking on a website project.

1. Should I build it myself?

Usually, this is quite an easy decision. Either you're excited at the prospect of developing a website yourself, or you're not. For those with no knowledge, experience or interest in web design and marketing, or no time to commit to it, it's unequivocally better to hire someone who has. A desire to save money is not reason enough to do it yourself. There needs to be some underlying motivation, passion or pursuit of knowledge to jump the many hurdles required to bring an effective website to fruition, or it won't happen.

For those with a burning desire to give it a go, rest assured that the world of DIY web design has come a long, long way. Once upon a time, the decision to build a website without a web designer meant acquiring a base-level knowledge of HTML and an offline website application like Dreamweaver, then agonising over snippets of programming code for months on end... only to scrap it out of frustration, or push through to a site that was probably more of a lead repellent than a Lead Machine.

Nowadays, there are a plethora of platforms available to get a website up and running without laying eyes on a snippet of code. Many of these are *hosted solutions* such as Wix or Squarespace, which roll web hosting and a web design platform into one paid service. Using a hosted solution makes it relatively easy to set up and produce a website, even as a total novice.[30] It involves setting up an account with the host company, registering a domain name and directing it to the host company's servers (usually offered for an extra fee during the account setup process), choosing a suitable web design template as a base, then getting down to business – styling and structuring the site and populating it with content.

But easy isn't everything. With a hosted solution, the end result of an amateur user's best efforts is often not as fast, functional or aesthetically-pleasing as the template's demonstration page. If you deviate slightly too far from a template's scripted layout, the website can become an eyesore. It's important to realise too, that the site can never be transferred to another hosting server – it's stuck where it is, at the mercy of the host company's customer support department and pricing policy.

The alternative to a hosted solution is a ***self-hosted solution.*** As the name suggests, this is a more autonomous option, requiring the selection of independent providers for domain name registration and web hosting, as well as a suitable web design platform, such as the open source **Wordpress** platform, available via *www.wordpress.org.* Self-hosting is the option advocated by most designers. It can be a little harder to wrap your head around in the beginning, but well worth it for the freedom and flexibility it provides into the future.[31]

Whether opting for a hosted or self-hosted solution, a critical step in DIYing a successful site is choosing the right web design template, referred to as a ***theme.*** Depending on your platform of choice, there can be tens of thousands of themes to choose from. Themes for most platforms can be purchased from sites such as *www.themeforest.net*, with completely free themes often only a Google search away. For Wordpress, free themes can be found at *www.wordpress.org/themes.* Before getting too excited at the prospect of a free site, however... a word of warning. Free themes tend to come with little, if any, technical support so you're largely on your own. They can be low-quality, buggy or just inflexible; inhibiting the implementation of the components necessary to create a Lead Machine. Given that a website is an SSB's greatest marketing asset, it's worth paying for a high-quality theme; one that's smart, flexible and modern with easy to install demo content, drag-and-drop design functionality, well supported updates and ongoing customer support to make designing and maintaining a professional site as seamless and stress-free as possible.[32]

No matter what DIY products or services you're considering, always check the online reviews associated with them. Never take a provider's word for how superior their platform or theme is. Instead, run a Google search for *[provider/platform/theme name] reviews* and delve into the feedback left by previous customers. Look for common threads and trends (positive or negative) for things like the responsiveness of the customer service team, search engine friendliness and server speed. A little bit of digging before signing up with a provider can prove invaluable; revealing flaws and failings that wouldn't have come to light until you'd spent an exorbitant amount of time or money trying to overcome them.

Building your own website can be the cheapest option. However, in assessing the viability of a DIY site, be sure to consider the opportunity cost of the time required to research platforms and themes, educate yourself about how to use them, build a site and troubleshoot it, let alone create compelling content. However many hours you think it will take... multiply it by 10 for a more accurate indication. Weigh that up against the hourly value of your time to determine if it really is worth doing yourself or if you would be better off outsourcing.

If you do decide to go it alone, don't get so focused on doing it for free that you sacrifice the opportunity to implement the Secret Service Website Formula. If nothing else, consider budgeting a small amount for the creation of high-quality content for the homepage; engaging a copywriter for the headings, calls-to-action and body content, and a photographer to shoot a few feel-the-love images. This will make a world of difference to the impact and effectiveness of an otherwise generic web design.

2. Should I Engage an Amateur?

For those of us with no interest in doing it ourselves but no desire to spend a lot of money either, asking for or accepting help from a tech-savvy friend or family member can be a tempting option... but also a troublesome one. As well-intentioned as the individual may be (having generously agreed to take on the project for free, a nominal fee or under a contra arrangement) the fact is that it takes a good deal of insight, time and effort to deliver an effective, polished website. Amateurs tend to lack the necessary insight or underestimate the time and effort required, which can obliterate our hopes of a finished site, let alone a high functioning Lead Machine.

The opportunity to work with an up-and-coming or hobbyist web designer may seem like a fantastic opportunity but it can have an array of unwanted side effects, such as:

- Lengthy delays (wasting time, while losing the chance to drive leads and sales);
- The use of outdated or inflexible platforms, technologies and programming methods (resulting in a site that's old and antiquated before it's even launched);
- Derailed projects;
- Disappointment with the resultant website... if there even is one;
- Awkwardness between the client and designer;
- A breakdown in any pre-existing personal relationship.

Given these risks, engaging an amateur can cost more than expected. That said, every web designer has to start somewhere. If you're willing to: 1) risk the project falling through, and 2) micromanage them with the aid of this book, then by all means, give it a go. It might just be the start of a long and happy, lead-filled union.

3. Should I Hire Offshore?

If after decisions one and two, you reach the conclusion to engage the services of a professional designer, another consideration emerges – to explore offshore outsourcing or support a local business.

Utilising online portals such as Upwork or Freelancer to hire offshore workers has become a popular way to get a website up and running with minimal expense. This is due to the oversupply of cheap, skilled labour in countries such as India, Pakistan and the Philippines. However, like working with an amateur, the potential benefits come with risks.

My experience with offshore freelancers has been mixed. It's been great for the technical/programming side of projects – fixing little bugs and installing updates – but not for the marketing and design components. I gave up on offshore outsourcing for website design due to the constant use of dated styling techniques. I'd become attuned at spotting 'offshore design', characterised by sloppy text formatting and spacing, a lack of marketing-mindedness and – the thing I found most painful – the overuse of gradients and shadows resulting in sites that would date prematurely. I also found that, unless clearly stipulated, many offshore designers would think nothing of using unlicensed stock images in their designs – plucking images from online obscurity without considering the very real risks to the website owner of fees, fines and lawsuits due to blatant copyright infringement.

On the other hand, what I found refreshing about working with offshore designers – initially, at least – was that they weren't at all self-centric. They saw web design as a job, not a means for artistic expression, so they were happy to do whatever was asked of them to get a project over the finish line.

I soon discovered, however, that the absence of an artistic agenda does not make a designer service-centric. Far from it. My offshore designers happily did what I asked but not much more. They had little service-centric initiative – no design suggestions to improve user engagement or conversions and no involvement with content beyond pasting it in place. For some time, I tried to educate them about my approach and expectations but nothing seemed to stick. Our approaches were so different that it required me to micromanage the graphic design of each and every project, which wasted time and caused a lot of angst and frustration. Eventually, I found a fantastic local agency who were amenable to my service-centric approach and budgetary constraints, enabling me to bring the work back to Australia. Despite the higher cost per site, this decision paid off in spades – saving me time and money in many other ways.

For me, there's nothing like the sense of stability, certainty and confidence that comes from working with a trusted local team, particularly for a convoluted service like web design. In a world of limitless options and technologies, it's reassuring to have a local hand to hold; someone you know lives nearby, has a verifiable track record and is available to meet face-to-face if need be. This reassurance is invaluable, which is why websites designed by local designers and agencies prevail over cheaper alternatives despite their extra cost.

This is not to say that offshore outsourcing is an avenue to explicitly avoid. It can work but – like working with an amateur – it requires significantly more input and involvement from an SSB owner or project manager to produce an effective website.

Although it feels more secure, it's important to know that working with a local web designer is, in itself, no guarantee of website success. In fact, the most distressing web design experiences tend to result from working with locals, not outsourcing offshore. That's because we tend to expect (and pay) more when working with a local, leading to a greater sense of disappointment and betrayal if it all goes wrong. The higher the expectations, the harder the fall when they're not met.

To avoid the pain of a web design project gone wrong, there's one final, crucial decision to make before settling on a course of action...

4. Should I Lead the Service-Centric Charge?

Creating a Lead Machine website takes something extra... or rather, *someone* with something extra: the willingness and capacity to take the service-centric lead. Without a dedicated project manager to lead the charge, the project will revert to its default self-centric setting and the opportunity to create a Lead Machine will be lost. The crucial 'step back' that's needed – to: 1) see the business for what it is and where it aims to be, 2) identify and collect the components required to connect, convince and convert, and 3) ensure these components are bolstered by great design – will be missed, preventing the business from putting its best online foot forward.

The role of Lead Machine project manager will most likely fall to one of two people – either us as the SSB/website owner or our web designer.[33] If choosing to DIY, work with an amateur, hire offshore or hire a local who's rigid in their approach, the role of project manager and the responsibility of bringing a Lead Machine to life will fall to us by default. Expecting an amateur, offshore or rigid local designer to produce a Lead Machine without any service-centric direction or micromanagement is like expecting to find a pot of gold at the end of a rainbow... it's not going to happen.

Managing the creation of a Lead Machine takes a combination of big picture thinking and precise attention to detail. It requires a crystal clear understanding of and commitment to:

- The **purpose** of the project (the creation of a Lead Machine)
- The **strategy** to achieve the purpose (the Secret Service Website Formula)
- The **functional competencies or disciplines** required to action the strategy (the four marketing amplifiers).

It also involves selecting the right functional technicians (copywriter, photographer, videographer and web designer) for the project, providing each one with a set of clear and concise directives and overseeing progress as it's made. Taking the time and initiative to explain the project's purpose, strategy and function-specific aims and expectations to each technician from the outset is essential. Equally important is making time throughout the project to check that the directives have been understood and are being implemented, that progress is being made in the right direction and that the site feels on track to fulfilling its purpose as a Lead Machine.

Just as a proficient wedding planner liaises with a bride and groom to determine their wishes, brings various elements together to create their ultimate 'big day' and coordinates the event so seamlessly that no-one notices they're there, so too is the role of a Lead Machine project manager. However, instead of food and flowers, the latter brings together compelling copy and connective imagery.

Briefing a Non-Service-Centric Designer

For those ready to step up to the project manager plate – whether it's to keep costs to a minimum, embrace the challenge of a self-developed site or give an amateur a leg up – never underestimate the power of a great brief. Briefing a copywriter, photographer or videographer can be as simple as recommending or lending them this book and referencing the applicable chapters, along with a meeting or two. Briefing a non-service-centric web designer (an amateur, offshore, self-centric or rigid local designer) is more challenging because it requires far more business-specific detail.

Every business is different, with a unique set of aces up its marketing sleeve. As a Lead Machine project manager, it's our job to work with content creators to see the makings of magic in a business, identify its aces and source the marketing amplifiers (copy, photos and video) required for the web designer to make the magic happen. For this to translate to a high performing website, however, we (the project manager) must be on the same page as the web designer, both literally and figuratively, through the provision of a crystal clear web design brief.

Without a comprehensive brief, a non-service-centric designer will be focused primarily on the creation of a 'pretty online face' for a business. A pretty face is fine for a stock-standard, under-performing website but to create a Lead Machine, we need more than superficial beauty... we need substance. Without conveying an SSB's substance in a web design brief, the designer won't know it exists, let alone that it needs to be incorporated into the design. The business' marketing magic will remain hidden and the opportunity to create a highly connective website will be lost.

The brief required to get more than a 'pretty face' website needs to stipulate the site's purpose, priorities and prerequisite features in an easily digestible format. To assist with this, the Secret Service Web Design Brief is available to download for free at *www.secretservice.biz/downloads.* This is a customisable template geared to ensure the bases required to create a Lead Machine are covered – boosting the chances of ending up with a website that works, without hiring a service-centric designer.

Finding a Service-Centric Designer

The alternative to managing the project yourself is to find and hire someone to do it for you; someone up to speed with the purpose and particulars of the Secret Service Website Formula, the contacts to create high-quality website content and the systems to bring it all together in a timely, effective way. Ideally, this would be a freelance web designer or small design agency with a service-centric approach, experienced in applying Secret Service web design and project management principles.

In reality, however, finding a service-centric web designer isn't quite that straightforward. Until the approach becomes more mainstream, it's a matter of clearly communicating your web design expectations to potential designers until you find one who is amenable to it. Bear in mind that while outsourcing the whole process will cost more, it will save a lot of time and energy and increase the chances of producing a highly professional, effective and long-lasting website.

Foundations of Lead Machine Design

Once settled on a broad course of action (be it to DIY or engage a non-service-centric or service-centric web designer), there are a few things to check to ensure your new website will have the underlying capacity to function as a Lead Machine. These are not decisions or options but rather foundational prerequisites – boxes that must be ticked, no matter who develops the site or what technologies are used.

First and foremost, an SSB website needs to be 'friendly' in four ways. Knowing and implementing this from the outset is crucial; giving the site a greater chance of making a positive first impression by avoiding the user red flags that will otherwise undermine its performance. In turn, the site will have a longer, more lucrative lifespan.

Figure 13: The Friendly Four – Essentials of an effective SSB website

Mobile Friendly

A mobile-friendly website is a site designed to display effectively on smartphones and tablets. Mobile-friendliness is crucial, not only for a positive user experience but because Google now excludes mobile-*un*friendly websites from displaying in search results for searches performed on mobile devices. Given that over 64% of all Google searches are now performed on a mobile device, not having a mobile-friendly site has dangerous implications for SSBs – cutting our chances of being found online by almost two thirds.[34]

Avoiding this is as easy as confirming that the designer and resultant website will utilise RWD technology. **Responsive web design** (RWD) is the current standard in mobile-friendly web design. Older mobile-friendly sites had two versions of the one website running alongside each other – one to display well on a desktop screen and the other to display well on a mobile screen. RWD rolls everything into one sophisticated website which morphs fluidly to fit the size of the screen it's being viewed on. Nowadays, spending time or money on web design that's not responsive would be like buying a computer with a floppy disk drive – not the wisest of investments.

Search Engine Friendly

Search engines such as Google and Bing are incredibly valuable marketing platforms for SSBs, with the capacity to provide streams of highly targeted traffic to a website for free – if our website is geared to cooperate with them, that is. Search engine optimisation (an optional but highly recommended marketing activity covered in Chapter 20) can be necessary to tap into much of this traffic, but for many SSBs a base level of search engine friendliness can be enough to outrank the tired, old sites of other local businesses – scoring the lion's share of traffic and leads.

A search engine friendly (SE-friendly) website is a site that's conducive to being 'crawled' (browsed or scanned), interpreted and indexed by search engine programs known as 'web crawlers', 'spiders' or 'bots', then displayed effectively to search engine users. No one knows exactly what a search engine looks for or prioritises in a website because its algorithm (the formula that determines where webpages should rank in search results) is constantly changed. This is done not only to keep unscrupulous SEO workers on their toes but to improve the quality, accuracy and relevance of search results, making the search experience better, faster and more effective for users.

What we know for sure is that, to present high-quality search results, search engines favour websites with high-quality content. When content is clearly written, rich with relevant keywords and of genuine substance to users, it's more likely to rank well in search engines – so long as the website is built to support the efficient and effective crawling, interpreting and indexing of its content. To facilitate this, website content also needs to be: 1) readily accessible – fast to load, mobile-friendly, clearly structured with a well-considered 'sitemap' etc, 2) uninhibited – free of page errors, broken links, viruses, messy code, rasterized text, etc, and 3) up-to-date and well maintained, among other things.

As complicated as it may seem, much of our site's SE-friendliness hinges on the web designer and/or platform we opt to build with. As a rule of thumb for SSB owners looking to choose or approve the platform on which to build a new site: follow the crowd. Select a popular platform with a track record of SEO success, such as Wordpress. Taking an alternative route – be it a trendy hosted solution or a built-from-scratch solution (upon the recommendation of a technically-minded, self-centric designer) – risks falling short of the SE-friendly baseline and getting stuck with a website that simply doesn't deliver.

Website Owner Friendly

Owner-friendliness is the extent to which a website can be accessed, updated, added to and optimised by us as the site's owner, our staff or professionals of our choosing, independent of the original web designer.

Once upon a time, any changes to a website had to be sent to a web designer to be actioned due to the technical nature of the work involved. These days, thankfully, managing a website is far less technical. With a decent underlying platform, a website's administration area is accessed via a password protected dashboard in an internet browser. There's no code to wade through and far less margin for error. Simple adjustments and additions (like changing page content, adding pictures to galleries, creating blog posts and basic SEO) can be actioned by us – if we so choose – with little technical skill and no out-of-pocket expense. To minimise the risk of breaking the site, it can pay to get a designer's assistance with certain things – such as platform or security updates and design modifications – but there should be nothing stopping us from changing web designers or hosting providers if we want to. As the site owner, we should be in complete control.

User Friendly

The number one prerequisite for the design of a Lead Machine is user-friendliness. It must be geared to meet the needs of users – to connect, convince and convert in an intuitive, user-friendly way. This is only possible through a well-considered user experience and interface.

When the Secret Service Website Formula is followed, with a service-centric approach to design, user-friendliness is typically par for the course. Unless the site has functional glitches, the structure or content is inadequate or you've forced a square peg in a round hole (using a template not conducive to the design of a Lead Machine), it will be friendlier than most SSB sites by default. For maximum user-friendliness, embrace and embody the Secret Service Website Formula and select a designer who does too; work as a united team and you can't go too far wrong.

Last but not Least... The Fine Print

Beyond the Friendly Four, there's another foundational aspect to consider when developing a website. Although it makes little difference to a site's effectiveness, the fine print required to adhere to applicable laws and mitigate legal risk is a vital consideration. Web designers don't typically advise on this. It's a website owner's responsibility to confirm and provide the legal wording required to legitimise their site.

As a general guide for Australian SSBs, two pages of legal content typically suffice:

Page	Purpose	When is it needed?
Privacy Policy	To explain how users' personal information is used and stored.	A Privacy Policy is legally required if a website has an enquiry, contact or subscription form through which users submit personal details.
Terms of Use or Terms & Conditions	To explain how a website should be used and help protect the website owner from misuse of the site's content.	A Terms of Use page is an important safeguard, particularly for a website providing information that could be relied on by users as 'advice'. Through carefully worded clauses, such as a disclaimer, clear Terms of Use help protect a website owner from the ramifications of their information and intellectual property being used or relied upon in unintended ways. **Important note:** If goods or services are sold through the website, a more comprehensive Terms & Conditions policy is legally required to address topics such as returns and refunds, shipping, warranties and compliance with consumer law.

In certain situations, extra pages or provisions may be required. If third parties are allowed to advertise on a website (excluding search engine advertising), contribute to the site's content or promote to its subscribers, for example, the fine print will need more detail to set legally enforceable boundaries. If engaging with or selling to the European Union, the stringent requirements of the General Data Protection Regulation (GDPR) must be met, including the use of a *cookie notice* and other specific protocols. The United Kingdom and other regions have similar standards. Be sure to check what's required in the countries where the intended users of your site are located to make sure you comply with applicable laws and regulations.

Unless you're a lawyer, a website's fine print is not something to write yourself. As with any legal document or contract, an amateur attempt is likely to be riddled with legal vulnerabilities, if it's enforceable at all. Engaging a lawyer to write policies from scratch can be expensive though, with no foreseeable return on investment, so it can be hard for small businesses to justify. A good middle ground can be to source a high quality, regionally appropriate pack of legal documents online. Search for *'website legal documents bundle for [your country]'* via a web browser to explore available options.

Once the pages of fine print required for legal compliance and risk mitigation are ready, they can be made accessible via links in your website's footer. Avoid including them in the main menu at the top of the site as they're likely to scare potential customers away.

The Quest for the One

Many SSB owners choose a web designer based on convenience. It's common to meet a designer at a networking event or elsewhere, assume it's 'meant to be' and engage them on their personality alone, without objectively assessing if they're a good fit. Much like in love, we can want the relationship to work so badly – often out of apathy, or the hope of ending a seemingly relentless search for 'the one' – that we can settle for less than we need; overlooking values, traits and tendencies that don't align with our own.

To determine the fit and friendliness of a possible course of action (be it engaging a specific designer, or using a particular DIY platform), we have to ask some serious questions and carefully weigh up the answers. This is the only way to make an informed decision and reduce the risk of website heartbreak.

Important questions include:

- 'What platform would you build my website with?' Be sure to note down the answer to research it later on.
- 'What is the platform's reputation in terms of search engine and site owner friendliness?'
- 'Will a base theme or template be used or will it be built from scratch?'
- 'Will the site be mobile responsive (i.e. built with RWD)?'
- 'Will it be able to incorporate the features/functionality of a Lead Machine (as detailed in Chapter 18)?'
- 'What country would my hosting server be based in?' This can impact a site's loading speed.
- 'What ongoing costs are involved?' These can include domain name registration, web hosting, theme membership, maintenance and security updates, etc.
- 'Will I be able to add extra pages, photos and features down the track, if needed?'
- 'Will I be free to do some DIY SEO or involve an independent SEO contractor?'

- 'Will I have direct access to my website files via a cPanel or equivalent?'
- 'Will I be free to change hosting providers if I ever choose to?'
- If evaluating a designer, 'What is your main focus when embarking on a website project?' The more they talk about business outcomes like leads and sales, the better.
- 'I want to apply the Secret Service Marketing approach – how can you assist me with that?'

Even if you're not 100% sure what these questions mean, they'll start to make sense once you ask them of different designers and platforms, and compare the answers you receive. Like when dating someone however, it's not what a designer or platform representative says, it's what they do that really counts. So, beyond asking questions, do some hands-on research. Start by Googling them and their responses to validate them, then ask for links to websites they've recently built or that have been built by platform users. For each site, assess the following:

- **How quickly or slowly does it load?** – If the speed frustrates you, visitors to your future website will be frustrated too.
- **How responsive and mobile-friendly is it?** – To test this, visit the website on a computer (desktop or laptop) and use the corner 'handle' of the browser window to adjust its size to medium (about the size of a tablet screen), then down to small (the size of a phone screen). Notice if the website morphs fluidly to suit the various screen sizes or loses its aesthetic appeal.

- **As a marketing tool, how strong or weak does it seem?**
  – Are you engaged by what you see? Does it have clear calls-to-action? Would you be inclined to take action?

If your opinion is unclear after visiting the provided sites, you can always reach out to one or more of the sites' owners, politely explaining that you're considering the designer/platform they used and asking if they'd recommend them/it and why.

Finding 'the one' (the ideal web designer or DIY platform) can be a project in itself, but it's a whole lot quicker with clearly defined expectations. Being upfront about what you want – a website geared to serve as a Lead Machine, which ticks the 'friendly four' and 'fine print' boxes – goes a long way to ensuring that's what you'll get. It's as simple as asking the right questions, reading between the lines and verifying what you're told to determine if a designer or platform is up to the task. Even if you're not completely sure what you, or they, are talking about, taking the time to ask meaningful questions is crucial. It helps attract and retain those who align with you and repel those who don't; reducing the risk of being taken advantage of and boosting the chances of establishing a blissful, lead-filled union.

CHAPTER 17.

THE BUSINESS END OF SERVICE-CENTRIC DESIGN

While SSB owners stand to benefit from knowing what it takes to build a Lead Machine, another group stands to benefit just as much, if not more. Website designers across the globe have a vested interest in learning to create Lead Machines for SSB clients as a means to grow successful web design businesses.

For struggling web designers, switching to the production of Lead Machines (away from websites that generate mediocre results) can have a profound effect. It can be the key to gaining sales momentum, systemising and streamlining operations, becoming financially stable and experiencing a greater sense of personal and professional fulfilment – all by helping fellow SSBs get the marketing tool they need most... a website that really works.

However, a few behind-the-scenes changes can be required to support this switch. With that in mind, web designers and SSB marketers, this chapter is for you. SSB owners and others, once you've read the myth below, feel free to jump to the next chapter.

The Sexy Site Myth

In the world of web design, there's a myth that keeps many web designers stuck in self-centric, starving artist mode. It's that to be successful, a website must be unique, sleek and sexy enough to stand out in a design portfolio or be admired by creative peers. This belief subverts SSB marketing efforts for several reasons:

1. **Unique design is the enemy of easily understood.**

   Uniqueness is essential for the creation of a Lead Machine... but there is a crucial difference between unique *content* and unique *design*. Unique content (in the form of feel-the-love photos and copywriting) is critical to the effectiveness of an SSB website. A unique layout – designed and developed from a blank canvas – is not. An overemphasis on unique design not only wastes an SSB's limited resources, it can completely undermine the purpose of the project, with the resultant website requiring too much interpretation to be easily understood by potential customers.

2. **Sleek and sexy can be a barrier to action.**

   The design of websites using a sleek, minimalistic style has become popular in recent years, and understandably so. Minimalistic websites can be beautiful, with their pale grey text, clean lines and white space. But being appealing in an artistic sense doesn't make a site an effective marketing tool. That's because the epitome of sleekness and sophistication can't be achieved without sacrificing certain design and formatting techniques, such as text highlighting or the use of hand-drawn arrows to direct attention to a call-to-action. These techniques may seem crass or primitive to minimalists, but they're invaluable to service-centric designers because *they work*. They contribute to the creation of a highly engaging, user-friendly and intuitive website interface that's more likely to drive leads. And at the end of the day, that's all that really matters.

3. **Creative peers are not end users.**

If designing an SSB website for the acknowledgement or admiration of fellow creatives, rather than to satisfy the needs of the site's intended users, you can't expect to produce a Lead Machine. Designing a site for anyone but the business' ideal customer (be it creative peers, yourself or even the site's owner) is a recipe for real-world disappointment.

The success of a website isn't determined by its uniqueness, sleekness or sophistication, nor how impressive it is to those in the know. What matters is that it's designed in the best interest of the business it represents – to serve and satisfy the needs of potential customers and drive leads. This doesn't take creative genius; it just takes some insight and empathy – the ability to put ourselves in the shoes of the site's intended users to determine what they need to see and experience to feel sufficiently connected and convinced, then be converted into leads.

Designing websites in the best interest of SSBs can require a dramatic change of heart and mind – from rigidity and resistance (founded in ego) to insightfulness and empathy (founded in service to others). It's a big mental switch, but well worth it, providing an opportunity to escape starving artist mode and forge a prolific web design career with more clients, more income and a greater sense of contribution and control.

The Content Conundrum

The biggest practical implication for web designers switching from self-centric design to the service-centric design of Lead Machines pertains to content; knowing what content is required to connect, convince and convert, how to procure it and at what point in the design process it needs to be attained.

With a traditional, self-centric approach to web design, the acquisition of content from the client (SSB owner) takes a back-seat to the creative part of the design process. A site is usually designed before any content is received, in a process like this:

The Self-Centric Web Design Model

1. **Sales meeting** – A preliminary meeting in which the web designer introduces themselves to a prospective client, explains what they do and shows a portfolio of work they've done. The designer enquires about what the prospect likes and wants in a website (both aesthetically and functionally) and, sooner or later, provides a quote for consideration.

2. **Transmission of essentials** – If/when the quote is accepted (and any pre-emptive requirements such as payment of a deposit are met) the designer requests the bare essentials they need to get started with design and development – usually a high-resolution logo file, domain name and/or web hosting details and a list of required website pages.

3. **Design** – When now in possession of the bare essentials, the designer gets to work, producing visual mockups of one or more pages, often referred to as 'wireframes'. As no website content has been received at this point, dummy 'lorem ipsum' text and generic stock photos are used as

placeholders wherever the designer envisions the final content to slot in.

4. **Feedback and revision** – Next, the designer sends the initial designs through to the client, along with a request for feedback. Depending on the feedback received, one or more rounds of changes may be required to reach a point where the client is happy to proceed with development.

   Unfortunately, SSB owners can be so overwhelmed with delight at the prospect of being represented in such a professional, corporate capacity that enormous, underlying issues can be overlooked. Insignificant errors such as spelling mistakes are often corrected, while catastrophic big picture issues go undetected, and a design that's not equipped to connect, convince or convert is set in stone.

5. **Development** – Once the client gives the go ahead, the designer develops the site, taking it from a static design to an interactive website, not yet visible to the public.

6. **Call for content** – When sufficiently developed, the designer informs the client that the site is ready to be populated with page content and requests it be sent through.

7. **Mad panic and major delay** – The client scrambles to get content together, suddenly realising it's a bigger, more time-consuming project than anticipated. They finally send it through (perhaps in dribs and drabs over a matter of weeks), unsure if it's up to scratch. The designer doesn't flag any concerns so the client assumes their content is fine.

8. **Content population** – By the time the designer receives the content, they've mentally moved on from the project, having long since developed the site. Relieved to be

able to wrap things up, they accept the content without consciously considering its quality. The content is regarded as *fixed and final,* or worse – a necessary evil. It's inserted into position, a process that can be as frustrating for the designer as trying to squeeze a crooked, square peg into a pristinely carved, round hole. There's often more or less text than anticipated, along with poorly shot images that pack nowhere near the same punch as the stock photos used as placeholders in the original design.

9. **The big reveal** – Once populated with content, the designer lets the client know that the site is ready to be viewed and checked, before being made live. The client logs in excitedly but is underwhelmed. It's hard to articulate exactly what's wrong but something doesn't feel right. It doesn't have the same 'wow factor' as the original design. A few changes are requested in an effort to improve the situation but, not wanting to waste more time or money on it, they reluctantly agree to go live.

10. **Launch and bug-fixing** – The site is made live and any residual issues identified and resolved. The client is somewhat excited but mostly relieved that the site is finally finished so they can turn their attention to the next pressing matter.

11. **Fallout** – A few months later, the client realises the new site hasn't generated the return on investment they had expected. The designer hasn't made any further contact, so they're left feeling abandoned and underwhelmed by the whole experience, wondering where it all went wrong.

Where the Self-Centric Model Falls Down

In no other service industry does the nitty gritty of constructive action commence without the content (instructions and/or materials) to do a comprehensive job. Imagine if a plumber tried to lay pipes at a construction site without detailed pipework plans or the pipes themselves, or if an accountant tried to process and lodge a client's tax return without receiving their bookwork. The outcome of the service would be disastrous – fraught with errors, omissions and costly repercussions, if it eventuated at all.

As counterintuitive as it is, the 'design first, get content later' approach to web design came about for a valid reason. As any web designer will attest, waiting to receive a polished suite of content from a client *before* kicking into creative action is a recipe for business disaster. Projects can linger for months or even years, opening up a can of operational issues – job scheduling headaches, strained customer relationships, cash flow conundrums and more... until it all becomes too much and the business goes bust.

In the web design game, the logical alternative to waiting for content from clients is *not* to wait for it – to launch into creative action, despite not having any content to work with. This gives projects a sense of momentum that moves them through to completion within a reasonable timeframe. While this approach isn't the best for SSB clients (resulting in websites that aren't as effective as they could be, if at all), web designers who use it can at least stay afloat. But, for those who aren't satisfied with the status quo, there is another way.

Doing a Web Design 180

For a long time, I accepted the self-centric status quo despite a nagging sense of discontentment. Although most clients seemed happy enough, deep down I knew that the websites we were building for SSBs (around 95% of projects) were not generating the results they could be, largely because the content we collected from them wasn't geared to drive leads. I also knew that to do anything about it, we'd need *better* content collected *earlier* in the design process. This inner knowing distorted my perception of customer satisfaction; I constantly felt as though my clients were bitterly disappointed in me.

Needless to say, I was miserable, unfulfilled and lacked the motivation to pursue sales. I desperately wanted us to design websites that really worked but couldn't see how to make it happen. Then, one day, the feeling of discontent became so paralysing that I could no longer ignore it. So I sat down with a pen and paper to figure out how to move forward. In my mind, there were only two options – the equivalent of being stuck between a rock and a hard place:

Option 1) Stick to the status quo – Keep the web design process the same; suppressing my feelings of doubt and dread, and pushing through my resistance to making sales in order to build a viable business. This would mean settling for less – accepting that I would never achieve the kind of results for clients that would make me, or them, truly satisfied.

Option 2) Switch up the status quo, by collecting content upfront – Flip the design process on its head; collecting content from clients *upfront* so we could showcase it in the best possible way. This would mean pressuring clients to create and send through their website content from the moment they signed on the dotted line. Sure, it would get client communications off to a rocky start, plus there'd be a huge risk of project lag, budget blowout and ultimate business demise... but hey, at least I could sleep at night knowing we were designing more effective websites... or could I?

Upon articulating these options, it became clear why I'd been fraught with anxiety and discomfort for so long. I'd been wrestling with a choice between my integrity and my business – my heart and my head... and I couldn't fight anymore. The status quo had to change or I'd have to bow out gracefully and go get a job.

Before I had a chance to hit up the job search websites, something miraculous happened. The simple act of outlining my options on paper led to a realisation... even if I *were* to flip the design process on its head, the success of a client's website would still depend on the quality of the content they supplied us, which was almost always substandard. Although we'd receive the content sooner, it would be no stronger. There would only be so much we could do with it without blowing our budget and making a loss on the project. Without investing more time and energy into each project, our websites would be no more effective than they would if I was to stick with the status quo (the more viable but soul-sapping option 1).

And that's when it struck me: Why were we forcing SSB owners to be content creators, if they didn't specialise in creating content? All that time, I'd been forcing brilliant technicians, consultants and professionals – masters in their respective fields – to do something that didn't come naturally to them... something I knew more about. In handballing the responsibility of content creation to our clients, I was acting in my own best interest, not theirs; prioritising operational convenience over the experience and results of the businesses we were supposed to be serving. While it might have been nonsensical of our clients to think that *we*, or any web designer, could produce a powerhouse website with little more than a logo file and a few paragraphs, it was equally nonsensical of us to assume *they* could provide a comprehensive design brief and compelling content when marketing and content creation were not their fields of expertise.

So, in Bucky Fuller fashion, I scrapped the first two options and came up with a third:[35]

> **Option 3) Switch up the status quo, by collecting TOP QUALITY content upfront** – A carbon copy of option 2 with a couple of crucial differences: no settling for substandard content and no waiting around to receive it. Clients would need to meet my high standards or I wouldn't work with them. Simple.

Making top quality content a prerequisite for working with you might seem like a scary prospect for many web designers but I was at the brink of walking away from web design anyway, which meant I had nothing to lose.

3 Ways to Collect Top Quality Content Upfront

Having settled on option 3, I had to figure out how to make it happen. As far as I could see, there were only three possible ways to procure top quality content at the start of website projects:

1. **Empower clients to create quality content themselves** by somehow teaching them the specifics of the Secret Service Website Formula.

2. **Direct prospects to third party content creators** to craft quality content (compelling copy, feel-the-love photos and videos) before coming to us for web design.

3. **Provide all-inclusive website packages encompassing the creation of top quality content**. This would mean managing every aspect of every project: subcontracting the content creation functions we weren't equipped to provide (photography and videography) and handling the rest in-house... taking the critical responsibility of content creation away from the client.

After a period of trial and error, the most feasible course of action became crystal clear. Empowering SSB owners to create their own content (the first method of content collection) was calling to me – and eventually prevailed with the decision to write the *Secret Service Business Series* – but it wasn't going to make ends meet in the meantime. Directing clients to third party content creators (collection method 2) sounded fine in theory but, in reality, it meant every project was delayed or derailed. Web design sales would be left hanging while prospects went off to work with third parties, only to get lured away by nice, 'normal' designers promising them a quicker, cheaper result. This wasn't in their best interest, nor ours.

With options 1 and 2 ruled out, it was clear: content-inclusive website packages were the way to go. This meant replacing the self-centric web design model we'd adopted by cultural osmosis with an entirely new, content-inclusive, service-centric approach, outlined below.

The Service-Centric Web Design Model

1. **Education session or sales meeting** – A new take on the preliminary meeting in which the web designer focuses more on understanding and educating the prospective SSB client than on conveying their own achievements and capabilities. The SSB owner's results and frustrations are identified, discussed and put into context using the Busy/Slow Cycle (presented in Chapter 2 of *Secret Service Marketing*), the crucial role of a website is explained using the Marketing Wheel (Chapter 2 of this book) and the differences between a run-of-the-mill website and a Lead Machine are outlined, followed by the process of creating one.

   NOTE: The meeting plan that worked best for me can be found in Chapter 18 of *Secret Service Marketing*, 'Supercharge Your Sales Meetings'. Essentially, instead of putting things back on the SSB owner by asking what they want in a new website, the designer takes control – outlining what content is needed for the SSB owner to achieve their desired outcome, as well as a course of action for creating it. For me, this meant walking them through three clearly defined website packages – Kickstart, Smartstart and Powerstart – with no negotiation on inclusions or price.

2. **Content collection** – If/when a package is selected or a quote accepted (and any obligations such as paying a deposit are fulfilled) the designer requests the bare essentials they need to get started with design and development – a logo file, domain and hosting details etc but *not* a list of required website pages as that falls under the banner of copywriting.

   If the designer is facilitating content creation, the

copywriter and photographer (and videographer if required) are involved at this point. They're introduced to the client and initiate their respective roles – the photographer contacts them to discuss and book a feel-the-love photoshoot while the copywriter contacts them to schedule a time for an interview (either in person or over the phone) to 'dig for the gold'.

NOTE: With the service-centric approach, any content or supporting materials received from the client are considered variables, not 'fixed and final'. They may be used, improved or disregarded completely at the discretion of the project manager, web designer or copywriter in the best interest of the project.

3. **Content creation** – The copywriter determines the page names, crafts the on-page and off-page calls-to-action (excluding summary sentences) and writes the content for the homepage. There's no rush for the remaining page content. In fact, it can be better to write the inner pages in situ – after the website has been developed – to ensure it sits well on the page and is formatted in an engaging way.

Meanwhile, the photographer conducts the feel-the-love photoshoot, edits the photos and sends them through to the designer (*not* the client), ready to be used in the design.

4. **Design** – Equipped with homepage content and feel-the-love photos, the designer can now get to work, producing a visual of the homepage geared to connect, convince and convert.

5. **Feedback and revision** – The designer sends the initial homepage design through to the client, along with

a request for feedback. Although a couple of rounds of changes may be required before development can proceed, any concerns tend to be less about the design and more about the copy (pointing out the inaccuracy or irrelevance of certain statements, for example). As the content is 100% authentic (no stock images or placeholder text), the client tends to be overwhelmed for the right reasons – amazed by how professional and authentic their business looks, without a trace of corporate fakery.

6. **Development** – The designer develops the site, taking it from a static design to an interactive website, not yet visible to the public.

7. **Content population** – Content for the inner pages is received from the copywriter or, if preferred, the copywriter logs onto the developed site to write/populate it directly.

8. **The big reveal** – Once populated with content, the designer lets the client know that the site is ready to be viewed and checked, before going live. The client logs in to a site that's strikingly different to one they would have received from a run-of-the-mill website designer. They find the heart and soul of their business, captured and conveyed on screen. A few content tweaks are required but on the whole, they can't believe how easy the process was and how little work they had to do.

9. **Launch and bug-fixing** – The website is made live and any residual glitches identified and ironed out.

10. **Google push and traffic chat** – The designer pushes the website into Google using Google Search Console and phones the client to reiterate that the success of the site hinges largely on getting traffic to it. Suggestions for

driving traffic (such as those outlined in Chapter 20) can be made and complimentary activities offered.

11. **Lead monitoring and traffic advice** – The designer monitors the leads flowing in through the site and, two to three months later, reviews the results. If leads haven't started flowing organically, it's suggested to the client that they pursue other marketing activities to drive more traffic. This doesn't require deep analysis or input – simply directing the client to *The Modern Marketing Arsenal* can be enough to make them feel valued and supported by their designer.

Why the Service-Centric Model Outshines the Status Quo

The service-centric web design model is superior to the self-centric model, first and foremost, because it produces a better outcome. It enables web designers to create websites that produce real world, quantifiable outcomes for SSB clients in the form of leads, customers and business growth.

But the benefits of the service-centric model extend far beyond the client's bottom line. By insisting on top quality content and coordinating its collection upfront, the service-centric approach cuts the frustrations of the self-centric model off at the knees. It transforms the dynamic of the designer/client relationship; ending the frustrations of the 'content conundrum' for the designer, while relieving the client of the overwhelming responsibility of content creation.

Under the service-centric model, clients tend to be much happier and relaxed, both during the web design process and afterwards. Not only do they end up with a website that actually works (or at least, has the capacity to), they tend to feel a greater sense of camaraderie with the designer and be more likely to look back on the design process fondly, given they barely had to lift a finger for the website to come to fruition. All most SSB clients want is for buying a website to be a streamlined, straightforward process with a semi-predictable outcome, like when purchasing other business assets. The service-centric model makes this possible; gently guiding them through the process with minimal stress and bringing all required elements together with minimal effort – something that savvy SSB owners are happy to pay extra for.

Obviously, web designers benefit enormously from the service-centric model too. When it's implemented well, they can experience:

- Easier, more productive sales meetings;
- Increased sales conversions;
- Higher-paying customers and increased profit margins;
- Smoother web design projects;
- Stronger customer relationships;
- Increased customer loyalty;
- Increased referrals and word-of-mouth;
- Stronger testimonials;
- Increased demand for web design services;
- Greater job security;
- Reduced anxiety;
- Increased motivation;
- The ability to save time and money by streamlining operations;
- Business growth and longevity;
- And more.

For me personally, the best thing about switching from self-centric to service-centric mode was the feeling of satisfaction that came from genuinely acting in clients' best interests. Designing websites with the capacity to make a real difference in the lives of SSB owners – propelling them forward in their business journey – is an incredibly rewarding pursuit. A deep sense of pride and purpose flows from it... a far cry from the anxiety and frustration of designing for visual appeal alone.

If the service-centric model was to become the status quo, the web design industry would be challenged. Fewer web design projects would be lost to cheap offshore and 'non-content' designers because the benefits of paying more for Secret Service mastery would be obvious. There would still be a place for offshore workers – particularly for site maintenance and updates – but they too would need to adapt. This would change the face of the web design industry for the better; paving the way for stronger small business communities with more local jobs.

Wide-scale adoption of service-centric web design would also have a tremendous impact on professional content creators and their respective industries. Making a decent living as a freelance copywriter, photographer or filmmaker is no mean feat, largely due to a lack of awareness about the valuable contribution they can make to SSB marketing. With a shift to the service-centric model, this would change. Work would flow from web designers and agencies to copywriters, photographers and videographers organically, providing consistent income. This would make the business of content creation more appealing, lucrative and sustainable, enabling the copywriting, photography and videography industries to flourish.

Beyond the professions involved in Lead Machine design and content creation, adoption of service-centric web design has the potential to benefit every service profession – from accounting to zoological consulting and everything in between. Equipped with a Lead Machine (the product of service-centric design), every SSB has the opportunity to benefit from easier, cheaper, more effective marketing, reduced price-based competition and the many other advantages of the Secret Service methodology.

Essentially, adopting a service-centric approach to web design means everybody wins. It's infinitely more sensical, streamlined, satisfying and sustainable for the individuals and businesses involved. But above all else, it just feels right... and for a struggling service provider, that can make all the difference.

CHAPTER 18.

THE NUTS & BOLTS OF A LEAD MACHINE

Web design is the fourth and final marketing amplifier, not because it's any less important than the other three but because it's contingent on them. The design of a Lead Machine is only possible once content has been created – when we've got compelling copy, feel-the-love photos and, optionally, a video to work with. Only then can a truly effective website be designed; one which puts the content on a digital pedestal for service seekers to see, feel, understand, appreciate and, most importantly, act upon.

Creating this digital pedestal is not rocket science but there is science to it. Service seekers' minds function in a relatively systematic way, which means they behave quite predictably on a website. On the whole, they'll respond more favourably when certain web design principles and practices are adhered to than when they're not. As SSB owners and web designers, we need to acknowledge this and adapt accordingly if we want to design sites capable of propelling businesses to a higher level of growth and prosperity.

Boiled down to web design basics, an SSB site requires certain elements to be useful and fit for purpose – much like a building. A building without doors and windows would be an uninviting, inaccessible box; without a roof and walls, it would be a cold, disorienting frame; and without a strong foundation, the entire construction would collapse. We wouldn't dream of building a physical business premises with anything less than these basic elements and yet, every day, scores of digital business premises (websites) are built and launched with the equivalent of just that – far less than they need to serve their intended purpose. So, let's break it down... the essentials of a Lead Machine, starting with a solid foundation.

A Strong Foundation

The foundation of a website is the platform or framework on which it's built. These range from DIY website platforms such as Squarespace and Wix – typically used by business owners with no web development experience – through to advanced frameworks like Ruby on Rails and Django – used by master programmers to create the most technically sophisticated websites and applications in the online world.

While a Lead Machine website is not complex enough to warrant the use of an advanced framework, it's too complex for most DIY platforms. The foundation of a Lead Machine must be versatile enough to include specific, custom-designed elements in certain places, in a way that looks professional and pleasing to the eye. To the best of my knowledge, none of the self-hosted solutions sufficiently fit this bill – at least not without the intervention of an experienced web designer (defeating the purpose of a DIY platform).

As introduced in Chapter 16, my pick of all platforms and frameworks for SSB website development is Wordpress, and I'm not alone. Wordpress is the platform of choice for over 43% of website owners from individuals to global corporations.[36] That's because it's more than a web development platform; it's a highly versatile content management system (CMS) equipped to handle the requirements of simple, static sites through to complex data-heavy ones. For this reason, a whopping 63.7% (almost two thirds) of sites with a known CMS are built with Wordpress – remarkable, given the internet's monolithic size and the plethora of web development platforms available to choose from.[37]

Wordpress is a worthy choice for several reasons.

1. **It's free** – Wordpress is a self-hostable platform, available free of charge to anyone who wants to use it. All that's needed to get started is a domain name and a web hosting account with SSL security purchased for a nominal fee.

2. **It's smart and secure** – Wordpress is open-source software, which means its original source code is available for use, distribution and modification by others. Unlike with closed-source or 'proprietary' software, the creators of open-source software deliberately grant rights to users that would typically be reserved under copyright law. Giving away your rights as a software creator may sound silly, but it's actually highly strategic. It can result in a vibrant virtual community of astute developers, actively working to improve and enhance the software – for their own use

and for the greater good – in a system that embodies the ideals of communism, as is the case with Wordpress.

The Wordpress community, headed by a core group of developers, work tirelessly to improve and update it. The platform benefits from millions of minds – each with a vested interest in its continual improvement. This enables it to stay at the cutting-edge of functionality and security, for the good of all users and their websites.

3. **It's SE-friendly by nature** – Wordpress was developed first and foremost as blogging software. Due to the richness of content associated with blogging, search engines are believed to favour blog-based websites. Although it's impossible to know how much of an innate SEO advantage a Wordpress foundation provides, one thing's for sure: it gears a site for search engine friendliness from the get-go. Installation of the Wordpress platform paves the way for the creation of a content-rich site and the optimisation of that content for maximum search engine exposure.

4. **No provider 'lock-in'** – Unlike with hosted solutions, the existence of a Wordpress website does not hinge on monthly payments to a proprietary software service. As a Wordpress website owner, you are in complete control of your website and what happens to it. You're free to change hosting providers or web designers at any time without losing the entire site and being forced to start from scratch.

5. **Easy-access admin area** – All Wordpress sites have an online interface for behind-the-scenes management and administration, known as the 'dashboard'. This area allows the site owner (and any other authorised users) to make content changes, perform maintenance and monitoring

functions and execute more advanced developmental updates as required. Gone are the days of requiring an FTP program to download and wade through HTML files to find the spot that needs to be edited. With Wordpress, the back-end of a website is as accessible as its front-end, making updates and additions possible from anywhere in the world with nothing more than an internet connection and web browser.

6. **Options and extensions** – One of the greatest benefits of a Wordpress site is its aesthetic and functional versatility, made possible through the use of themes and plugins.

A *theme* is a set of template files that determines how a website appears to users. The files work together to establish the design and layout of pages and posts so they display in an appropriate, consistent and aesthetically pleasing way. As such, the task of designing or redesigning a Wordpress website predominantly involves the design and installation of a new theme.

A *plugin* is a piece of software that extends the functionality of a Wordpress site in a particular way. As it stands, there are over 60,000 plugins available for Wordpress, providing features and functions from contact forms, security filters and SEO frameworks to image galleries, shopping carts and appointment scheduling systems... just to name a few. Some are free, others are paid and many are a blend of both (offering a free version and a more comprehensive, supported version for those willing to pay for it). While too many plugins can slow a website down, a handful of strategically selected ones can provide all the bells and whistles a Lead Machine could need.

Framework, Façade & Fitness for Purpose

The theme and plugins used in a Wordpress site are equivalent to the framework and façade of a building. They determine its look, layout, structure, flow and functionality, as well as its fitness for purpose – how suited the site will be to performing as a Lead Machine (subject, of course, to the quality of content it's populated with).

Wordpress themes can be purchased premade or created from scratch but, for SSBs, neither is an optimum solution. The vast majority of premade themes simply don't support the design requirements of a Lead Machine. They tend to be too specific (designed for a particular type of business), too generic or too difficult to implement and modify. But a custom theme designed and developed from scratch isn't ideal either. The development of an entirely original theme (often referred to as 'bespoke' web design) is overkill for an SSB and a poor allocation of limited website funds. Custom design and coding waste time and money that could be invested in things that would have a far greater impact on the results produced by the site; namely, feel-the-love content (copy, photos and videos).

The optimum means of producing a Lead Machine lies in a blend of both options… using a premade Lead Machine conducive theme as a base for producing a customised website.

There are two ways for SSB owners to obtain a Lead Machine conducive theme:

1. **Hire a web designer with a Lead Machine template** from which they customise themes for individual SSB clients. Working from a base template allows a designer to keep design and development time to a minimum, so they have the time and budget to apply the Secret Service Website

Formula. It's what makes the development of a Lead Machine possible without charging tens of thousands of dollars for it.

2. **Use – or hire a designer who uses – a well-supported drag-and-drop page builder theme and/or plugin as a base**. A drag-and-drop page builder plugin is an extension that allows Wordpress site owners or designers to create, edit and customise web pages by dragging and dropping required elements into place... no programming code required. A page builder *theme* takes this a step further by providing a range of layouts/templates to select from as a starting point, avoiding the need to build from scratch. These layouts are designed to work seamlessly with the page builder plugin's drag-and-drop functionality, which makes them highly customisable and more amenable to the creation of a Lead Machine than other premade themes on the market.

   Whether you're planning to work with a designer or go it alone, the right page builder theme can change the game, producing a website that's far more adaptable and user-friendly at both the front and back-ends.

   For links to Wordpress page builders and other tools I use and recommend for designers and DIYers, visit *www.secretservice.biz/toolkit.*

Had it existed back then, I probably would have explored using my favourite page builder as a base for the development of our websites templates. Instead, we developed our own, which worked just as well. They just took a bit longer to design and refine, and were a little more rigid.

For me, the development of website templates was key to creating a service-centric, results-oriented web design business, finally capable of turning a profit. If we'd stuck with bespoke design, the development of Lead Machines wouldn't have been a viable pursuit. There would have been too much work involved for website projects to be profitable at a price acceptable to the SSB market. We would have had to increase the price of our packages so much that they'd have been out of reach – and we'd have been out of business.

So, templates it was – or should I say, 'template'. The original Cyberstart package (long before the Secret Service Website Formula was conceived) had a choice of six templates – a result of me assuming our clients needed a range of layouts to choose from. As my thinking evolved, so too did our templates, which gradually distilled down to just one. This final template generated such excellent results for our SSB clients (in conjunction with the service-centric design model and Secret Service Website Formula), that we used it as the basis for each and every site, without giving clients any other option.

At first, I felt nervous about not giving clients a choice of layouts, but that didn't last long. I soon realised serious SSB owners didn't care about having a choice, nor did they care if their website had the same basic layout as other sites. Whether it was built from scratch or from a template, they just wanted a website that worked; one with the capacity to drive leads. As it was my field of expertise, they were more than happy to be guided by me on how to make that happen. Once I explained that we used one particular layout as a starting point for every SSB site due to its demonstrated ability to generate leads, no further convincing was necessary.

Our final high performing theme, then called SmartStart, now referred to as the Lead Machine theme, consists of two design layouts or 'blueprints'; one for the homepage and one for the inner pages. As the homepage is the longest and most crucial to the site's performance, let's start there.

The Lead Machine Homepage Blueprint

Figure 14a: The Lead Machine Homepage Blueprint (top half)

Figure 14b: The Lead Machine Homepage Blueprint (bottom half)

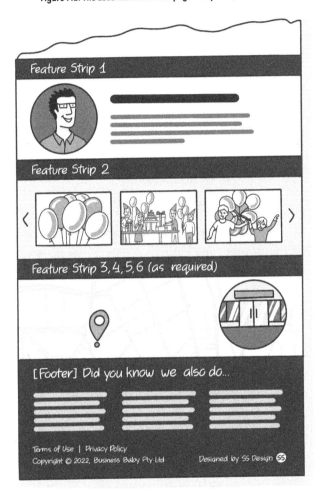

This is longer than the homepage of an average SSB site but for good reason. For SSBs, the homepage is where the game of marketing is generally won or lost. The content featured on it, and how that content is presented, determines the level of connection and curiosity experienced by website visitors – whether they form a favourable first impression and are driven to explore more of the site or not. Beyond gold standard copywriting and photography, this hinges on the function of design. Without great design bringing the various elements together into a highly engaging, user-friendly interface, even the highest grade marketing gold will fail to impress.

The 7 Segments of a Strong SSB Homepage

A Lead Machine homepage has seven segments, each requiring careful consideration and purpose-driven design. From the top of the page to the bottom, they are as follows:

1. Header
2. Navigation menu
3. Scrolling photo banner
4. Call-to-action form
5. Body content
6. Feature strips
7. Footer

Each of these has a specific purpose and set of design criteria that contributes to the creation of a Lead Machine. There's more to some segments than others but all play a critical role. The instructions and insights for each one are the nuts and bolts holding everything together, outlined segment by segment below.

1. Header

A Lead Machine's header is the equivalent of a fascia sign on a commercial premises. Both identify a business and let visitors know that they've come to the right place. Only two elements are required to achieve this: a logo and an off-page call-to-action block (essentially, the business' basic contact details).

Logo

A logo in the header gives a website a sense of identity – replicated on each page for congruence and consistency. Through a concise fusion of words and graphic detail, a logo has the power to communicate a lot about the business it represents (explained in Chapter 12 of *Secret Service Marketing*, 'The Truth about Branding'). A strong logo gets the user experience off to a solid start, giving visitors confidence they've arrived at the site of a professional entity that's applicable to their needs.

The optimum location for the logo is at the left of the header (top left of the page). This is conducive with how the eyes of website users typically scan a site – starting from the top left, moving to the top right, then down the page in an 'F' or 'Z' formation, looking for worthy places to linger and land.

Off-page call-to-action block

Calls-to-action are like the doors on a building – they're the means by which potential customers 'enter' our business. Just as a business premises without a front entrance will receive few walk-in enquiries, an SSB website without prominent calls-to-action will facilitate few online leads. The vast majority of potential customers will pass right on by.

As explained in Chapter 9, a Lead Machine needs two types of call-to-action, on-page and off-page. The on-page call-to-action (a 'stepping stone to service' offer and enquiry form) doesn't come into play until further down the page, once an emotional connection has been sparked. An off-page call-to-action block, however, consisting of a *phone* and *place* call-to-action as applicable, needs no emotional introduction. It should be visible immediately, at the top right of the site. This makes it easy to locate and access – not only for repeat customers looking to retrieve the business' phone number or address in a hurry, but for first-time visitors who (having seen them in the first instance) will know to scroll to the top of the page to take off-page action if/when they're ready.

Other than the logo, the phone call-to-action should be the most prominent aspect of the header. While this prominence can be achieved through elaborate design, it's not necessary. Simple text formatting, making the phone call-to-action large and brightly coloured, is all it takes. 'Phone', 'Call us now' or a telephone icon preceding the phone number is adequate wording for the phone call-to-action, while 'Visit us at' (or similar) is ideal for the address of a physical premises.

Figure 15: Header with off-page call-to-action block (starred)

2. Navigation Menu

A website's navigation menu is the means by which visitors explore what a business has to offer. This makes it a crucial consideration.

In Chapter 11, we covered the importance of the page names listed in the navigation menu, but equally important is its placement and style. In years gone by, positioning the menu vertically down the left-hand side of a website was commonplace. But times have changed and so too have the expectations of internet users.

Although user expectations will continue to evolve, a horizontal menu is preferable for a SSB site when viewed on a computer screen, and a *hamburger menu* when viewed on a mobile device.

On a full-size screen, a horizontal menu positioned directly under the header provides the most efficient and intuitive user experience. It's quicker and easier to interpret than a vertical menu, more aesthetically pleasing, less distracting and feels more natural to use.

A horizontal menu is also more conducive to the creation of a well-organised, content rich site through the use of *drop-down menus.* Drop-down functionality is an important aspect of both user-friendliness and owner-friendliness. Not only is it key to making pages of content easily accessible for website visitors, it gives us the freedom to alter the size and structure of our site as we see fit; adding or removing pages when we need to, with minimal effort and no expense.

Figure 16: Header with drop-down navigation menu (starred)

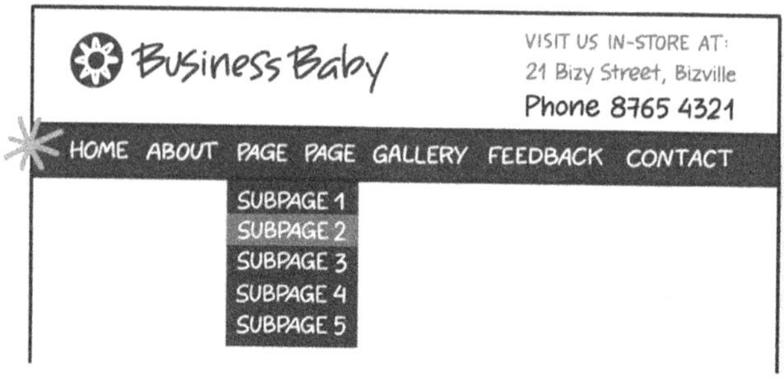

While a full-width, horizontal menu with drop-downs is optimal for visitors accessing our site from a computer, it's not conducive to smartphones or other mobile devices where screen space is at a premium. The solution lies in ***responsive website design (RWD)*** – specifically, the incorporation of a hamburger menu, which displays on small screens and browser windows only. A hamburger menu is a vertical menu, represented by an icon consisting of three stacked lines which looks a bit like a hamburger. When touched or clicked, the icon 'toggles' the navigation menu – making it appear and disappear as required – thereby saving space. Hamburger menus have become sufficiently mainstream to include with confidence on SSB sites, but only for mobile devices. Despite the trendiness of the hamburger menu, a full-width horizontal menu provides a far superior user experience on a laptop or desktop screen... so don't abandon full-width navigation bars just yet.

When designing a navigation menu, bear in mind that you're designing a control panel for end users to access and explore a website. It needs to facilitate accessibility and encourage exploration, not hinder it. This is achieved by making it as logical and user-friendly as possible, remembering it's not how flashy a menu is, but how functional it is that counts.

3. Hero Image Display – Scrolling Photo Banner

As we've explored in depth, much of a Lead Machine's connectivity comes from its images – in particular, photographic images of people and, to a lesser extent, products.

But the existence of connective imagery is not enough. Great photos can only be of connective benefit if they can be seen and appreciated by website visitors. This responsibility doesn't fall to the photographer; it falls to the web designer. As the one to decide what images to include and exclude, where to display them, how big they'll be and if they'll be modified in any way, the photographic buck stops with them. The designer's discretion and discernment when selecting, placing and processing hero images goes a long way to determining their impact on website visitors, in turn going a long way to determining the success of the site itself, so it's critical that the designer has the insights required to make strong image decisions.

The single-most important place to display photographs on an SSB website is a large scrolling banner (often called a rotating banner, image carousel, slideshow or slider) on the homepage; a designated area under the navigation bar geared to rotate through a selection of hero images.

To be clear, the banner is *not* for bombarding visitors with promotional offers. It's to give them an instant, commitment-free glimpse into our working world – like the front window of a shop. It's a controlled means of allowing service seekers to visually validate who we are and what we do and to form an unconscious connection with us within seconds of landing on our site.

Figure 17: Hero image display with scrolling photo banner (starred)

A scrolling photo banner is preferable to a single, static image because it displays and communicates much more without taking up any more room. The multiplicity and movement of images in a scrolling banner generates attention, interest and intrigue while giving the site a sense of depth and dynamism. A single static image can't possibly have the same effect.

However, tapping into the benefits of a scrolling photo banner is contingent upon certain design decisions. It must:

1. **Appear above the fold** – For maximum visibility, the banner must be positioned to appear predominantly above 'the fold', which means most of it is visible to users arriving on the homepage without them having to scroll down. This can be challenging to achieve across all devices but it's important to strive for. If the banner is below the fold, it won't be visible in the first instance, which means the images may not get the chance to influence the all-important first impression.

2. **Be responsive** – For maximum impact, the banner area needs to be wide enough to fill the browser window on a large computer screen but responsive so it adapts appropriately and fluidly when the browser window is minimised or when viewed on a small mobile device.

3. **Transition naturally** – The transition from one image to the next in a scrolling banner doesn't need to be decorative or dramatic to draw the eye. In fact, it's better if it's not. Fancy banner transitions such as 'fly in', 'flip', 'wipe' or 'shape' might seem clever to begin with, but they date quickly. What's more, they can detract from the images themselves, impeding them physically and connectively. A more natural transition such as a subtle 'fade' effect is a better choice. Not only will it keep the emphasis on the images, it will continue to look fresh and modern for years to come.

4. **Pass the speed test** – Just as a fancy transition effect can stand in the way of visitors connecting with images, so too can a scrolling photo banner that doesn't load quickly enough, or transitions too fast or slow. Speed issues can cause immense frustration and a high *bounce rate* (the proportion of visitors who abandon a site without engaging with its content), so it's vital to sort them out before going live. Note that there's no one-size-fits-all transition speed for a scrolling banner. Simply test it out, and ask others to do the same, to determine what feels comfortable.

5. **Be a highlight reel** – A scrolling banner is not intended to showcase scores of images, just the strongest. The optimum number of images is about five; enough to tell an engaging visual story without causing frustration or overwhelm. Even with a small number of images, it's

good to ensure users have the ability to navigate back and forth between them by clicking directional arrows. But the most crucial thing to know about the design of a homepage banner is that it is *not* a photo gallery. It's more like a digital photo frame, reserved for the best of the connective best.

6. **Need no interpretation** – The images in the homepage banner should be selected and formatted for connectivity and relevance, not for artistic appeal. That means excluding photos that look cool but communicate little (such as visual signature shots), in favour of people and product shots that are the most authentic and engaging. It also means resisting the urge to spice up the photos with artistic effects, such as decolourisation (from full colour to black and white, for example), saturation or the overlaying of multiple images to create a collage style banner. When working with a feel-the-love photo or high-quality product shot, it's best to let the original image speak for itself. Artistic intervention will only undermine its ability to communicate and connect.

7. **Stamp, don't sell** – While most forms of third party proof are best displayed in feature strips further down the homepage, the scrolling banner is the prime position for showcasing an accolade. Overlaying official (legitimately-earned) award insignia on one or two applicable banner images can amplify their impact exponentially. A feel-the-love photo of a builder and a professional shot of a home they've built is one thing; those same images stamped with a *Master Builders*

Association: Winner – Excellence in Building Awards logo is quite another (as shown below). It gives the images a whole other level of meaning and credibility which can cause website conversions to sky-rocket.

Figure 18a: Homepage banner - Authority shot with stamped accolade

Figure 18b: Homepage banner - End result shot with stamped accolade

These are real-world examples courtesy of Beveridge Constructions *www.beveridgeconstructions.com.au* and Master Builders Association NSW *www.mbansw.asn.au* | Photography by Michelle Ridland (18a) and Andy Warren *www.hunterimagebank.com.au* (18b)

A banner can also be stamped with a word, phrase or slogan to emphasise a business' point of difference or specialisation. This can be highly effective – concisely communicating why the business is unique and/or better than others in its niche.

Figure 19: Homepage banner - Close-up shot with a service specialty statement

Real-world example courtesy of SA Irrigation & Landscaping
www.sairrigation.com.au | Photography by Drawcard Photo
photo.drawcard.com.au

That said, it's important to distinguish between 'stamping' and 'selling'. The scrolling banner on an SSB website is **not** the place to spruik products or services with corporate-looking promotional offers. This causes ***banner blindness*** – a condition in which visitors skip over then ignore the banner area, unconsciously knowing they're being sold to. Banner blindness can affect all types of businesses, but for SSBs it can be particularly detrimental. If service seekers ignore our banner area on the basis of one or two promotional images, the opportunity to connect with and visually validate us via the other images will be lost. So, stamp banners but never use them to spruik or sell.

4. Call-to-Action Form

For SSBs, an on-page call-to-action form is the equivalent of a business premises' main entrance; it's how website visitors access our business – making themselves known to us so the sales process can commence. Even with side entrances (a phone call-to-action, a general enquiry form on the Contact page or a fancy chatbot), an inviting main entrance is critical. Without a prominent, inviting call-to-action form, taking action by any means will feel more daunting for visitors, so fewer will, stifling the site's performance. It can only perform as a Lead Machine if it has a prominently positioned, well designed facility to drive leads.

The location of the call-to-action form is of utmost importance. Visitors should never have to search for it. It should appear in a consistent, prominent position on *every page* of the website, maximising the chances of it being seen at the crucial moment when they consider taking action, whenever and wherever that may be. The only exception is the Contact page, which requires its own unique enquiry form suitable for more general enquiries.

To have the desired effect, the call-to-action form needs to be both obvious and enticing. Beyond the development of an enticing lure line (explained in Chapter 9), both of these factors hinge on design. The form is made obvious through its placement on the page (consistent from one page to the next) as well as the use of colour and contrast to make it stand out. It's made more enticing through the formatting of the box, background, lure line, text fields and submit button as well as the inclusion of extra imagery.

In a full-size browser window (on a computer), the most practical location for the call-to-action form is the right hand sidebar. Here, the user's eyes are naturally drawn to it, whether they're initially scanning the page or reading the body content to the left. The form can become even more of an eye magnet when customised with appropriate imagery – be it an isolated photo of the owner, a product shot, an icon or other graphic element. A well-considered image or two not only makes the call-to-action more prominent, it makes it more palatable – injecting the form with a sense of approachability, friendliness or even fun.

Figure 20: Ideal position of the call-to-action form (starred), alongside the body content

In the small browser window of a mobile device, the call-to-action form is ideally designed to 'fly-out' from the right of screen when a button containing the lure line is clicked or pushed.

As mentioned in Chapter 9, an on-page chat mechanism can be explored as an extra 'side entrance' call-to-action but it's not essential to the creation of a Lead Machine. If implemented and managed well, a live chat feature or chatbot can be a beneficial addition to an SSB website, as an extra means to generate leads. However, it should be used in addition to a call-to-action form, not as a replacement for it. Without the call-to-action form, a chat box can do more harm than good – confusing, distracting or frustrating users and driving perfectly good leads away. For that reason, it's worth holding off on the installation of a chat plugin until the base performance of the site has been assessed.

5. Body Content

While the words comprising the body of the homepage are a crucial consideration (discussed in Chapter 11), so too is the positioning of the body content segment, the formatting of text within it and the means by which we bring attention back to our call-to-action once we've said our piece.

The perfect position for body content (on a full-size screen) is underneath the scrolling banner, to the left of the call-to-action form. If the form occupies one third of the page width, two thirds of the page width is left for body content. This is ideal for several reasons: 1) it's easier and less daunting to read than text spanning the full width of the page, 2) it's reminiscent of the width of a book or online article, therefore more comfortable and familiar for users, and, most importantly, 3) it allows the call-to-action form to remain in a user's peripheral vision as they read, making it more likely to be seen and actioned.

Figure 21: Ideal position of the body content (starred)

As explained in Chapter 11, the written portion of the body content segment ideally consists of three parts: a heading, the body copy (approximately three paragraphs) and a summary sentence. These not only require great wording, but great formatting to ensure they're visually stimulating and easy to read. Although the copywriter might format the provided copy, the responsibility of selecting fonts, colours, sizes, line spacing, and more, ultimately falls to the web designer. They have the power to *make* the body copy – through user-friendly formatting – or *break* it – through artistic over-indulgence.

The main indicator of user-friendly formatting is legibility. Every aspect of the body content – the heading, body copy and summary sentence – must be clearly readable. This may sound obvious but, when designing a website, it can be tempting to select decorative fonts for artistic appeal. While the occasional fancy font is fine, it must be considered not only aesthetically but practically. Is it a web safe font, such as a Google Font, fit for the purpose of online display? Will it be used in a large font size, for small amounts of text (i.e. for headings)? When formatted in the chosen font, are all letters clear and comprehensible? Can the eye move quickly and smoothly through the words without getting tired or stuck? If the answer to any of these questions is no, the artistic appeal of the font will be lost on website visitors and won't be worth the risk.

Other text formatting temptations that can hinder a site's user experience, involve colour, size and styling variations – or lack thereof. One of the most common mistakes is the selection of a pale colour (such as light grey) and smaller-than-average size for paragraph text. This, along with the avoidance of bold, italic or coloured text highlighting, is often done in an attempt to camouflage text or make it appear sleek or 'sexy'. But text isn't supposed to be sexy. It's supposed to communicate. The harder or more boring we make it to read, the more difficult it is for the words to connect, convince and convert. For this reason, it's best to stick with conventional paragraph formatting: a standard serif or sans serif font (whichever best suits the brand), in black or dark grey and a comfortable font size (usually 16px). However, emphasis should be given to important words or points through the considerate use of bold, italic, highlighting or other text variations. This adds visual interest and draws the reader's eye through the text, reducing the chances of them abandoning the site out of boredom.

Above, below and between paragraphs on the homepage, the formatting of the heading, subheadings (if applicable) and summary sentence can add even more visual interest. The heading and summary sentence have a particularly important role to play, sandwiching the body copy with large, colourful text. They not only help catch the eye, but give the body content a clear start and end point, making the paragraph text more palatable. A strong, clear font is necessary for headings, subheadings and summary sentences – limited to a small range of colour and size options via the site's stylesheet to prevent it from looking cheesy, messy or amateur.

When selecting fonts for a website, online tools such as *www.grtcalculator.com* (Golden Rule Typography Calculator) can come in handy, facilitating the preview of fonts, then determining, displaying and outputting optimum heading sizes, line heights and more.

Beyond the formatting of text in the body content segment, there's a small graphic component to consider which subtly encourages visitors to take action, thereby helping the site drive more leads. All it is, is a brightly coloured, hand-drawn arrow, floating between the summary sentence and the call-to-action form at the bottom right of the body content segment. This creates a visual bridge from the body content to the contact mechanism (the form), steering visitors to take the desired action.

Figure 22: Hand-drawn arrow, directing visitors to the call-to-action form (circled)

6. Feature Strips

Feature strips are horizontal, full-width sections, located underneath the body content on the homepage. They're designed to showcase a business' most authenticating, validating content in a succinct and highly visual way.

Up to six feature strips can be included in the feature strip segment, depending on the nuggets of marketing gold available to choose from (determined in conjunction with the copy-writer). Each strip conveys one of four points:

- **Who** owns/operates the business
- **What** the business does
- **Where** the business premises is located (if applicable)
- **Why** the business is genuine and trustworthy

Who, *what* and *where* feature strips are optional but, if they're applicable to a business, highly recommended. *Why* strips (at least one but preferably more) are essential. They're applicable to every SSB site, no matter who owns it, what the business does or where it operates.

THE WHO FEATURE STRIP

A *who* feature strip is an introduction to the business owner, comprised of:

- A title (such as 'Meet the owner' or 'Meet the Queen of Clean');
- A short written statement with a button to 'Read more' which links through to the About page; and
- A feel-the-love authority shot.

Recommended for skill-based businesses dependent on the technical expertise of the owner, a *who* feature strip helps establish a foundation of authenticity, accountability and trust.

Figure 23: *Who* feature strip

A *what* feature strip is a visual representation of the various services a business offers or what projects it's recently completed. The strip contains an interactive image carousel beneath a title such as 'What we do...' or 'Recent projects', with a series of labelled images depicting various services or end results. When clicked, each image links through to a relevant page of content.

Figure 24: *What* feature strip

A well-considered *what* strip is highly beneficial, as it puts a business' capabilities into context with photographic cues. It also adds a sense of contrast to the bottom half of the homepage which can help draw the eye down through more text-heavy feature strips.

THE WHERE FEATURE STRIP

As the primary *place* call-to-action, a *where* strip is only applicable for SSBs requiring customers to attend a physical premises, such as restaurants, clinics and salons.

The ideal *where* strip consists of:

- **A title**, such as 'Visit us at...' or 'Find us at...'
- **The street address** of the premises, in written form
- **Trading times**

- **An interactive map** with the location clearly pinpointed, and/or
- **A photo of the premises' front façade** so customers know what to look for when they arrive.

Figure 25: *Where* feature strip

THE WHY FEATURE STRIP

Why feature strips are for the display of the crème de la crème of convincers – third party proof, as well as the odd logic lever. The idea is to have multiple *why* strips on the homepage, capitalising on multiple convincers – accolades, accreditations, affiliations, appearances, attestments, logic levers or a combination thereof.

Accolade strips

While the prime position to showcase an accolade is the scrolling photo banner, a feature strip is a great place to reinforce it or to display multiple awards, as shown in the mock-ups below.

Figure 26: *Why* feature strip - Single accolade

Figure 27: *Why* feature strip - Multiple accolades

Accreditation strips

A feature strip is also the best place to display an accreditation, such as an industry association membership or compliance certification. Like accolades, accreditations can be presented individually or collectively and have the greatest impact when represented by official insignia.

Figure 28: *Why* feature strip - Single accreditation

Figure 29: *Why* feature strip - Multiple accreditations

Affiliation strips

It can be tricky for an SSB owner to find ways to capitalise on affiliations with respected entities – either suppliers or commercial customers – but a feature strip is the ideal spot. Designing it is as easy as displaying the logos of affiliated entities (with their permission) beneath a suitable title.

Figure 30: *Why* feature strip - Multiple affiliations

Appearance strips

An appearance feature strip is used to capitalise on a business' appearances in the media. A strip featuring a scan or screenshot of the publication (article, video, etc) – linking through to the full article or video on an 'In the Media' page – is ideal for one-off appearances. For multiple appearances, it can be more effective to display a row or group of media body logos, titled 'As seen on...' or 'As featured by...'

Figure 31: *Why* feature strip - Single media appearance

Figure 32: *Why* feature strip - Multiple media appearances

Attestment strips

Feature strips containing attestments (testimonials) are one of the most valuable design elements on the homepage of an SSB site. A featured testimonial ideally consists of a pull quote (the most glowing portion of a longer testimonial), the customer's name, business name, location or other information for basic context, alongside a photo of the customer or end result. Multiple testimonials can be displayed in a single feature strip by utilising a testimonial rotator or slider plugin. Alternatively, they can be stacked on top of each other with the feature photo on the left, then the right, and so on, for visual stimulation.

Figure 33: *Why* feature strip – Attestments

Logic lever strips

Lastly, *why* feature strips can be used to establish or reinforce a point of difference in the market, through the presentation of a logic lever: a service specialty statement, numerical evidence statement, security statement (guarantee or other promise) or sale sweetener.

Figure 34: *Why* feature strip – Logic lever (service specialty statement)

Figure 35: *Why* feature strip - Logic lever (security statement)

Designed well, *why* feature strips of all types validate a business and reinforce its service offering. They help website visitors feel safe and secure at the prospect of engaging the business' services; like they've come to the right place and would be silly to go elsewhere.

Feature Strip Tips

For a feature strip segment with strong visual impact, the following are essential.

- **Colour and contrast** – Colour and contrast are vital to the design of strong feature strips. Alternating background and foreground colours from one strip to the next is an effective tactic. Not only does it clearly define each one, it's visually stimulating, helping to draw visitors' eyes down the page.

- **Words and pictures** – Feature strips are most impactful with a combination of concise wording and visual elements, such as photographs, logos, illustrations, icons or other insignia. Each feature strip needs carefully crafted words (kept short, sharp and shiny) reinforced by applicable imagery.

- **Full colour images** – Photos and logos are best displayed in full colour, not black and white or with coloured filters. While images might look elegant in grayscale or sepia, they'll have a far greater connective impact in full colour.
- **Responsiveness** – As with other aspects of an SSB site, the quantity and composition of feature strips can't be set in stone across all size screens. Some strips may need to be removed or their content scaled back when displayed on mobile devices to prevent the homepage from overwhelming smartphone users.

Beyond looking the part, it's important to ensure that a feature strip segment is easy to modify. A site should be flexible enough for feature strips to be overhauled in-house by a novice site owner or editor – giving us the ability to add and remove strips, change the order in which they display, switch background colours, insert text and images, etc. This gives a homepage the ability to evolve over time, just as the business it represents will.

7. Footer

The footer is the final segment of the homepage and one that can serve a special, functional purpose at the discretion of the designer.

Once upon a time, the footer of a website was reserved for a secondary list of links to the site's main pages, but times have changed. Now – as long as the site is built using a modern framework (with a navigation menu comprised of text, not images) – there's no need to replicate the menu in the footer, which frees it up for something far more valuable: SEO.

The footer provides a rare opportunity to squeeze valuable *long tail keyword links* into a website. Long tail keywords are highly specific, three or four keyword phrases that play a crucial role in the SEO of SSB sites. They're the terms serious buyers or service seekers type into search engines on a quest to find particular goods or services. By injecting long tail keywords into a site, linking to applicable inner pages of content, we increase the site's chances of ranking well for those terms on Google, in turn increasing its chances of being found by those who are actively seeking what the site is promoting.

Of all sections of a website, the footer is the best place to inject long tail keyword links as it doesn't compromise content quality or user experience. Although it's ideal to write them into headings and body copy, the length and structure of long tail keywords can make them difficult to include without the content sounding awkward or unprofessional. While the inclusion of keyword links in the footer won't compensate for injecting them into the body content, it ensures they're included on the site at least once, which, for most SSBs, is once more than they otherwise would have featured.

The most unintrusive, user-friendly way to factor long tail keyword links into the footer is to list them under the title 'Did you know we also do...' as in the example below:

Did you know we also do...
- Pest inspections Barossa Valley
- Building inspections Barossa Valley
- Termite inspections Barossa Valley
- Pest inspections Nuriootpa
- Building inspections Tanunda

Three columns of five longtail keyword links fit nicely into the footer. This provides 15 uninhibited opportunities to inject the names and locations of a business' services into its website.

Beyond keyword links, other elements worth considering for inclusion in the footer are:

- **A copyright notice** (e.g. Copyright © 2024, ABC Building Pty Ltd) – Technically, website content is protected by copyright law whether a copyright notice is displayed or not but it's still worthwhile including it as a deterrent to those with devious intentions.

- **Links to the fine print** – As explained in Chapter 16, certain pages (such as Terms of Use and Privacy Policy) can be required from a legal standpoint but can be off-putting to visitors if listed in the main menu. The footer is the ideal spot for listing and linking to these pages. It's a means of making the fine print accessible without scaring away visitors who are yet to feel connected enough to take it at face value.

- **Basic contact details** – Sometimes, website visitors can scroll to the bottom of a website for a phone number or physical address. If the website adheres to the Lead Machine blueprint, they shouldn't need to resort to this but some still may. For this reason, restating the *phone* and *place* calls-to-action in the footer can be worthwhile... no fancy formatting required.

- **The web designer's logo/link** – For sites designed professionally, the inclusion of the designer's logo in the footer is a nice final touch. Being seen to have invested in professional web design subtly implies that the business is a considered pursuit (as opposed to a fly-by-night operation). It also throws the designer a bone in the form of a link to their site. Before going live though, just check that the link is set to open in a new tab of a visitor's internet browser, so it's not a means for traffic to leave the site.

With these and the 'Did you know we also do...' links factored in, the footer will be larger than that of many other websites but with good reason; it will be geared to contribute to the functionality and effectiveness of the site, not just take up space.

Figure 36: Footer

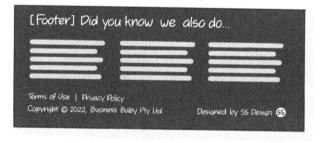

Due to the pivotal role the homepage plays in sparking and reinforcing a positive first impression, it tends to be the longest and most intricate page of the entire site. In terms of design, it warrants extra time, consideration and effort but, once it's finalised, the design of the inner pages can fall swiftly into place.

The Lead Machine Inner Page Blueprint

Figure 37: The Lead Machine Inner Page Blueprint

The 6 Segments of a Strong Inner Page

Over half of the seven essential *homepage* segments belong on a Lead Machine's *inner pages* too, with no adjustment. These are the header, navigation menu, call-to-action form (with the exception of the contact page, as explained earlier) and footer. Keeping these four segments consistent from the homepage to the inner pages is important; setting the stage for an intuitive user experience.

The *feature strips* segment has no place anywhere but the homepage. Every inner page – be it About, Contact or any other – needs to have a designated focus and intention. Adding feature strips beneath the body content would only muddy the waters, detracting from the focus of the page.

This leaves two segments: the hero image and body content. Both of these are as critical to inner pages as they are to the homepage but with a couple of distinguishing features.

Hero Image Display – Static Photo Banner

Unlike on the homepage, the hero image display on inner pages should be singular and static, not scrolling. A single, static image, matched to the topic or focus of the page, sets the scene for the content that follows. It also ensures the page gets off to a visually stimulating start, while differentiating it from all other pages.

As well as being static, the hero image display on inner pages needs to occupy less space than on the homepage. While all hero images should span the full width of the browser window, those on inner pages should be about half as high as the homepage banner, forming more of a panoramic strip. This takes up less room above the fold, making it obvious to users that the image is a prelude to the page content, not the main event.

Cropping certain shots (particularly those of people) to a half-height panoramic strip can present a challenge. That's why it's so important to brief the photographer about the intended use, placement and specification of images prior to a feel-the-love photoshoot. If they know what's needed design-wise, they can factor it into the shoot and produce shots fit for their intended purpose.

Although hero images on inner pages are restrictive size-wise, they provide greater artistic freedom than those on the homepage. As long as they're relevant to the content, inner page hero images can be selected for aesthetic (not connective) appeal, so visual signature shots and extreme close-ups are welcome.

Body Content

While the body content segment of an inner page can look similar to that of the homepage, it's usually longer and more detailed. As well as a heading, paragraphs and a summary sentence, a typical service page may contain:

- Subheadings
- Many more paragraphs
- Bulleted or numbered lists
- Images
- An image gallery
- Videos
- Pull quotes
- And more

Ensuring these elements are presented in an engaging, functional way is an important part of web design. This is primarily achieved through the well-considered placement and styling of text and digital media. The aim is to transform the content on each inner page from a mind-numbing wall of text to a visually stimulating user experience.

Room to Move

The blueprints and mock-ups in this chapter have been kept simple and generic for a reason – to provide just enough guidance to produce a Lead Machine, without inhibiting a designer's creativity. For some designers, it may be tempting to ignore these suggestions and apply the Secret Service Website Formula in an entirely different way. While that's certainly an option, deviating from the prescribed layouts without mastering them first isn't recommended. It's better to get a few runs on the board with the original layouts, then, when producing sites that effectively drive leads, adapt and evaluate them from there.

Adhering to a pre-set layout may appear repetitive or restrictive but it's more stimulating than you might think. Within the boundaries of the Lead Machine blueprints, there's plenty of room to move, with infinite scope for design customisation and creative exploration.

Despite following the same basic structure, there's no reason every Lead Machine can't look unique and custom designed. Just as two homes constructed with the same floor plan can end up with a vastly different look and feel due to the selection of different materials, fixtures and finishes, so too can two websites built with the Secret Service Website Formula.

Although the page segments remain the same from site to site, there is infinite scope to customise them through the selection of colours, shapes, fonts, images and other elements. As long as these selections are made in the best interest of the business a website represents, it can't go too far wrong. Just be sure to stand back and view the proposed design through the eyes of a potential customer. How does it look? How does it feel? What elements draw the eye? Do these elements aid in connecting, convincing and converting? If not, what needs to be done to shift the focus to those that do? Putting yourself in the shoes of intended customers in this way, while being as honest and objective as possible, is key to creating a website equipped to outperform others in the market. But if that doesn't appeal, there is another way...

CHAPTER 19.

MAKINGS OF A POWERHOUSE PARTNER

While the tactics outlined in the last chapter can be applied by anyone with the tenacity to tackle a web design project, there are three disciplines or skill sets that – when explored and honed – can make the world of difference to the final outcome. The equivalent of a 'triple threat', a designer with expertise in these three areas is likely to be a powerhouse web design partner; someone you want in your corner when building a Lead Machine, especially if you don't have the capacity or desire to become heavily involved in the project.

Figure 38: The 3 disciplines underpinning Lead Machine design

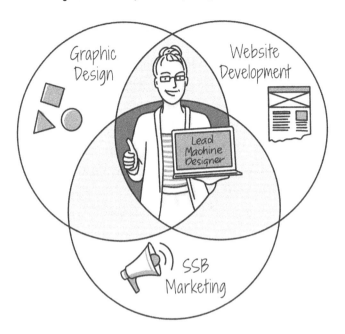

The first of these disciplines is *graphic design*. An understanding of the fundamental principles of conventional graphic design (long-standing rules and theories that guide the effective selection and use of shapes, images, typography, colours, contrast, white space, balance, etc) is important when designing websites. Subtle alterations to a web design wireframe to better adhere to graphic design principles and practices can have a huge impact on the feel, flow and professionalism of the end result.

The second discipline is *website development* – the technical know-how to transform a visual wireframe into a fully functional website. While it's possible to make a website with little to no concept of the code or complexities going on behind the scenes, it certainly helps. A small change to a site's layout or functionality that might take an experienced developer a few minutes can take a novice a few days... let alone the development of an entire site. To save time and frustration, and produce a polished site, website development skills are key.

Last but certainly not least is the discipline of *SSB marketing*. This is concerned with the needs and expectations of small skill-or-service businesses and those they exist to serve. Marketing insight is pivotal to the design of a Lead Machine, because it tells us when to adhere to graphic/web design convention and when to break it, in the interest of visitor engagement. In conventional graphic design, for example, white text on a black background may be fine, but for the design of a Lead Machine it's a bad idea – inhibiting readability, thereby inhibiting the site's capacity to connect, convince and convert.

Marketing insight is what makes the difference between an 'okay' designer and an exceptional one. When cultivated (by reading the *Secret Service Business Series*, tuning in to marketing research and trends, and prioritising user experience above all else), marketing insight is what gives a designer the ability to make informed decisions and do truly rewarding, result-oriented work; producing websites with the ability to make a real difference in the lives of their owners.

With *Secret Service Marketing* and *The Secret Service Website Formula*, mastery of all three disciplines is not necessary to become a powerhouse Lead Machine designer, but an awareness of them – and an interest in developing them – is imperative.

For web designers and marketers, an applied interest in graphic design, web development and SSB marketing is a springboard to professional fulfilment and a lucrative career as a freelancer, contractor or entrepreneur.

For SSB owners embarking on the development of a single Lead Machine, finding a web designer whose focus spans these three disciplines means you're probably onto a good thing. Just be sure they can walk the walk, not just talk the talk. An ideal designer will be guided by Secret Service principles and values. They won't need to be asked about their marketing focus or service-centric approach, it will shine through when discussing previous sites they've built and their intentions for your project. Most notably, they will:

1. **Embody the principle content is king** – Knowing that a pretty face can't make up for a lack of substance, Lead Machine designers care about the quality of the content they work with. They'll talk about the importance of content, stipulate what content is needed and – in one way or another – help facilitate its attainment. Upon receiving content, they'll review it and intervene if necessary, knowing they alone have the power to influence and improve it before setting a web design in stone.

2. **Prioritise leads over looks** – Lead Machine designers talk less about how websites *look* and more about how they *perform*; the experience that sites offer users and their capacity to drive leads. They will draw attention to elements of designs that connect, convince and convert, such as calls-to-action, banners and feature strips, rather than artistic details that have no bearing on user experience.

3. **Channel their inner service seeker** – The needs and expectations of a site's intended visitors are top of mind for a Lead Machine designer, which means they can't help but talk about them. Every conversation about design or

content will refer to the feelings and behaviours of users, and words such as *users, visitors, user experience, engagement, impact* and *results* will feature heavily in discussions.

If you think you've found a Lead Machine designer, listen out for these values, do your due diligence (outlined in Chapter 16) and expect to pay extra for the privilege. Remember, the hub of your marketing efforts is an asset worth investing in – be it financially or, if going it alone, the investment of your own time.

A Word of Warning for Web Designers

Building websites is not what it once was. It used to take a double whammy of technical expertise to bring a website to fruition: the creative fortitude to design an attractive site and the coding abilities to turn that design into a functional interface. But with the upsurge of drag-and-drop page builders, the tide has changed. A flare for creativity and code is no longer enough to survive as a web designer – at least not with SSB clients.

As drag-and-drop technologies become more sophisticated, the barriers to entry on web design are falling away and the floodgates have opened. Graphic designers, marketers and those with no knowledge of coding whatsoever are able to thrive as web designers if they take the right approach.

For freelancers and web design agencies with SSB clients, it's a matter of *populate or perish*; become service-centric, content- and marketing-minded and results focused – genuinely caring about the outcomes achieved for clients – or struggle to survive. There will come a time when self-centric design no longer pays the bills. Freelance web designers will be faced with a choice: to quit, forgoing the freedoms of self-employment to work for a big business or creative agency, or to make the leap to conscious web design, working in the best interest of SSB clients. On behalf of the scores of small businesses seeking the expertise of service-centric web designers, I urge you to choose the latter. Use the tips and techniques in this book as a basis to reinvent yourself and become the powerhouse web design partner you were born to be... principled, passionate and prosperous.

PART THREE

SHARING THE LOVE: FOR LEAD MACHINE MAGIC THAT LASTS

CHAPTER 20.

TO GOOGLE, WITH LOVE: FREE TOOLS TO GET SEARCH TRAFFIC SOONER

Once a site has launched, SSB owners and web designers alike tend to assume the work is done and that it's safe to focus on other things. But stopping there leaves some major opportunities on the table – functional finishing touches that can make or break a site's performance. Failing to follow through with these is like expecting a marriage to work without investing any time or energy into the relationship beyond the 'big day' – a whole lot of expense and fanfare, celebrating a union destined for divorce.

Without question, the most valuable and accessible marketing opportunities for SSB website owners are provided by the search engine Google.

Google is an incredibly powerful marketing mechanism for SSBs – a modern-day business directory, on steroids. Through Google, we have the opportunity to tap into a continual flow of high-quality internet traffic to drive leads and sales. But it doesn't happen automatically. Like pumping water from an underground stream, syphoning traffic from Google requires infrastructure and groundwork – the performance of certain preliminary tasks using purpose-built online tools. This *Google groundwork* doesn't need to be executed by a web designer. It can be done by anyone with a live website and an interest in that site's success.

For SSB sites, Google groundwork consists of three preliminary tasks, utilising three different tools. Although these will be introduced in detail, note that the provision of step-by-step instructions has been deliberately avoided. Not only would they date this chapter prematurely (due to the constantly evolving nature of online applications), they may also inhibit each tool from being used to its full potential by those with the drive to delve beyond the basics. In lieu of step-by-step instructions, website links and keyword search prompts are supplied as starting points for sourcing thorough how-to guides online. And if any other concepts seem confusing or unclear, a quick Google search will help fill in the blanks.

Google Groundwork Task #1:
Use Yoast to Create a Sitemap & Kickstart SEO

One of the many benefits of building a website with Wordpress is the availability of plugins to help facilitate SEO (search engine optimisation). The right plugin can take much of the guess-work out of the optimisation process; guiding, streamlining and simplifying it so that – with concerted effort – any one of us is capable of getting our website to rank better on Google and other search engines.

By far, the most popular SEO plugin for Wordpress is Yoast SEO. Yoast is an excellent, user-friendly application, used by amateurs and professionals alike. It can be downloaded from *www.yoast.com/wordpress/plugins/seo/* or installed directly, using the plugin search function in a website's Wordpress dashboard. While a paid version is available for users seeking more features and flexibility, Yoast can be used to achieve excellent results without paying a cent.

That's not to suggest however, that optimising a website to perform well in search engines is easy. Even when using Yoast, search engine optimisation takes time and tenacity. Some of us have that, others don't. And that's okay. As explained in *The Modern Marketing Arsenal,* Search Engine Marketing is one of 10 types of marketing activity available to SSB owners. It's up to each of us to determine what combination of activities is right for our business. Choosing activities that align with our strengths, objectives and resources is the best bet; focusing on those with the capacity to provide the biggest bang for our marketing buck. SEO often fits this bill, but not always.

Whether we have the drive or dollars to walk the SEO path or not, Yoast is worthwhile. Beyond paving the way for future SEO exploration, this handy Wordpress plugin has the ability to streamline a particular task that Google Groundwork Task #2 is contingent upon – namely, the creation of an ***XML sitemap.***

An XML sitemap is a file that tells search engines what pages a website contains to help them navigate and index those pages appropriately. As well as the URL addresses of the site's pages, it can detail how important each page is, how often search engine spiders should crawl it and which pages to exclude (enquiry form 'thank you' pages, for example).

Because sitemap creation is such an important aspect of the SEO function, the Yoast plugin contains an automatic sitemap generator. Rather than producing one manually (which can be quite confusing for novices), Yoast allows us to produce an XML sitemap at the click of a button via the Wordpress dashboard; streamlining the process and making it quicker and easier to move on to Task #2.

GOOGLE IT: For Yoast installation and optimisation instructions, type *How to install Yoast in Wordpress, How to generate a Sitemap with Yoast* or *How to get the most out of Yoast SEO* into a search engine. If your website isn't built with Wordpress, you'll need an alternative means to create a sitemap. Start by typing *Easy way to generate a sitemap for* [*your platform, e.g. Shopify*] *website* and take it from there.

Google Groundwork Task #2:

Use Google Search Console to Get Crawled on Command

Google Search Console (previously known as Webmaster Tools) is a free platform provided by Google for webmasters (site owners or creators) to manage, monitor and optimise how it views, interprets and indexes their sites in the Google search engine. Although Search Console has a plethora of advanced optimisation tools, the most handy facility for SSB owners and web designers is the ability to prompt Google to crawl and index a new website. Through Search Console, we can submit a site's core details and XML sitemap directly to Google, drawing its attention to each page. This saves us from waiting around for weeks or months for Google to realise that a new website exists and is ready to be crawled. Essentially, it pushes the site into the Google system, so it gets indexed for inclusion in search listings quicker than it otherwise would.

Located at *https://search.google.com/search-console*, Search Console can be accessed by anyone with a Google user account.[38] Once logged in, adding a new website is as easy as clicking the *Add Property* link and following the prompts. The domain name will then need to be verified to prove it's legitimately owned and managed. This can be more complicated but thankfully, the Yoast SEO plugin helps streamline this too, with a designated field in which to paste the Google HTML Tag generated during the verification process. From there, a link to the sitemap (created earlier) can be submitted for Google to process and index accordingly. Once complete, the website will then have the capacity to appear in search listings for relevant Google searches.

GOOGLE IT: For more detailed instructions to set up and use Google Search Console, type *How to use Google Search Console* into a search engine, or visit Google Search Central at *https://developers.google.com/search.*

Note that a website will rarely rank well for relevant searches from day one and, if it does, it probably won't stay there. Ranking consistently can take time. For unique keywords, such as a business name, it can happen quite quickly and easily but for more competitive terms (such as 'Canberra builders') it can take a lot of time, commitment and concerted SEO effort to rise through the ranks.

Google Groundwork Task #3:
Create a Google Business Profile to appear on Google Search & Maps

Google Search and Maps were developed to make it easy for internet users to find, connect with and review businesses in their local area, and it works like a charm. When a user searches for a business through Google – by name or type and location (e.g. 'restaurants near me') – applicable business profiles appear as listings toward the top of the search results, along with a map showing their geographic location and a host of other handy details.

Due to reliance on Search and Maps across the globe, these listings – called *Google Business Profiles* - present the single greatest free marketing opportunity for SSBs today. Through them, we have the ability to generate high-quality local traffic to our websites with no ongoing effort or out-of-pocket cost. As far as marketing activities go, they provide an unbeatable return on investment.

Most established businesses have a pre-existing Google Business Profile, whether their owners know it or not. That's because – in the interest of providing the most comprehensive user experience possible – Google acquires business data from many sources. If a business has been listed in a public telephone directory, for example, it will more than likely have a Google Business Profile, ready and waiting to be claimed.

It's easy to determine if a business has a pre-existing, claimable profile or if one needs to be created from scratch. Simply Google the business by name and suburb in Search, Maps or Google Business Profile Manager (accessible via *www.google.com/business*). If a profile exists, it will be quite obvious. A listing with basic details will appear, providing the option to *Claim this business* or *Own this business? Claim it now.* If a profile doesn't exist yet, an option to *Add a missing place* or *Add your business* will be available instead. From there, prompts can be followed to add or edit the profile, thereby adding or editing the business' Search and Maps listings.

All it takes to make the most of any exposure generated by Google Search and Maps is to create a thorough Google Business Profile and update it occasionally. Search and Maps listings have the capacity to present an enticing overview of a business, with photos, contact details, a website link, open times, customer reviews and more. To derive maximum benefit from it, think of it as a mini website. Complete all fields accurately and upload high-quality images and photos where indicated, using feel-the-love photos for greatest impact.

Once a profile has been added or edited, check it from the front end (via Search or Maps) to see how it will appear and be perceived by Google users. View the listing critically and click your website link – as a potential customer would – to make sure it works, then edit it again if necessary. Once satisfied, check the listing every couple of months (or when responding to a review) to ensure all details are still correct.

For many SSBs, the combination of a Google Business Profile and a Lead Machine website can be instant and astounding. Sometimes, it can be all the marketing effort a business needs, generating scores of leads per week and saving hundreds or thousands of dollars a month in paid marketing activities. But even if the impact of a Google Business Profile isn't quite that extreme, it at least boosts your chances of getting found and noticed by service seekers in your local area... which is often half the battle.

GOOGLE IT: For further information about getting listed on Google Search and Maps, type *How to create a Google Business Profile* into a search engine.

Bonus Opportunities
(Extra Groundwork for Go-Getters)

For go-getters who find themselves relishing the challenge of the three Google groundwork tasks... don't stop there. A plethora of other free opportunities are available to support the performance of an SSB website, to pick the low-hanging fruit off the internet traffic tree and to track and monitor results. Some of the most worthwhile of these are outlined below.

Bonus Opportunity #1: Other Links & Listings

In addition to Google Search and Maps, listings can be claimed or created on the following platforms and directories:

- Bing Places (the Bing equivalent of Google Business Manager at *www.bingplaces.com*)
- Yellow Pages
- Yelp
- TrueLocal
- Facebook Marketplace (classified advertising platform)
- Gumtree (classified advertising site)
- Craigslist (classified advertising site)
- Member directories on industry association and other applicable websites

- And more (type *best free business directories in [your country]* into Google as a starting point)

The accumulation of online listings serves two valuable functions:

1. **Backlink generation** – With the exception of classified advertising platforms, most sites offering free business listings provide the opportunity to include a website link. These links – known as ***backlinks*** – help bolster a business' online presence by improving the perceived authority of its website. Website authority (or domain authority) is a metric used by search engines to help determine how high a website should rank in search results. The more backlinks it has on *reputable* sites, the better. Note that backlinks on *disreputable* sites (link farms, etc) can have the opposite effect – reducing a site's authority, causing it to rank lower or be dropped from Google altogether. When it comes to link building, the slow and steady accumulation of backlinks on reputable sites wins the race.

2. **First page domination** – Online listings help a business dominate the first page (or more) of search engine results for its business name. Instead of appearing once or twice on the first page of Google amid a sea of other businesses with a similar name, every listing is likely to lead the searcher to the website and contact details of the correct business. This helps alleviate the risk of mix-ups between a business and others with a similar name (which happens surprisingly often).

362 THE SECRET SERVICE WEBSITE FORMULA

Bonus Opportunity #2: Google Analytics

One of the greatest benefits of the current technological climate for businesses is the ability to track and monitor marketing performance with incredible speed and accuracy. Thanks to Google, this opportunity is available to the owner of any website via its Analytics platform.

Google Analytics enables us to monitor the performance of our marketing with a level of detail that marketers of old (including those with the biggest budgets) could have only ever dreamed of. With Analytics set up, we can easily see how much traffic our site is getting, where that traffic is coming from, what devices it's being accessed on, where those devices are geographically located, how long visitors are remaining on each page, what the conversion rates are and much, much more – all for free.

Note that linking Google Analytics with Google Search Console opens up more opportunities for tracking and monitoring. However, for most SSB owners, Analytics is more than enough – providing all the statistical insights we need to keep track of our site's performance.

GOOGLE IT: To get started with Analytics, type *How to use Google Analytics* into a search engine.

Bonus Opportunity #3: Bing Webmaster Tools

Despite having a tiny market share in comparison to Google, the search engine Bing is still a worthy consideration for SSB owners and internet marketers. Google may get the lion's share of search traffic but it also gets a lot more businesses seeking to capitalise on it through SEO and paid advertising, which can make these activities expensive. Bing has less competition, so it can present a cheaper means to explore Search Engine Marketing and drive some extra leads.

Whether interested in exploring paid marketing opportunities with Bing or not, it's a good idea to sign up for Webmaster Tools. **Bing Webmaster Tools** (accessed via www.*bing.com/webmasters*) is the Microsoft equivalent of Google Search Console, where a site's details and sitemap can be submitted for crawling and indexation by Bing. Although less traffic will flow through to a website from Bing than Google, a little extra traffic is better than none... and every little bit helps.

GOOGLE (OR BING) IT: For instructions to set up and use Bing Webmaster Tools, type *How to use Bing Webmaster Tools* into a search engine.

Bonus Opportunity #4: Mobile Friendliness Tools

With over half of all website visits occurring on a mobile device, mobile-friendliness is more important now than ever. As such, many free tools are available to help website owners determine how mobile-friendly their websites are and improve them if possible:

- *https://developer.chrome.com/docs/lighthouse*
- *www.bing.com/webmaster/tools/mobile-friendliness*
- *https://pagespeed.web.dev*

The first and second tools test the mobile-friendliness of a web page, displaying a list of issues that could impede a site's Google and Bing rankings on mobile devices. The third tool, *PageSpeed Insights*, allows you to hone in on a site's loading speed on desktop and mobile devices separately. With mobile loading speed being such a crucial determinant of user experience, it's worthwhile running the mobile loading speed test, alleviating any issues, then resubmitting the site into Google and Bing via Search Console and Webmaster Tools.

Search Engine Sweet Talk

An English poet called John Donne once wrote 'No man is an island', and the same can be said of a website. An SSB site can't serve as a Lead Machine in online isolation. It requires connection to other sites – particularly those with the capacity to send substantial streams of traffic to it... namely, search engines. As you've read, forging these critical connections isn't difficult – it just takes a bit of time and initiative.

It's in the best interest of both a site's owner and its designer to ensure the tasks outlined in this chapter – particularly those relating to Google – are actioned. Obviously, a site that performs well in search engines benefits its owner, through increased traffic, leads and sales. But it also benefits the designer, who can capitalise on the results to promote his/her services into the future. A track record of real-world results is so beneficial to designers that it's worthwhile offering to action Google groundwork tasks free of charge for SSB clients, just to make sure they get done.

Making use of the free tools provided by Google to drive traffic to a website is one of the most pivotal yet overlooked aspects of running a modern-day SSB. It's a small, one-off outlay of time and energy for a potentially enormous reward; a means for us, the little guy, to stand on the shoulder of the giant and whisper sweetly in its ear... prompting it to relay our marketing messages to those of its loyal subjects actively seeking the services we offer, day or night, in our local area. This is an incredible opportunity; one that can literally make or break a service business. So, once equipped with a website, ensure the three Google groundwork tasks (at a minimum) get done. Then, cross 'launch website' off your to-do list and move on to other things, which may include ironing out some kinks.

CHAPTER 21.

TROUBLESHOOTING: FAILURE TO LAUNCH OR TOO MUCH OF A GOOD THING

As Shakespeare once noted, the course of true love doesn't always run smooth. Upon launching a website and 'sweet-talking' Google, leads *can* start flowing in at a nice steady rate but, more often than not, they'll flow in at a rate of knots, a not-so-steady trickle, or not at all.

At the upper extreme of Lead Machine performance, it's not uncommon to be flooded with leads where before there were none. This outcome may be enviable and exciting but it can also be overwhelming and stressful, particularly for those who don't need a lot of customers to make ends meet, such as a builder or B2B service provider. A flood of leads presents a great opportunity but only if it's anticipated and navigated carefully, as covered later in the chapter. Endeavouring to go with the flow when a business is not equipped for fast growth can cause it to capsize and sink in a stormy sea of disgruntled customers, suppliers and staff... not an enviable predicament.

The opposite of a lead flood is a lead drought; when the leads that are expected to flow in through a newly developed website don't arrive. While it's okay to wait around for a few weeks in the hope that the site will kick into gear, anything longer than that wastes time and money. At some point – preferably sooner rather than later – steps need to be taken to identify and overcome the problem.

A Lack of Leads

There are four main reasons why a site following the Secret Service Website Formula won't generate enough leads.

1. **Technical glitches** – Like with a physical machine, one small bug, error or oversight in a website can jam the whole system, preventing it from performing as it could. For SSB sites, performance problems often stem from a call-to-action error – an enquiry form that no longer works or an incorrect phone number, for example.

   Checking and testing your website regularly is important to avoid losing leads through technical errors or accidental oversights. Enquiry forms and other features that worked fine to begin with can break as a result of security updates or design adjustments; blocking leads from that point on. To catch errors and minimise their impact, be sure to periodically review your site and test its calls-to-action.

2. **Insufficient traffic** – The most likely reason a site geared as a Lead Machine doesn't drive leads is a lack of traffic. No matter how well a site is crafted to connect, convince and

convert, if no one is visiting it, no one can be converted. This is where Google Analytics comes in handy, showing how many visitors are landing on a site and where they're coming from.

There is only one solution to a lack of traffic... getting more traffic. This starts by actioning the basic Google groundwork tasks outlined in Chapter 20, followed by other 'no-brainer' marketing activities revealed in the third book of the series, *The Modern Marketing Arsenal.*

3. **Weak content** – If a site has no technical glitches and is receiving a steady flow of traffic from quality sources, its content (words and images) might be missing the mark; failing to connect, convince or convert. If built in accordance with the Secret Service Website Formula this is less likely, however it is possible – particularly for DIYers who've avoided hiring a professional copywriter or photographer to keep costs to a minimum.

To help identify any issues, consider: 1) seeking the opinions of individuals who fall within your target market, via business groups on social media sites, or 2) consulting with an SSB savvy marketer or copywriter. This can expedite the process of assessing and overhauling a site's content to make sure it's on point.

It's in modifying a website to improve its performance that 'split testing' can come into play. ***Split testing,*** or ***A/B testing***, is the process of testing slightly different variations of a web page (two different headlines, calls-to-action or colours for example) to determine which has the greater impact on website users.

Split testing can be highly beneficial to sites selling physical or digital products online, however its net value to SSBs is unclear. There's a steep learning curve and quite a bit of work involved – from the selection and implementation of a suitable split testing application to the ongoing creation of variants for testing and monitoring. However, for digitally-curious entrepreneurs, it's an option worth exploring.

4. **Business model blues** – If a technical glitch, lack of traffic and poor content have been ruled out and a website still fails to perform, it may be that the business model underpinning it doesn't resonate with potential customers. As impressive as a website may look, if the underlying business model is weak, the site's content won't align with the needs of those who visit it. Something will feel 'off' and they'll leave the site as quickly as they arrive.

   With a weak business model, an SSB's website won't be the only thing that struggles. Acquiring and retaining customers by any means will be a battle... the stress and strain of which may eventually force the business to close. To avoid such a fate, start by identifying what your current business model is, why it's not working and how it could be improved – a framework for which is provided in Chapter 11 of *Secret Service Marketing,* 'Agility: Use it or Lose it' – The 8P Business Model.

Once a website is working, it can be largely 'set and forget'. A decent Lead Machine can reliably generate leads for years with little intervention. While a few planets need to align for this to happen – a strong business model, high-quality content, service-centric web design and an effective combination of marketing activities – it is certainly achievable.

To be clear though, *largely set and forget* doesn't mean *happily ever after.* The internet is continually evolving, which means websites must evolve too. It would be unrealistic to expect a single site to serve as the hub of an SSB's marketing efforts forever. Every site requires an occasional overhaul to move with the times. Adhering to a tried-and-tested blueprint such as the Secret Service Website Formula, however, means it won't need overhauling as often; every 6+ years, instead of every two or three.

Although Lead Machines can exist without much intervention, they benefit enormously from regular updates. A bit of input and effort – taking the time to add new images, reassess the structure and content of pages, write the occasional blog post, test contact forms and perform routine maintenance – can go a long way, both literally and figuratively; helping the site perform optimally for a longer period of time.

But, as mentioned at the start of the chapter, what to do if a newly developed website *doesn't* work is *not* the only contingency plan to have in place.

Too Many Leads

At the opposite end of the spectrum, it's important to know what to do if a Lead Machine works too well... generating more leads than anticipated. In this seemingly ideal but actually quite dangerous situation, most of us are likely to respond in one of two ways:

1. **Ignoring the problem** – Diligently responding to enquiries and actively pursuing sales but failing to deliver a high standard of service, due to a lack of preparedness for growth.

2. **Ignoring leads** – Burying our heads in the sand; avoiding and/or ignoring website enquiries as if they never existed.

Pursuing sales without adequately following through (as in response 1) is bad for business – inciting complaints, negative word of mouth and damaging online reviews. Ignoring leads (response 2) may seem preferable but can be equally as damaging, causing prospects to experience a sense of rejection, which can have similar repercussions. Although the latter response may seem like the lesser of two evils, the reality is that both cause disappointment to innocent service seekers, leaving them to conclude that the business they found so connective and convincing online is fraudulent in the real world.

Luckily, there's an alternative response to the problem of too many leads, contingent upon the answer to one seemingly simple question: 'Do I want to grow my business?' Many SSB owners aren't interested in growing beyond a certain level of revenue or responsibility – and that's perfectly okay. Shooting for the stars isn't for everyone. Many of us want little more than to provide for our families; earning an adequate, relatively consistent income while doing what we love and enjoying the perks of self-employment. There's absolutely nothing wrong with that... as long as we consciously recognise and prepare for it, before our default response to an influx of leads kicks in, causing us to disappoint those we set out in business to delight.

Business Maintenance Mode

If seeking to maintain a set level of revenue and responsibility (as opposed to significant business growth), leads need to be managed carefully: accepting those that align with the business' objectives and areas of expertise, and rejecting those that don't.

There's a wrong way and a right way to reject a lead. The wrong way is to reply in a harsh or condescending manner or not reply at all, leaving a sour taste in the prospect's mouth.

The right way does the opposite, leaving them with a positive lasting impression that can be as powerful a marketing force as the delivery of an exceptional service outcome; boosting their perception of the business, rather than undermining it.

Connective Lead Rejection

Turning the negative of rejection into a positive, connective experience is simple. All it takes is a swift and courteous reply, by phone or email, comprised of the following:

1. **Recognition** – A brief acknowledgement of the enquiry and the importance of the job/project, e.g. 'Thank you for getting in touch regarding the renovation of your home. It sounds like an exciting project and we are honoured you've considered us.'

2. **Explanation** – A short spiel about why the requested service is not available or suitable, e.g. 'In order to maintain a high standard of service, our workload is capped at a maximum of X projects per year – a limit we have reached for this year' or 'Due to high demand for our services, we are fully booked until June'.

3. **Suggestion** – A possible course of action or next step for the enquirer to take, e.g. 'You might like to try contacting Ollie Gallagher at O.G. Building [phone number and email address] instead. He is a trusted associate of ours and I'm sure you'll be delighted with the outcome, if you decide to proceed with him.'

   Note: If interested in trying to retain the prospect in the short-medium term, an offer can be made to add them to a waiting list.

4. **Appreciation** – A final note, thanking the enquirer again for their time and consideration and wishing them all the best for their job/project.

Suggesting an alternate course of action (point 3) serves a double purpose. Not only does it lessen the blow for service seekers – gently steering them elsewhere rather than bluntly turning them away – it's a means for us to steer the course of our business. Referring leads onto other trusted providers enables us to cherry-pick the jobs or projects we want (those that align with our business model and areas of expertise) and handball the rest. This can be particularly liberating for those who've found themselves regularly doing work they don't enjoy or that isn't profitable enough.

Good things tend to come from referring unwanted leads to alternative providers. Giving intra-industry referrals is an act of service that generates goodwill (essentially, good business karma) by demonstrating that a business is customer-focused and an industry player. The development of such a reputation tends to have a chain reaction; attracting inbound referrals from others in the industry (including businesses previously regarded as competitors) and the opportunity to be involved in bigger and better projects with customers who are less sensitive to price.

Referring leads to fellow businesses can also provide a direct benefit in terms of passive income. With a bit of groundwork, deals can be struck: a finders fee or commission payable on leads that successfully convert into sales, for example. Initiated and managed well, such arrangements can prove mutually beneficial and lucrative for both parties, making them well worth considering before handballing leads willy-nilly.

Note that any providers you refer leads on to, should be ones you've personally connected with, vetted and verified as suitable; bearing in mind that the outcome of their service – good or bad – may reflect back on you.

Business Growth Mode

If seeking to make the most of a high-functioning website – growing a business rather than merely maintaining it – more is needed than just being open to extra leads. For an increase in sales to be sustainable, we must pave the way to higher levels of productivity and profitability; actively preparing for and nurturing it. This requires three concurrent and continuous activities.

1. **Learning** – Growing a business sustainably isn't possible without growing yourself, both personally and professionally. That means continually striving to learn new things – be it facts or findings to share with customers, ways and means to achieve desired outcomes, or lessons from negative situations. Being committed to learning makes a world of difference to a business owner's attitude, outlook and intuition, and is key to unleashing a business' potential.

   Sources of information, advice and inspiration that can be of particular benefit are:

   - **Books** – Having a non-fiction book on the go at any given time is a simple, low-cost way to prioritise continual, life-long learning and mental expansion. The sister books in the *Secret Service Business Series* (*Secret Service Marketing* and *The Modern Marketing Arsenal*) are an ideal place to start, followed by other business and self development publications.

- **Videos and podcasts** – A wealth of amazing insights are available online, in the form of videos (via YouTube) and podcasts (via iTunes, Spotify and other podcasting services). For those prepared to do a little digging and practise the art of discernment, a world of free online learning awaits.

- **Professional associations** – Business centres and industry associations can provide excellent resources for SSB owners seeking to prepare a business for growth. They typically offer individual consultations, group workshops on topics of interest, networking opportunities and more, for a nominal fee and/or annual membership.

- **Business mentors** – Mentors are individuals who support others in navigating the twists and turns of their business journey; offering insights and advice to expedite the attainment of technical, entrepreneurial and/or self mastery. They do this *not for payment* but for the pleasure of paying it forward or giving back.

  The two main ways to get a mentor are to participate in a voluntary, orchestrated mentoring program or to approach someone directly. Either way, the ideal mentor is someone you respect and admire, who has achieved goals similar to those you intend to achieve, with values similar to your own. They needn't provide continual input or a constant presence – just intermittent insight and inspiration. A coffee catch-up once every few months can be enough to unlock crucial pieces of the business puzzle, springboarding you to personal and professional growth.

- **Coaches** – Coaches differ from mentors in that they provide more structured guidance for a set period of time and a predetermined fee. Engaging a coach can be extremely beneficial, providing the direction, motivation and accountability to achieve a desired result. However, for most SSB owners, the assistance of a coach is not something that's needed all the time, nor is it essential to succeed in business. The best time to engage a coach is when you feel stuck or limited in your capacity to break through to the next level of personal or business growth, having tried other modes of learning to no avail.

- **Courses and coaching programs** – Investing in a course (be it formal education or training, or a less formal online program) can be one of the best investments possible; developing your knowledge or skills in a certain area, or attaining a framework to achieve a certain outcome. A good coaching program can be equally as valuable, if not more, due to the inclusion of periodic support and accountability sessions with a designated coach; boosting the chances of implementing what you're taught.

However, it's important to vet coaching programs and online courses (particularly those promoting one-on-one or group coaching) carefully. While many are brilliant, others are downright dangerous. A healthy dose of scepticism and critical online investigation *before* signing up is vital to avoid being sucked in by a money-making scam or worse – a commercial cult.

2. **Planning** – Business growth doesn't come easy, even with a constant supply of leads. To be sustainable, growth needs to be planned and prepared for; ensuring your business is equipped to meet increasing customer demand.

A good place to start is by asking yourself a question: 'As it stands, what would stop my business from making the most of a sudden influx of leads – our capacity to convert leads into sales (sales capacity), our capacity to physically deliver on our marketing/sales promises (operational/ logistical capacity), or both?' From there, you can drill down into the deficiencies – identifying what they are and how they would impact the business and its customers if not addressed. Then, determine what information, systems and resources are needed to overcome the deficiencies, and strive to implement them before an influx of leads occurs.

If you could physically cope with more work but couldn't keep up with the sales function (following up on leads, preparing quotes, etc), then increasing the business' *sales capacity* should be the focus of planning. After identifying the deficiencies, you might decide to refine your Lead-to-Sale Strategy (explained in Chapter 17 of *Secret Service*

Marketing, 'Make the Most of Fresh Leads'), create a suite of sales document templates and canned email responses, and implement customer relationship management (CRM) software, for example.

If you could handle an influx of leads but couldn't cope if those leads converted into paying customers, then increasing the business' ***operational capacity*** should be the focus of planning. Comparing your business' systems and resources with those of well-established businesses in your field or industry can be the quickest way to identify operational deficiencies. While replicating their infrastructure is unlikely to be feasible, knowing what systems and resources they've invested in over the years can be invaluable intel, and something to aspire to.

While it's possible to 'wing it' instead of actively planning for growth, it's less likely to work out well. Sustainable growth isn't possible without having the systems and resources in place to support increased demand for your goods or services. Getting these ducks in a row doesn't happen by itself. Each one requires anticipation and analysis of the business' needs, consideration of various options, a decision and coordination (aka planning). Without planning, a business can't evolve and without evolving, it can't graduate to a higher level of growth and profitability – no matter how many leads it gets.

3. **Implementing** – All the learning and planning in the world equates to nothing if the ideas, systems and strategies you decide on aren't implemented. Business growth, like change of any kind, requires action.

Implementation can be difficult for SSB owners due to limited time and resources. We can't possibly implement everything we intend to – at least not all at once. Prioritisation is essential, as is perseverance. Visible business progress comes in fits and starts and requires persistence and resilience. Making mistakes and bad decisions, spending time and money actioning things that don't pay off and experiencing a rollercoaster ride of emotions are par for the course. It's hard… but it's also the most thrilling and rewarding challenge you'll ever face.

Learning, planning and implementing is part and parcel of building a viable business. It's what's meant by *working on your business, not in it*. While working on your business 100% of the time might be a laughable proposition, striking a healthy balance between working *on* and working *in* it, shouldn't be. Not only is it entirely possible to give equal priority to both, it's crucial to capitalise on the sales opportunities a Lead Machine generates and build a sustainable, satisfying business.

FOR LOVE OR MONEY

Now that you've almost finished the book, the Secret Service Website Formula might seem all too easy. Take some well-considered words, add a few heartfelt photos, format and display them in accordance with the Lead Machine blueprints, then push the site into Google. Job done. While the formula is simple, it's not necessarily easy. And it's not for everyone.

Some SSB owners will be repelled by the formula or find themselves unable to follow through with it. These fall into three main groups:

1. **Those who aren't open to self-growth**

   The Secret Service approach to business is simple but broad in scope (hence being spread over three books). Being receptive to it takes a thirst to do better and be better, in business and beyond. SSB owners who take a short-sighted, get-rich-quick, know-it-all or woe-is-me approach to business are unlikely to experience this thirst and will have no inclination to explore or activate the Secret Service Website Formula.

2. **Those who aren't open to business growth**

Successfully implementing the formula not only requires a willingness to grow and evolve personally, but to grow and evolve in business. Many SSB owners are content to coast at their current pace and trajectory, with no desire to grow their business, move with the market or with the times. For them, the formula may feel irrelevant or surplus to requirements.

Others might be keen to grow their business but aren't willing to evolve it. For a Lead Machine to work at full capacity, three things need to align: what our target market wants, what we promise via our marketing communications and what we have the capacity to deliver. This alignment doesn't come instantly or automatically. Even SSBs following a long-standing operational formula, such as cafés or real estate agencies, need to evolve their business model over time; tweaking and transforming it as the business matures and the market environment changes. That is no mean feat.

As explained in *Secret Service Marketing*, developing a strong business model takes adaptability, foresight and fortitude. Many of us give up before reaching that point or can be so used to struggling that we're blind to possible remedies and resources, let alone strategies like the Secret Service Website Formula, designed to drive business growth.

3. **Those with an unharnessed ego**

Injecting our human identity into the marketing of our business takes a degree of courage and vulnerability not possessed by everyone. It requires us to put our personal insecurities aside for the sake of those seeking our services

– not getting so hung up on our perceived imperfections and inadequacies (physical and otherwise), that we can't put the connective needs of our customers first. SSB owners who can't bring themselves to do this will forgo or dilute the formula, thereby forgoing or diluting its benefits.

Along with courage and vulnerability, creating a Lead Machine takes integrity and humility. An SSB owner may be excited at the prospect of injecting their identity into their website but, if fuelled by selfish intent such as fame or fortune, it won't have the desired effect. Either the website will fail to connect with service seekers or the owner will inadvertently sabotage themselves (ignoring leads or providing subpar service) until the business is no longer viable; an unconscious reflection of the inauthenticity of the business' marketing. If not done for the right reason – to meet the connective needs of those seeking our services – lending our face to our marketing won't work... not for long, or not at all.

The life-changing, long-lasting benefits of the Secret Service Website Formula are contingent upon a healthy ego. Only those who can strike a balance between rising above their insecurities and keeping their feet on the ground will experience them.

Although it might seem unfortunate that the formula isn't for everyone, it's a good thing. It sorts the wheat from the chaff of service providers, leaving the spoils for those of us who are open to the evolution of ourselves and our businesses, have genuine integrity and mastery, and are in business for the right reasons. If you've had the foresight and open mindedness to invest in this book and read to the end, you're one of these individuals. You have what it takes to action the formula and join a powerful, growing minority of SSB owners rising up against the under-performing, overpriced marketing strategies of big business to thrive in the service of others.

The natural next question is: 'But what if too many SSBs apply the formula? Won't all our sites look the same?' The answer is no... quite the opposite. A website that applies the Secret Service Website Formula will look and feel different to other Secret Service sites, because it'll be geared to capture and convey the unique image, identity and personality of its owner. An SSB is merely an extension of the human at its helm, and its website a reflection of that. No matter how many sites apply the formula, they will be as distinct as their respective owners.

Even if every SSB in a given industry were to adopt the Secret Service Website Formula, there would be more to celebrate than to worry about. Some businesses would benefit a lot and others a little, depending on the strength of their business models, how well they implemented the various aspects of the formula and the amount of high-quality local traffic flowing to each site. For those that tick these boxes, price-based competition would be all but eliminated. Service seekers would have the information and elements they need to choose a provider based on intu-ition, rather than price and practicality alone. They would form a subjective, emotional connection to a particular provider and justify paying a higher price for the privilege of working with them (within reason, of course) due to a perception of greater value. This would result in a fairer distribution of work and pave the way for a more united, supportive and resilient industry. Toxic price-based competition would be superseded by healthy service-based competition, for the good of all.

If just 25% of all SSBs adopted the formula, the face of business would be changed. No longer would SSB owners feel compelled to mask their business' size with a cold, corporate façade, nor to constantly compete with others on the basis of price. Instead, we would feel privileged, proud and steadfast in our smallness – secure in the knowledge that bigger does not mean better.

Feel the Love to Live the Dream

The key to successfully applying the Secret Service Website Formula is quite literally 'feeling the love' for what you do and who you serve, over and above the money you stand to make from it. While some businesses are successful with money as the main driver, it rarely works for SSBs. For us, an overemphasis on money tends to have the exact opposite effect – blocking our capacity to earn it by stifling creativity, inhibiting attention to detail, and attracting price-sensitive customers who prove more trouble than they're worth.

It's in feeling the love for our business and customers, and influencing service seekers and stakeholders to feel the same, that we have the power to create a truly successful, sustainable and satisfying SSB. Activating and amplifying our connective energy – via our website, interactions and operations – creates an energetic foundation for money and other rewards to flow; giving us the capacity to elevate from merely surviving to sustainably thriving.

This doesn't happen overnight, and it's no romantic stroll in the park, but it's unequivocally worth it. As confessed in the first few pages, many years of my life were plagued with chaos, confusion, self-doubt and struggle, as I wrestled with honouring my integrity (working in the best interest of those I served) or making money. Thankfully, my integrity won out. Rather than succumbing to internal and external pressure to prioritise profits over people, I evolved my business model – time and time and time again – until I finally struck the love/money equilibrium; integrity intact *and* money flowing in proportion to my contribution. If my struggles as a *lost SSB soul* resonated with you, rest assured that the heartache I experienced for so long pales in comparison to the sense of contentment I enjoy as a result of striking this balance.

Turns out, integrity isn't the weakness I thought it was. It's our greatest strength and most lucrative business asset. With integrity, the Secret Service methodology and a website geared to connect, convince and convert, there's no need for SSB owners to choose between love or money. Not only can we have both... we should settle for nothing less.

YOUR MICRO MISSION

Congratulations! You finished *The Secret Service Website Formula* – book two of three in the *Secret Service Business Series*.

To help the Secret Service approach gain momentum, there are a few things you can do:

1. **Share the love** – Post a short review of this book (complete with a photo or two) on your social media platform of choice, or wherever you bought it online. This is one of the best ways to help others discover the series for themselves.
2. **Lend, gift or recommend** the book to a struggling SSB owner, designer or content creator.
3. **Look local** – Ask your community bookshop or library to stock the Secret Service Business Series, if they don't already.
4. **Loop yourself in** – Join the Secret Service revolution by subscribing to occasional updates via *www.secretservice.biz* (scan the code and sign up now).

See you in book three (*The Modern Marketing Arsenal*) where you'll discover SSB-specific tactics to attract new customers and get the most bang for your marketing buck.

Laura de Lacy
Author & Secret Service Marketer

ACKNOWLEDGEMENTS

Producing the Secret Service Business Series was a mission made possible by many. A huge thank you to Isabelle Russell, Gianna Grbich and Tatsiana Teush for your dedication and expertise; David, Jessica and Keely at Green Hill Publishing for your patience and professionalism; Nett Hulse, Natasha Pintaric, Gianna, Michelle Ridland, Jason Lehman and Thomas Le Coz for your support and valued contributions over the years; the small business owners I've had the privilege to work with – each one instrumental in nutting out the Secret Service approach; Graham McGuiggan; Peter Daniels and Brett McFall for your trust and tutelage; Gordon Kay for proving that integrity and generosity **do** belong in business (when I was starting to doubt it); Brad, Corinne and Caro for your strength and inspiration, in life and from above; Billy for believing in me before I was ready to; Ellie and Evie for being our village; Lovell and Jacqui (my earth angels) for paying it forward; the de Lacy and Braithwaite clans – my family and best mates; And last but not least, William Devlin... 'I may have given you life, but you gave me mine'.

INDEX

ENDNOTES

1 International Telecommunication Union (2020), *Measuring Digital Development: Facts and Figures 2020*, ITU Publications www.itu.int/en/ITU-D/Statistics/Documents/facts/FactsFigures2020.pdf

2 Telstra (2020), *Telstra Business Intelligence 2020: Digital Marketing*, p8, via https://www.smarterbusiness.telstra.com.au/trends/customer-trends/Introducing-Telstra-Business-Intelligence-2020

3 Estimate calculated from: Australian Bureau of Statistics (2022), *Counts of Australian Businesses, including Entries & Exits, July 2018 - June 2022*, Data Cube 1, Tables 1 & 13a

4 Graduate Careers Australia (2018), *GradStats: Employment and Salary Outcomes of Higher Education Graduates from 2017* www.graduatecareers.com.au/files/wp-content/uploads/2018/01/gradstats-2017-3.pdf

5 Explained in detail in Chapter 3 of the first book of the series, *Secret Service Marketing*.

6 Hopkin M (13 Jan 2006), *Web users judge sites in the blink of an eye*, Nature www.nature.com/news/2006/060109/full/news060109-13.html

7 James MB (30 Jul 2013), *Conscious of the Unconscious*, Psychology Today www.psychologytoday.com/blog/focus-forgiveness/201307/conscious-the-unconscious

8 If considering costly rebranding, assuming a fancy new logo is the key to skyrocketing sales, don't be fooled. For the do's and don'ts of SSB branding, refer to Chapter 12 of *Secret Service Marketing*, 'The Truth About Branding'.

9 Human needs and their implications on SSBs are explained in depth in Chapter 14 of *Secret Service Marketing*.

10 Anderson K (2008), *Victorian Advertising of Gloucester*

11 Chapman G (2016), *The 5 Love Languages*, Strand Publishing

12 Garber M (19 May 2012), *The Tao of Shutterstock: What Makes a Stock Photo a Stock Photo?*, The Atlantic www.theatlantic.com/technology/archive/2012/05/the-tao-of-shutterstock-what-makes-a-stock-photo-a-stock-photo/257280/

13 For examples of poor stock photography, and a giggle, perform a Google image search for 'worst corporate stock images'.

14 Due to the comparative insignificance of stock photography, any reference to photos or photography from this point on, refers to the *genuine* variety – not the generic stock variety, unless otherwise stated.

15 Refer to Chapter 11 of *Secret Service Marketing* for guidance.

16 Insider Intelligence (12 Jun 2017), *Video will account for an overwhelming majority of internet traffic by 2021*, Business Insider www.businessinsider.com/heres-how-much-ip-traffic-will-be-video-by-2021-2017-6/

17 Goodrow C (27 Feb 2017), *You know what's cool? A billion hours*, YouTube Official Blog https://youtube.googleblog.com/2017/02/you-know-whats-cool-billion-hours.html

18 Sensis (2018), *Yellow Social Media Report 2018*, p8

19 Sensis (2020), *Yellow Social Media Report 2020*, p7 www.yellow.com.au/social-media-report/

20 Explained in detail in Chapter 4 of *The Modern Marketing Arsenal*.

21 Wikipedia's definition of 'documentary film'.

22 O'Nolan J (21 Sep 2009), *The Difference Between Art and Design* www.webdesignerdepot.com/2009/09/the-difference-between-art-and-design/

23 Sugarman J (1999), *Triggers: 30 Sales Tools You Can Use to Control the Mind of Your Prospect, to Motivate, Influence and Persuade*, DelStar Books, United States of America

24 Janse B (2020), *Zig Ziglar*, Toolshero, https://www.toolshero.com/toolsheroes/zig-ziglar/

25 Note: Detailed information about niching (complete with step-by-step instructions) can be found in Chapter 9 of *Secret Service Marketing*, 'Unleash the Niche', and the development of a slogan or subline is covered in Chapter 12 of the same book, 'The Truth About Branding'.

26 Koehn E (23 Mar 2017), *Top five regions where Australian businesses are at most risk of failure revealed*, SmartCompany www.smartcompany.com.au/finance/top-five-regions-australian-businesses-risk-failure-revealed-theres-bad-news-food-services-sector/

27 Note: The method used to identify the Active Distress Point of Cyberstart clients is detailed in Chapter 9 of *Secret Service Marketing*.

28 Note that underlining should only be used to present a hyperlink, not to emphasise a word or phrase.

29 Zinsser W (2016), *On Writing Well: The Classic Guide to Writing Nonfiction*, 30th Edition, HarperCollins, United States

30 Note that a hosted version of Wordpress is also available via www.wordpress.com.

31 The term **open source** denotes software for which the original source code is made freely available and may be redistributed and modified.

32 Many DIYers get stuck wondering why a newly installed theme-based website doesn't look like its demonstration site. If that sounds familiar, the installation of 'demo content' might be the missing link. Be sure to install the theme's demo content before adding any other content.

33 If working with a web design agency, note that the service-centric driver is more likely to be the project manager or account manager who briefs the design team, rather than the designer themselves.

34 Merkle (2020), *Merkle's Digital Marketing Report: Q2 2020*, p16 www.merkleinc.com/thought-leadership/digital-marketing-report

35 Richard Buckminster Fuller was an architect, inventor, author and futurist famous for stating: 'You never change things by fighting against the existing reality. To change something, build a new model that makes the old model obsolete.'

36 Wordpress.org (24 Dec 2022), https://wordpress.org/about

37 W3Techs (24 Dec 2022), Usage statistics of content management systems https://w3techs.com/technologies/details/cm-wordpress

38 If you don't have a Google user account, it's a good time to consider signing up for Google Workspace (an IT gamechanger for SSBs, as per Chapter 7 of *Secret Service Marketing*, 'From Chaos to Control: IT for SSBs'). Otherwise, a Google account can be created from the Search Console login screen.